l a n d s c a p e (s)

está dedicado

a la memoria de

Juan Downey

{ 1 9 4 0 – 1 9 9 3 }

FELIX: A JOURNAL OF
MEDIA ARTS
AND COMMUNICATION
VOL. 2, NO. 1, 1995

EDITORS *Kathy High + Liss Platt*

DESIGNER *Diane Bertolo*

ASSOCIATE DESIGNERS *Nora Fisch + Annie West*

ASSISTANT EDITOR *Jason Livingston*

AD SALES *Sang Lee + Kristin Stuart*

EDITORIAL ASSISTANCE *Claudia Manley*

STANDBY PROGRAM
DIRECTOR *Maria Venuto*

EDITORIAL CONSULTANT *Marshall Reese*

PUBLISHER *Kathy High/Standby*

Program, Inc.

FELIX gives voice to alternative media makers, encouraging discourse and exchange from within the media arts community, analyzing questions of aesthetics and current political issues, and furthering the development of radical and experimental images of our own.

During this period of social conservatism, **FELIX** calls upon media artists to speak their minds and speak about their art. The name **FELIX** was inspired by the original 1920s TV hero, Felix the Cat, whose image was one of the first transmitted. The mystique around 1928 mechanical television and its potential uses created a magic in the air. Felix was transmitted by technical pioneers and amateur inventors working independently and testing the limits of their medium. Those early days of "pre-television" represent the spirit of what we envision **FELIX** to be: one of sharing ideas, tools and technology and of redefining the nature of the medium. I call on this mascot to be an emblem to us, guiding us through this time of experiementation and exchange, when camcorders are common recorders of our lives, and networking is (for now) decentralized and available through phonelines.

FELIX is published irregularly by Kathy High/ The Standby Program, Inc., P.O. Box 184, Prince Street Station, New York, NY 10012, USA. Office phone for subscription information: (212) 219-0951 (Tel.) Editor's phones: (212) 431-5442 (Tel.), (212) 431-4608 (Fax). The Standby Program, Inc. is a non-profit media arts organization dedicated to providing artists and independent producers access to state-of-the-art media post-production services at discounted rates.

Funding for **FELIX** was provided in part from The New York State Council on the Arts, The National Endowment for the Arts, The John D. and Catherine T. MacArthur Foundation and by generous donations from our subscribers.

Subscription prices: Individuals: 1 volume (three issues) for $30; Institutions: 1 volume (three issues) for $34. Canada and Mexico: add $5 for delivery. For all other international deliveries: add $10 dollars for surface mail and $30 dollars for airmail.

FELIX welcomes responses, letters to the editor. Please feel free to call the editor to verify that material is appropriate. We regret we cannot return unsolicited materials unless accompanied by a self-addressed envelope with adequate postage.

FELIX is distributed by Autonomedia, the publishers of Semiotext(e), 55 South 11th Street, Brooklyn, NY 11211 USA. **FELIX** is printed by McNaughton and Gunn, Inc., MI.

ISBN: 1–57027–051–1.

FELIX
landscape(s)

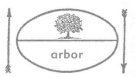

arbor

M A P

ELECTRONIC LANDSLIDE

PREVIEWS/REVIEWS

AND...

PAGE ONE: FROM <u>THE LOOKING GLASS</u>, 1981, BY JUAN DOWNEY
FRONT/BACK COVER IMAGES: PRELINGER ARCHIVES

ARTIST PAGES
(listed in alphabetical order):

(Pre)text

A Landscape Dialogue with Kathy High, Rick Prelinger, Liss Platt and Jason Livingston

Almost alone among the key players of this century's history, the landscape remains silent. But in truth it may be the most expert witness of all. In its broadest sense, "landscape" is a stage on which struggles occur — where humans extract resources from the earth, suburbs drain people and wealth from cities, and territory is contested between warring groups. Landscape is also a kind of slate upon which the evidence of culture, habitation and labor is written and may be read.

— OUR SECRET CENTURY/LANDSCAPE DISK, PROGRAM NOTES,
BY RICK PRELINGER

KH: This issue of FELIX looks at diverse notions of landscape including interpretations of place and home, and the architectonic, electronic and political boundaries that surround them. Recent struggles for decentralization or separatism throughout the world have redefined the notion of "locale" and increased the importance of "place," infusing it with passionate new meanings. The landscape of the body is also constantly being reshaped by current political regimes and biomedical procedures. In this issue there are discussions of the psyche and construction of boundaries, the landscape of the family and familial terrain, how the body occupies space, and the very real problems of "mapping" a place with moving pictures.

What is picturing the landscape? How does one mediate a particular landscape, moving through it, making visible what is usually invisible? What does the landscape of the psyche look like? How do I picture it when it is my *own,* or when it is *foreign* to me?

Landscape images become a vehicle for talking about history and invention. This mediation is also about technology, the ability to record what we witness. The landscape images of, say for example, my grandparents' old farm (now sold and only existing to me in photos) invoke aesthetics and memory: how I remember and want to remember certain land shapes, the garbage pit, burned-down barn, flocks of guinea hens, and ways my grand-parents struggled to keep the farm together. And how do I fill in the details in the years to come? Landscape grounds a story, shapes a way of seeing.

> *The virgin gaze is a utopia... Even before stepping foot on a plane or getting into a car, we often have a vision, a truly precise image, of the place we are going to and its contents. This is true to such an extent that in many cases one travels merely to verify that which has already been seen, in order to convert that which is already remembered into a souvenir.* [1]
> — "LEANDRO KATZ: REVISITING THE RUINS" BY CUAUHTÉMOC MEDINA

This area of landscape, and media's interpretation of it, is of utmost importance right now as people redefine their borders. There are new devel-opments in both our electronic links to our neighbors, and in our own site of the body. Cyberspace has no sense of "place" in the world, yet it is referred to as a highway. Human eggs are escaping the confines of the "vessel" that once carried them and can be exchanged for money. And the question of locale is still crucial in the mapping of our human genes. So, at once we will become (potentially) grounded in our genetic makeup, but floating without boundaries through fiberoptics, unified through one big network. As we move closer to a consumer-driven organization of space how do we as media makers define the obscuring of boundaries, how do we visually treat an ever-growing theme park of a landscape in this country and elsewhere?

> *The 'design' of television is all about erasing differences among these [edited] bits, about asserting equal value for all the elements in the net, so that any of the infinite combina-tions that the broadcast day produces can make 'sense.' The new city likewise eradicates genuine particularity in favor of a continuous urban field, a conceptual grid of boundless reach.* [2]
> — VARIATIONS ON A THEME PARK: THE NEW AMERICAN CITY AND THE END OF PUBLIC SPACE, EDITED BY MICHAEL SORKIN

 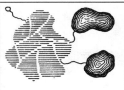 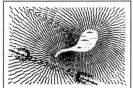 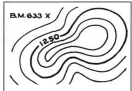

fig. 07   fig. 08   fig. 09   fig. 10

Two television ads struck me as rather odd lately. One was an airline ad featuring a very pregnant young woman. The ad opens with the woman collapsing into her seat, grabbing her husband's hand, and telling him in a breathy voice that she thought she was in labor. Suddenly there was lots of commotion and jerky hand held camera shots of the woman's pained face, the couple being ushered to first class, and a stewardess-assisted delivery taking place. All of the people pictured were white except one stewardess (a black African) who was in the background and clearly, by her framing, an underling. The woman successfully gave birth and everyone was depicted as happy. The final image was an idyllic shot of the plane flying through the clouds high in the sky with the pilot's voice-over announcing a welcome to "the newest member of this flight on *South African* Airlines" [ed.'s italics].

I speak about this commercial in the context of a depiction of another landscape — the sky. This final shot of the plane soaring through the clouds seemed so overwhelming: with the tense build-up of the birth, an emotional cry of a newborn white baby, and then a picturing of the smooth sailing vessel (much like the successful Mom) in the *sky*. Perhaps if it had been another airline I would not have been so keenly suspicious. This ad read uncomfortably for me, ringing of a new kind of wish, perhaps a recent desire to sire (a race) in the skies?

Another TV ad that has me wondering recently was made by Coca Cola. Created through computer graphics, digital imaging, this exquisitely drawn ad has coke bottles growing off a tree, a tree which startlingly resembles a baobab tree (indigenous to Africa). The coke bottles grow and fill up with brown liquid and then eventually the seeds (the bottle caps themselves) fall off and sprout new baobab/coke trees all around.

This ad seems a bizarre mixture of high tech and low, culture and nature combined to produce a new synthesis of the most ancient and magical with the most delicious and delightful. Ahhhh, computer graphics! Now, we can create a landscape that draws upon our imagination to isolate, to incorporate, to picture our acculturated desires and fears: coke is as natural as a fruit; coke is as old as the baobab; coke is plentiful and always available.

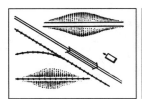 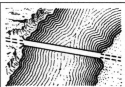 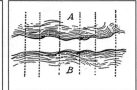 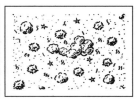

| fig. 11 | fig. 12 | fig. 13 | fig. 14 |

These numerous possibilities leave la mestiza floundering in uncharted seas. In perceiving conflicting information and points of view, she is subjected to a swamping of her psychological borders. She has discovered that she can't hold concepts or ideas in rigid boundaries. The borders and walls that are supposed to keep the undesirable ideas out are entrenched habits and patterns of behavior; these habits and patterns are the enemy within. Rigidity means death. Only by remaining flexible is she able to stretch the psyche horizontally and vertically. 3
— BORDERLANDS: LA FRONTERA—THE NEW MESTIZA, BY GLORIA ANZALDUA

RP: Some notes re: a proposal for a landscape video/film:

Using 35mm stock material, outtakes and process plates, travel throughout the United States (generally from East to West, generally from past to present, and on land).

Image quality will be high; the intention is to present as much detail as possible and recreate the notion of a hyperreal, intensified journey. The look of the stuff will not be home movies, but rather 35mm Hollywood production quality, locked-down, relatively long shots. (Though there could be a home movie sequence to recreate the Roadside America feeling). Most of the time, the video/film will stay in motion, and attempt to maintain a continuing, hypnotic movement through space, in such a way as to invest the surrounding landscape with an ephemeral quality. There will be breaks and codas in which the camera is still, or just pans, or does something unpredictable.

Some themes to include:

- The development of the U.S. from 1900 to approx mid-1960s, though these dates can change... changes in settling and arrangement of the country as viewed in these clips.

- Changes in transportation modes... from riverboats, horses, trolleys and elevated trains to railroads, to the ascendancy private cars, and from utilitarian private cars to highly styled private cars.

- The movement from East to West, and from North to South, beginning with immigrant New York (or even perhaps New England) and culminating with the West Coast and South, the multiculturalized regions of the 1960s.

- The growth of the middle class, especially the traveling middle class, and its attempt to universalize its vision of landscape, travel, other peoples. The continuing invisibility of marginalized groups in the United States. (slums in the 1920s, still slums in the 1950s).

- The development from multi-family urban housing to single-family suburban housing.

- Other changes as evidenced in the film (it would be nice to show social atomization, reduced opportunities for public assembly as time went on, spread of TV transmitters and TV antennas, movement from outdoors to indoors, and so on).

- The goal of the video/film will be to present evidence leading towards an understanding of the changes in the American landscape throughout the first 50 or 60 years of this century, and to ground this understanding in visual language and experience. We are eschewing words and traveling through time and space concurrently in slow, long takes.

LP: Reading Rick's passage, I can't help but bring up my all time favorite Hollywood film , *Over The Edge* (which also happens to be a favorite of Rick's). This movie is set in a non-place, a planned community in the California desert. The story centers on the teenagers who have virtually nowhere to go and nothing to do. They are subjected to living in this non-place because their parents bought into a concept — if everyone goes there, then something will be there. But it doesn't actually work that way, because a landscape of groomed roads and affordable spacious cookie-cutter houses does not necessarily provide a room of one's own. But the parents are too alienated themselves to actually feel alienation. They've sold out everything, so when prospective developers find the teen recreation center "undesirable," they close it down, unwilling and unable to recognize that it represents the only teen turf in town. To the background of such pumping angst-ridden bands as the Kinks and Ramones, the teens revolt and torch the highschool while the parents are inside discussing the "delinquency problem."

I've never found a scene so gratifying. Even after repeated viewing, it still delivers. There's a profound pull to wanting to have a place, a context, somewhere that feels real. The teens violent refusal to let their 'place' be taken away (read as both the rec center and their subjectivity) has, for so long, represented an empowering proclamation of territory. The film was made in 1979, it was Matt Dillon's first film. He was 14 years old. So was I.

JL: Kathy, I've seen that weird South African Air ad. Did you know it's based on an actual event? Apparently, they've made a few different versions. They found the "multi-racial" version tested best in the U.S. I could have this wrong. I think I read something about it in the *Voice.* Unfortunately, I haven't seen the Coca-Cola ad. It sounds like one of those moments of ideological nakedness you can only imagine as scripted.

Here are some words. There's a lot more to say specifically about this issue: like how so much of the writing takes the form of original stories (I am who I am as evidenced by where I came from and how I got to where I am now); also, the surprising (!) lack of environmental concern given the topic of landscape. This must say something...

If only we were like our own best friend, the dog, and satisfied ourselves by sniffing and pissing on trees.

It is perhaps predictably ironic that there is now a rallying in post-industrial societies for the transcendent promises of information technologies just as locality, ethnicity, and identity take on violent manifestations in the long shadow of the Cold War. Of course, it should not be forgotten that the earliest reports of atrocities in the former Yugoslavia reached an audience via the internet. However, I can't help but wonder, will this internationalism be bound to digital terrain?

In our exodus to the much-heralded global village (which might prove to be a forced march), will we become a population of consumer refugees, displaced from our lands and yet dreaming of that new and improved utopian landscape?

(P a u s e)

K H : I would like to thank some of the people who helped with this current publication. Liss Platt was of enormous value in putting this issue together, not only her energy and enthusiasm which helped us get through this double issue, but also her interest and constant questions and discussions around the topics which emerged. Diane Bertolo was also essential in creating the brilliant design, completion and details of the publication. My thanks to her for her patience with this project, her ever intelligent input, and her friendship.

I would also like to thank the entire staff at Standby for their undying support: Nora Fisch for her fundraising contribution and also for her captivating design assistance; Maria Venuto, who so gracefully handles the business end of *FELIX*; and Marshall Reese for his constant attention and consultation. I would also like to thank Sang Lee, Kristen Stuart and Jason Livingston for coming to our aid so willingly and for volunteering so many hours of dedicated and gifted work. Thanks to Tom Damrauer and the staff at EAI for always rescuing us in a pinch. I would also like to thank Shani Mootoo for her insightful editorial guidance and many needed suggestions. And Rick Prelinger, thanks for valuable input and the use of archival images and long hours of discussion around the definition of "a landscape."

This issue is dedicated to the memory of Juan Downey who had been a friend, and a supporter to the Standby Program and to FELIX from its inception. Juan's steadfast encouragement was essential in the continuation of this publication. His life and work as an artist were always an inspiration. In the spirit of always pushing the boundaries, we remember you Juan and hope wherever you are you are still laughing.

In the sixties, Juan Downey was the first artist to propose using space satellites as a medium in a global performance piece. Always a multimedia artist, in the 70s Downey quietly absorbed video technology into his work, and snakes too! "Now where <u>did</u> I leave that Anaconda?," Juan wondered seriously. Always exploring for new mediums of creative expression, Ambassador Downey turned to diplomacy for his innovative Yanomami initiative. In his role as "The Ambassador of Art", Juan converged avant-garde diplomacy with cultural communications. Juan was "Multi-Cultural" before multi-cultural was cool. ¶ Now Juan is working on the ultimate performance piece... He has become invisible.

— FROM A DEDICATION TO JUAN DOWNEY
"LIKE A DOLPHIN" BY DOUG MICHELS

Yanomami cameraman from **The Laughing Alligator**, 1979, by **Juan Downey.**

1. Cuauhtémoc Medina, "Leandro Katz: Revisiting the Ruins," *Poliester Tourismo*, Vol. 3, Num. 10, Fall 1994, México, p. 33.
2. Michael Sorkin, ed., *Variations on a Theme Park: The New American City and the End of Public Space*, NY, Hill and Wang, The Noonday Press, 1992.
3. Gloria Anzaldúa, *Borderlands: La Frontera — The New Mestiza*, aunt lute books, San Francisco, CA, 1987, p. 79.

Notes about Hard Times *and* CULTURE:

PART ONE: *Vienna 'fin-de-siecle'*

BY Juan Downey

Decline, disease, decadence, d e m i s e .
The demise of an empire.
Decadence of a crown, an apex of power.

X-rays of a dental d e f i c i e n c y .
Still inside my mother's womb, I was X-rayed.
A field of electromagnetic waves, passed through me as a fetus
Since before my birth, I decay.
Inside the dark warm womb, already back then, Frequency X-waves
penetrated m y u n f i n i s h e d b o d y .

"I hide my face behind my fan and my umbrella, to allow a
nation of death to peacefully grow within me"
The Empress had bad teeth.

X-rays transversed my unfinished brains. Since then,
downhill stumbling towards death; obscure undeciferable death.
D o w n h i l l d e c a y .
I am attracted towards cultures in breakdown, d i s i n t e g r a t i n g
societies, families in collapse. As a child I was astonished by

the lack of beauty of famous
writers, accomplished musicians looked common.

Even Mozart died in misery. What do you expect then?
What do I expect then if the genius of Mozart was ultimately trashed
in a common-grave. Just thrown in a mass pit.

Is a famous pianist ridiculous because he is short? Or writers
ridiculous because of their eye glasses and big noses?

Not even Mozart convinced Vienna.

He was dumped in a big hole. Just trashed: one of the best brains
ever! If Mozart couldn't succeed, why could we?

Malaria twelve years ago. A Yanomami told me once that he
loved me so much that he would eat my ashes if I died of Malaria.

Economic crisis and a major breakdown in the self esteem, in
the self evaluation, breakdown of the self. Disease as signifier.

V i e n n a   c a m e   t o   a n   e n d .   W e   a l l   d o .
But there's a beauty to ending. A flowering from the breakdown,
the crumbling, the collapse, the demise.
"If the grain doesn't rot..." Like those who fall, those who loose control,
loose power, loose health, those who gradually rot.

Face death!

My oldest brother used to like the Mozart requiem. We both heard it first
in the fifties in a French movie: "Un condamne a mort c'est
echape." Un condamne a mort... Death row. One condemned
to die. Condemned to die. While everything decays it flowers. Kubler wrote
" f l o w e r e d   i m p e r i s h a b l y . "

An attraction towards families in decay: the morbid, the purple lace, the
purple veil, the crumbling, the crumbs of power. An ugly pianist
who's too short and poorly dressed, but she can articulate harmonies of
mysterious beauty on the keyboard. Her dark hair shooting in all directions.

Something broken emanates beautiful sounds, inspiring smells.

From Chile, from the end of the world, I observe Vienna decay,
beautiful decay. From Mapuche territory I observe. Charles V the Emperor who
conquered, imposed his double headed eagle. Oh, eagle crowned twice you were

inscribed over the chest and heart of indian women. From New York I observe Vienna with my chilean eyes. With third world eyes I observe the first world decay through the lens of decaying New York. From a song

by Quilapayun: "Black Eagle you shall fall." Oh, double headed Eagle of my indians! Oh, eagle! Imperial Eagle!

From the Third World looking at the Second World look at the First World. Arnold Toynbee said that the U.S. went from pre-history to decadence with no t r a n s i t i o n .

This ease = Disease
the "K" = Decay

Flowered imperishably, the flowers that do not perish.
Flowers that do not perish,
f l o w e r e d .
My garden is flowering this April of 1990: forsythias, daffodils,
crocuses, tulips...
Flowering.
And Jesus said: " I f t h e s e e d d o e s n ' t r o t . . . "
Mozart flowered in his music but he rotted in a mass grave. The flower was thrown in a d a r k p i t , a b l a c k a b y s s .

Thomas Bernhard: " Two hundred friends will come to my funeral and you must make a speech at my graveside, Paul had said to me."

Kubler: "For the 17th century in Spain was an epoch of staggering economic difficulties above which painting, poetry and the theatre flowered imperishably."

The day shall come when I'm alone. The sun is setting. Or is it a f t e r t h e s u n s e t .
Glorious flowering while decay!
To reveal an interior collapse that has begun to manifest exterior signs.
Franz Joseph was descendant of Charles V.
The cracks on the crust of a decaying society. A crumbling society's crust cracks allowing gaps for free growth. The crumbling allows oxygen. From a Carlos Gardel tango:
" C o m o t o c í a e n e l b o u l e v a r d ! "

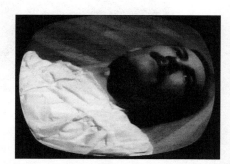

Still images from *Hard Times and Culture: Part One: Vienna 'fin-de-siecle'*

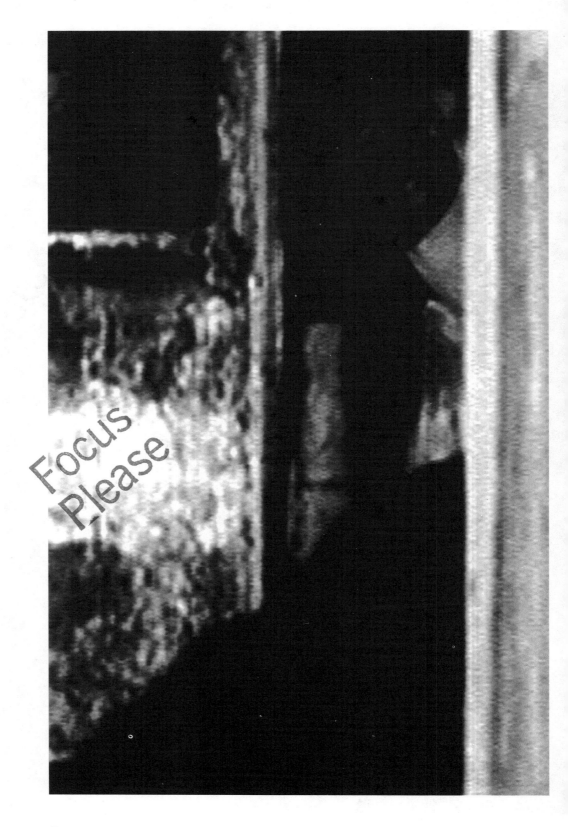

Yau Ching

Sara Diamond

Sandi Dubowski

Mindy Faber

Raul Ferrera-Balanquet

Richard Fung

Laura Marks

Shani Mootoo

Ridge Line

A

C

E

40

136

130

RE-MARKING TERRITORIES

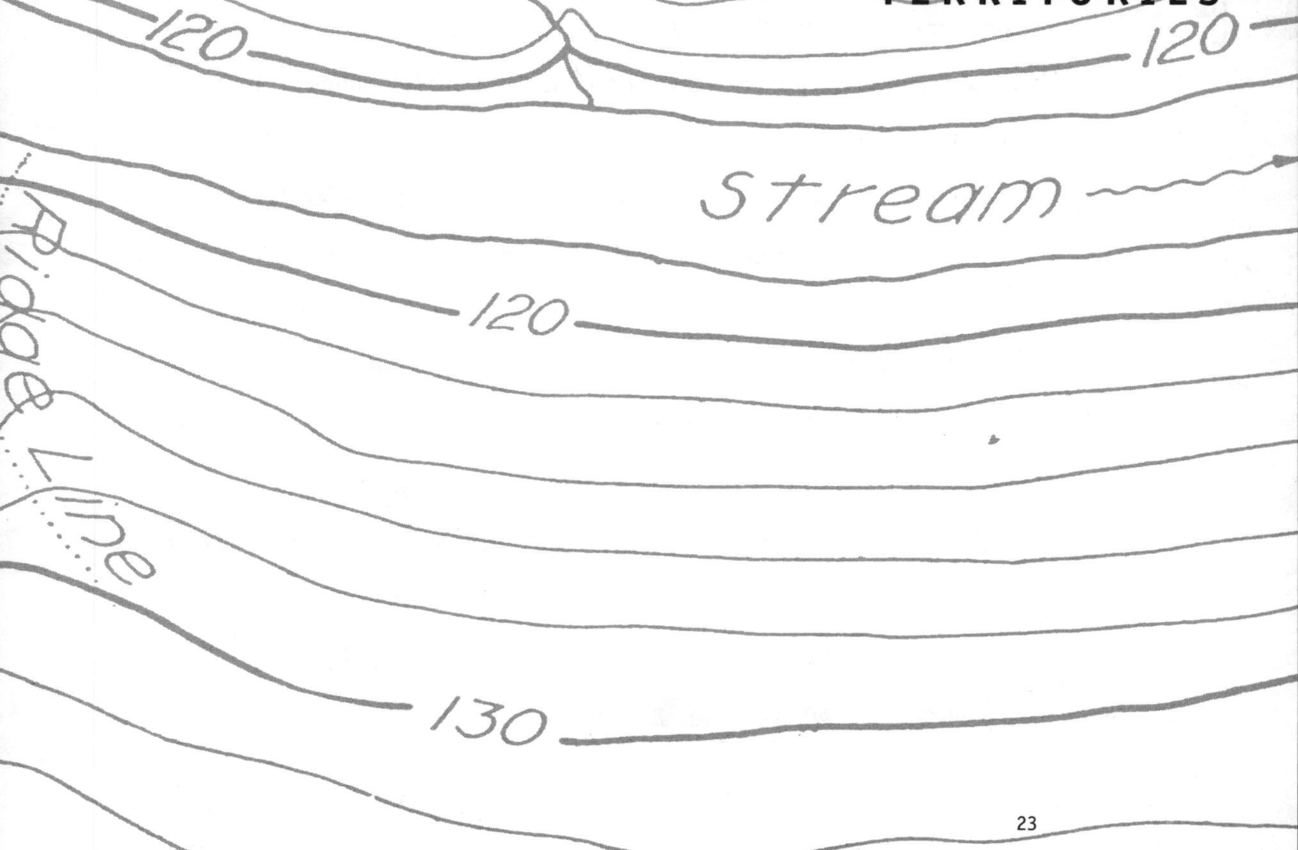

120

120

Stream

Ridge Line

120

130

KH: You know, my grandfather was a landscape architect. I suppose my memory of him centers around his love for nature. He was intrigued with the odd and unusual adornment in nature: besides building waterfalls, he also liked to raise peacocks and guinea hens. I remember a film he took of my mother and her mother at a highschool graduation or some such ceremony. My grandfather panned the camera around to "frame" the characters, his family. But then he continued to pan away from them, onto the bushes and trees around the park setting. In the 2 and 1/2 minute piece, there was perhaps a 15 second image of the women. My grandfather seemed much more interested in what was *behind* them. He allowed the camera to drift up and away from their familial poses to focus on these *giant* lilac bushes, trees really, which were surrounding the scene and were in full bloom. There the camera paused and watched intently: the lilacs were quite picturesque, swaying madly in the wind, quite sensuous in their blossoming and almost erotic. When I remembered this film, I thought of this issue of FELIX and this discussion I want to have about imaging landscape. **KH/LP:** What is a landscape if not a place, a setting, a site, a trace of light, a piece of ground? Memories and marks... Can we see the mark of particular landscapes in how their specific memories are worn—through accents, tastes, politics, sensations? How do different experiences of landscapes—relocations and dislocations, exile, concepts of home(land), family—construct complex identities and identifications for each of us? ¶ What memories do we carry with us that shape our interpretations of landscape and the terrain around us? How does one landscape feed into the reading of another, like a ghost image, or a shadow? **KH:** I know that, even today, I carry with me the silence and seclusion of the suburbs where I grew up, and that memory shapes my sense of the New York urban environment around me (where I live now). The quiet control of neatly rowed houses and groomed yards infuses and informs my reading of the chaos and disorder of the city. As I ride the subways and regard this place of anarchy, I can't help but remember my childhood of refined, predictable spaces, cultivated gardens, and polite scenes. Now my own imagined images are cacophonous and dense like the city, working to disrupt the order, the ease and assumptions of the privileged diorama, poking holes in the old insulated vista, and feeding off the energy of this cityscape. As a result, I am attracted to aggressive verticals as opposed to docile horizontals. I try to re-picture my youth's landscape of restraint and reserve with loud slashes of defiance in obstinate, objective scenes. I carry these contradictions with me, and I work against that order of my past. Or maybe I move

towards it... LP: I can't help but laugh a little, considering my own tendency to be a total control freak. And as I sit here and conjure up images of your manicured suburban spaces, I can't help but think of the rural apartment complexes and the acres of woods that comprised my upbringing. I think of stealing cigarette butts out of the ashtrays in the laundry room and running far out beyond the scrub bushes to the abandoned concrete foundations of more apartment buildings that never got built. I think about following streams to see where they go and getting totally lost as the late afternoon slipped into twilight. And I think, gee, wasn't anyone watching me? What was I doing without supervision? So now I supervise myself. I gravitate towards structure. I like things to be predictable, quiet, ordered. I too easily suffer from sensory overload. New York City has too many smells...

Dear Shani
Hiya Richard

A Dialogue by/with
Richard Fung and Shani Mootoo

DEAR SHANI,

As we launch our dialogue on landscape, I think not only about our mutual interest in the land as the principal icon of Canadian national identity, but also of our actual journeys across geography. I'm truly convinced that our sensitivity to the political construction of landscape comes out of these displacements.

Our trajectories mirror each other: you, born in Ireland, growing up in Trinidad, then arriving in Ontario to study; I, born in Trinidad, finishing high school in Ireland, then also coming to Canada. This movement continues the nineteenth century journeys of our ancestors to the Caribbean,

HIYA RICHARD,

Just to let you know, man, South Trinidad is not "dry and hot": when I am asked up here about Trinidad seasons (not "seasonings" as the Fung culinary mind might well read), the "do you have winter in Trinidad?" type question, I immediately think of the coldest time down in that particular south when the temperature drops to about 70 degrees and we pull out sweaters and wool blankets and walk around hugging ourselves, necks tucked deep into shoulders. The strongest image that comes to mind actually is that first year when I planted string beans in a Styrofoam cup and transplanted them to the back garden when they were about ten inches high. Every morning before school I would go and look in awe at their new height and then in the evening I would carefully dribble water on them, making sure not to give too much too heavily. Then before the plant was a good foot and a half rain came, (we too could see it coming—around the corner and up the road) and it came and it came and it was as if it would never stop. That time, I watched my string beans from up by the dining room window as they were first beaten down by heavy rain, and then with helpless quiet panic I watched the water in the yard rise inch by inch. Rich black manure from the flower beds slid into the rising water. I watched the lawn disappear into it and saw my string bean plant first float on the black coffee-coloured water, then get totally submerged. I have another memory of a different time when the street flooded from heavy rain, and people's belongings were just floating down the street. That yours from across the black waters in India, mine from Southern China. Our histories are so overlapped, yet when we talk about Trinidad — still at the heart of both our work — it is such a different place for us. A lot of this is social — the differences between your family's South Trinidad Hindu culture and the creolized Catholic Chinese of Port-of-Spain that is my family. But in an island barely fifty miles long even the land itself is different, almost as much it seems as between your Vancouver and my Toronto.

My house in Port-of-Spain was at the foot of the Northern Range. You could see the rain showers moving down the Cascade valley and everyone would go around shouting "rain coming," closing all the windows and putting out buckets and basins for the leaks. I think of San Fernando as dry and hot. Although hilly, I associate the town with the long drive (probably

happened often, but this particularly striking memory was of a man in half an oil drum paddling down the street grinning, quite pleased with himself.

So, Mr. North Trinidad, keep in mind that it's not so dry in the South!

And another thing: you had to mention the hills, of course! You northerners just love to heckle us about our hills in the South, eh! "How can you tell a person from San Fernando?" "By their calves" (meaning that muscle at the back of the lower leg. . . not the little animals that one does indeed see just about everywhere — except on hillsides — in the southern country landscape). Do you think it's scripted that you would choose to live on fairly flat terrain in Toronto and that I have settled in hilly Vancouver, content with the familiarity of forever developing my calves?

The photo that you sent is terrific. Its dimensions and the particular hues of the emulsion are exactly the same as a whole batch of photos that I have of back-home. You know, the memories of the events that many of my old photos mark are so very fixed in time, their beginnings and endings fixed right there in the emulsion. Your photo brings back to me memories, not of Trinidad per se, but of my photos, the little 4 x 5 pieces of paper. My childhood is now like a muddled and fading dream: here, my Trinidadian past has been exoticised away (by myself as well as by others), and I am afraid that I am losing my grasp on what I once considered *banal details*, but which now I long to snatch back as precious specificities that might keep those early Trinidad days alive in me — banal details which I tended to omit because they were not easily translatable to the uninitiated. Most of what is left now is photos that speak to me only of themselves. Precious moments with, at best, a blurry context.

I could also just imagine you and Nan inventing yourselves in the heat of a lazy afternoon. It's not much different from the time that my sisters and I were on holiday in England with our parents.I was about 14 and they were younger. For some reason, (I want to invent the reason—but something holds me back, perhaps the fear of that unfortunate practice of reconstructing events to ensure specialness, to inscribe a politic) we found ourselves, the only children, on a busy street corner, very much aware of our difference in skin colour and clothing. Gray and all of one hour) across the Caroni planes, first rice then sugar fields, dead flat, the horizon broken by temples and mosques and oil rigs. Returning to Trinidad as a birder, I'm struck that even the wildlife is different in the South.

The picture I'm sending you was taken in our back yard in the early seventies, just before I left for Dublin. It shows my sister Nan, who died about six years later. Nan was the closest in age to me and at this point we were the only two siblings left in Trinidad. All of the others had already gone abroad to study — none of us returned to live in Trinidad. Nan and I were often bored and that afternoon we had decided to play model and photographer with her instamatic. This photo is part of a series with Nan in different mod outfits — hot pants, minis, flares — taken mostly from

cream coloured public buildings surrounded us, and fashionably suited severe looking white adults were hurrying by us. I remember feeling small and... well, invisible — a word we might not have used then. It was as if we were failing, not matching up, to the promises our colour held. Until the three of us spontaneously broke into a language we invented right there and then, a language made up of words, mostly nouns, strung together in sentence-like structure, words brought to Trinidad by it's immigrant populations from India, parts of Africa, and those that were sewn into a patois that included Spanish and French elements. We thought that this language would turn us into toucans like the ones in the Central Range back home. We thought that we'd be truly exotic, not just brown children who didn't even have a language of mystery, an intrigue to compensate for their browness. Not long ago I wrote a poem based on that memory:

Hurdi aloo, "Sita Gita Meethai!"	Tumeric potato, "Sita Gita sweets!"
Payme pone koorma.	Coconut dessert flour and sugar candy.
Joovay dhal tabanka?	Jour ouvert splitpea soup love-sickness?
Baigan peewah, junjhut mamaguy.	Eggplant fruit, confusion sweet-talk.

Jeera jhundi, "Gulab jamon chokha,"	Cumin prayer flags, "great dessert! chokha,"
Anchar roti, pelau bull jhol bayta!	Pepper roti, rice saltfish dish daughter!
Chunkay datwan taria paratha?	Fried garlic toothbrush brass pot bread?
Pomerac jook chataigne peewah.	Red pear shaped fruit poke fruit fruit.

Richard, your Trinidad culture seems so much different from mine. In a word, richer, actually. It intrigues, and infuriates me that my fifth generation family is not in touch with local bush remedies, barks of trees, teas from plants, that your mother has passed on to you, and that your mother knows how to speak patois, while none of my family for as far as I could remember knew more than a word here and there, and that one tying up the tongue on its torturous exit. I wonder where is the "creollised" part of the, or rather, my, Hindu Indian identity. When a phrase in patois glides out of your mouth I admit to a feeling of having been robbed of authenticity, a feeling that I don't remember having had in Trinidad, but experience here, in Canada. Here having a language of one's own can be a low angle and with the camera tilted to one side.

Nan is wearing a piece of cloth tied in the front; if you look carefully you can see where the un-hemmed end of the fabric hangs down the middle. Suffering from thalassaemia major from birth, Nan had left school when she was about ten. Dress design was one of several courses that my parents financed to keep her active mind occupied. As a result she had a large stash of cloth, waiting to be turned into clothes whenever she could muster the energy. This fabric reflects the African vogue of the black power period. First generation, middle-class and Chinese, Nan and I were nevertheless both distant supporters of the rise in black consciousness. At about this time she also delighted in owning a copy of Mao's *Red Book*, given to her by a cousin visiting from New York. Her other favourite books includ-

double edged sword: exoticisation on one edge, dismissal and banishment on the other. Patois is not a living language and so is no threat to anyone, inflicting then the edge of exoticisation, and sometimes, Richard, with your knowledge of things Creole you do seem so much more exotic than I! I am wary of falling into an easy stereotyping when I attribute the multiplicity of Trinidads to race and its specificities in relation to region, and/or to class. *The Chinese in Trinidad. . . or Northerners were more. . . than. . . Indians in the South tend to. . .*

In Trinidad race, culture, class and region has so many jumbled up permutations! Trinidad with all this complexity sure is a mirror for the possibility of Canada. Now, what we really must begin to emulate here in Canada is that line from our Trinidad and Tobago national anthem: "every creed and race"— by allowing everyone to celebrate each religion's festivities with a different national holiday for each and every one, don't you think?! Not just Christmas and Easter, but how about Eid, and Divali, and Chinese New Year, and Yom Kippur, and...

It's so ironic that you and I come from such different Trinidads where the crossing of our worlds might only have resulted in muddled collision, and here in Canada, I almost always think of *you* as my primary audience, in spite of the fact that I often feel pressured to respond positively to the assumption that the South Asian woman, and in particular, lesbian, is my true audience.

Take a look at the photograph I have sent you, Richard. It was taken at Chung's Photo Studio by the Library Corner on Cipero Street in San Fernando. It is a classic formal studio pose of the time, made all the more ceremonious with the Greek column on which I stand, taken to send to my parents who were living in Ireland at the time. Can you puhleeze tell me what my Grandmother is doing in a Chinese style dress with her Indian orinee, which she never left the house without wearing, dutifully draped over her head and tucked in at the waist! Only in Trinidad! I remember the dress well: dark-cream coloured heavy linen. The bamboo plant and Chinese characters were printed in brownish black to suggest ink and brush work. This is way back in 1962. Just down the road from our house, next to the San Fernando Mosque, was a Muslim Indo-Trinidadian family who frequently received suitcases of linen from China which they sold from

ed the work of Lopsang Rampa, the Tibetan monk born into the body of an Englishman, and *The Prophet* by Khalil Gibran.

The other notable fashion elements in this photo are Nan's half-bangs which were fashioned after a character in a tv western, and the chain and medallion Nan had bought me as a souvenir from Carnaby St. in London. It is actually quite a long chain — about a foot is hanging down her back, out of view — and went with a brown turtleneck sweater. Neither got much wear from me: the sweater either because it was too hot for the climate, or, more likely, because I was very self-conscious about being skinny and it exaggerated my boniness; the medallion I didn't wear because I was already victimized for being a sissy, and I didn't want to call more attention to myself with such a flamboyant fashion statement.

their house. (Did they *receive* these suitcases, or did they actually go to China, I wonder?) I remember the whiter than white tea towels we took home and the pillow cases with invisibly attached mint-pink flowers, mouth-freshener-green leaves and dots of egg yellow stamens. And the crocheted doilies my grandmother liked to give away as wedding presents. There was such a fascination with things Chinese then. On the other hand as far as I can remember there were no signs of attachment to India or Indian identity in my grandparents' house. Sure Ma wore an orinee and we ate food of Indian origin as if there were no other, but there were no colourful pictures in our home of deities like the ones I like to use in my art work nowadays, and no ornaments from India, no fabric, or filigree furniture from over there. I know that Ma had a lot of heavy gold jewelry that was passed on to her from her ancestors in India, but she preferred to wear colourful costume jewelry, clip on earrings and the like. What we "other," privilege and exoticise then, as now, had everything to do with where and how precariously, or firmly, rooted our culture and "place" were — case in point is my not-too-long-ago born again Indianness here in Canada.

(Ma went to the Open Bible Church three times a week. Which may well have had something to do with the erasing of Indian ties and the creation of a vacuum yearning to be filled with the richness of someone else's culture.)

Check me out! I was about five years old here. So many years later I can still feel the scratchiness of the stiff frilly crinoline under my dress. I don't remember this occasion specifically, but I bet that the dress wasn't easily put on me. I kicked and screamed pathetically whenever they tried to get me to wear one. (Not much has changed!) Even then I preferred shirts and pants — and nothing in pink! — clothing as signifiers that didn't confine me and mark me as different from my boy cousins who, unlike me, were not discouraged from running wild around the yard, and from falling, or climbing. In spite of the wide platform of the pedestal, Ma's hand is placed protectively behind me. Years later, this gesture still means the world to me. She died about two years after this picture was taken. Looking at her image now, I can all but smell her cool, always slightly damp, fleshy skin, and even though this is a black and white photo I clearly recall her light yellowish colour, a paleness prized in my

Nan is standing in front of our lime tree, behind which was a Jamaica plum and an orange tree whose fruit was too sour for anything other than juice. I would be sent out to harvest limes from under the prickly branches whenever Nan or my mother was baking. A curl of rind would always be beaten with the eggs for a cake. In this instance, we obviously decided that the lime tree wasn't exotic enough, because amidst the shiny green leaves we had arranged red blossoms from the Flamboyant tree down the street in front of the Mahabir's house.

These photographs were not intended for eyes other than our own; certainly any Trinidadian would see through our transvestite lime tree. What is striking to me now is how we set out so self-consciously to exoticize the Trinidadian landscape — and my sister. As an adult I recognize the aesthetic of forced hybridity from tourism

family. With perverse pride she had always been teased that perhaps her mother, my great-grandmother, had been visited by the white overseer on the sugar estate that she and my great-grandfather had worked on. A truly perverse pride. But not entirely improbable — this allowance is not a reflection of anything that is known about my great-grandmother, but putting aside prudishness, who really knows what goes on behind the closed doors of ordinary mortals?

When I look at this photo with my grandmother now, and think that her body might well be a map for mine, images of the outdoors and outdoor sports come charging at me as if in reaction. In her fleshiness is marked her gender and her class as a woman, and even though this very flesh was my security and assurance of being loved, it's flabbiness and softness, verifying the feebleness ascribed to her from childhood, has always been the marking that I have tried to avoid. *Outside* of that institution called home — first the garden, then later, mountains, rivers and lakes with faraway shores — has long been a refuge for me, and I speculate now that my passion since youth for the outdoors is an instinctual recognition that here my desperate need for the freedom to self determine, to be, and to become can most be fulfilled. I am constantly battling with the deeply inscribed memory in my body of umpteen generations of gendering. I agree with you that "our sensitivity to the political construction of landscape comes out of... displacements" — through "our actual journeys across geography." But may I include *gendering* as a displacement for those of us who cannot, will not be placed inside its structure, and landscape as a significant haven and site of reinvention and imagining?

In my late teens, on countless hikes to Mount El Tucuche and to Maracas Waterfall in Trinidad's Northern Range I was the only girl, and at Maracas Beach I dared to go where no girl would go — beyond the breakers where I would rise precariously with the swell of each wave and when it subsided bob there amongst a sprinkling of men. Even there, at the beach, I must admit, the unwelcome attentions of adult men on this little girl sent me swimming even further and further out to sea. What I remember well, now, but have never before admitted, was how terrified I was of snakes and scorpions and land slides in the hills, and of not being able to get back to shore, or of being publicity, restaurant menus and hotel decor I've seen in many neo-colonial tropical countries: elements of Hawaii are blended into the Caribbean by way of Mexico and Indonesia until any cultural specificity dissolves into one big fantasy of (first world) escape. I'm not sure from where we devised our ideas of "tropical island beauty." It could have been from the British or American popular culture that saturated the country, or it could have come from Trinidad's own self-promoting publicity. In any case, when I look at this picture now I see the struggle of the newly postcolonial subject to represent her or himself. In the search for visual signifiers of specificity, English-speaking West Indians rummaged through the international clothes chest, trying on, borrowing, discarding. In the quest for authenticity one remains entangled in the mediation of imperialism; so even the physical body of the nation is

sucked under by a current. (My mother often chided me for "showing off." If only she knew how scared I was of hurting myself when I preformed my anti-girliness stunts! In those days I was a tom-boy. You and I would have been quite a team!)

These risks that I took were not to defy the outdoors or its elements (which were sites of opportunity in fact), but to defy the boundaries that I was expected to be contained within, to prove that my body was alive and capable, and to rebel against this body taking definition and direction from elsewhere. Going deep into the land, or beyond the breakers was something that cowards would never do, and dirty old men proved to be perfect cowards! My childhood fantasies of adventure invariably involved severe challenges to my body, and challenges to other's perceptions of my body, and they always took place away from cities or even towns, across vast continents and expanses of land, the land itself and my closeness to it being of utmost importance. Riding a bicycle from the tip of the North West Territories all way down to Tierra del Fuego. Canoeing up the Amazon River. Trekking over the foothills of the Nepalese Himalayas. In my teens, after I had successfully defied normalcy by playing cricket in the streets with the boys, by helping them build a house in a mango tree, and refusing to wear dresses, my fantasies began to include a girl whom I would rescue, never from the elements or from nature, but from family, from men, from society.

Recently, barely able to stand against an icy and menacing wind in a wide dried out bed of rocks uprooted by ancient glacial action just below Yoho Glacier in the Rockies, I was struck by my own vulnerability in this almost barren landscape. Because of the turning weather I was at the mercy of this wild and fierce environment and had no strength or reasoning against it. But in a place like that everyone is equally at its mercy. When in a wilderness park I cross a tiny plank over a raging river, and am terrified almost to the point of paralysis, the only one who sees my body cowering, and my face crumbling is the woman who respectfully does not rescue me, but holds my hand and passionately tells me that she has every faith in me that I can do it. (Here I am back in my apartment in Vancouver safely writing this to you, so of course I crossed that one successfully—*twice*, there and back!)

viewed through a thick lens. The prominence of the beach in public representations of the Caribbean can't be seen outside of the economic need for tourism, for instance.

This photo may simply come from the antics of one boring afternoon, but the elements in its composition indicate a far larger social and historical context. I think for both of us our work is fueled by this constant going-over, a continuous reevaluation of what we once took for granted, a look at the past as a way of understanding the present. My invocation of Trinidad is a way of understanding Canada: lands apart, lands connected — like your Vancouver and my Toronto.

Love,

Richard

As I become intimate with geographic regions of the country and their specificities, as I pour over topographical maps, and learn to distinguish the details of flora and fauna, as the land takes me in I find that my yearning for the details of Trinidad quietens. It is not about the details of either landscapes but more about rummaging through the country, past its towns, its people and all its constructs to find that safe place. The Canadian landscape has consequently begun to replace precious imitations of the Trinidad landscape in my work, have you noticed? Significant elements still exists, but the Canadian version of them. Magnolias instead of hibiscus. Evergreens replace coconut and poui. "Red canoes on a glacial jade and turquoise lake"[1] instead of the Banana Quit in the tropical broad leafed bush in front of a hot blue sea.

In all of this, I am wary of the risk of a new colonising and exoticisation of this land by those of us who are fairly new immigrants — even if we are immigrants of colour — to the country seeking refuge in land, in one form or the other. On questioning my desire to know and so to *own* this land, I recognise a need for it to be that necessary place where I fortify myself, and am unconditionally welcome. *As I am*.

Sorry to stop so abruptly, but rain comin and I have to run and close up windows and look for a basin!

I look forward to your reply. Soon, I hope. Keep well. Love, etc., etc.

Shani

---

1. From *A Paddle and A Compass*—video by Shani Mootoo and Wendy Oberlander, 1992.

Media Becoming NOMAD

by Sara Diamond and Laura U. Marks

This exchange is a response to NOMAD, a year-long thematic residency. Sara Diamond was Director of the Banff's Centre Television and Video Program during that year. She is currently Executive Director of Media, Television and Visual Art. Laura U. Marks was a Banff resident in March 1994.

The Banff Centre sent out this call for proposals in fall 1992:

The Banff Centre Television and Video program is calling for proposals from artists, directors, producers, and writers. Accepted projects will begin development or production during 1993 or 1994. Projects which fit the theme NOMAD are of particular interest, but we might also consider strong imaginative proposals for television co-production which might fall outside of this theme. In addition to those artists selected on the basis of their project submission, additional participants may be curated directly by the program.

Resident artists will engage in various aspects of television or video practice, and will dialogue about the themes of the residency, their own and other artists/writers/directors' work. NOMAD will also involve artists and projects in several other programs at The Banff Centre including Media and Visual Arts. This is a unique professional development opportunity to evolve scripts, critical writing, studio and field production, post-production practices, and the interface between concepts and new technologies.

NOMAD incorporates several related concerns:
- Beliefs and identity are no longer stable. Artists and institutions are not exempt.
- Transculturalism, whether experiences as diaspora, border culture or difference, affects cultural practice and how we see ourselves.
- Technologies play a key role in reshaping perception, mobility and possibility.

> *The model in question is one of becoming and heterogeneity, as opposed to the stable and eternal, the identical, the constant... only nomads have absolute movement.*
> (Gilles Deleuze and Félix Guattari, *"Treatise on Nomadology—The War Machine,"* A Thousand Plateaus)

NOMAD can be imagined as the shifting and constant movement that alters economic, spiritual, and geographic categories and hence our understanding of the world. NOMAD represents varying concepts of space and time that inform relationships between and across cultures, between gendered and culturally different individuals. It investigates what happens to an image, a story, a

theory that moves from place to place. NOMAD challenges truth, thus allowing
that certain essentialisms can be made useful.

> *Nomads are known to be rooted in myth, legend, and folklore...*
> *To them, art has two essential factors: the ability to*
> *consolidate the community through ritual and performance, and*
> *collective participation in the dramatized, spoken, and*
> *artistic forms...The impact of their art and their way of life*
> *has two important aspects: the fundamental idea that all*
> *life, experience and existence is without frontiers or bound-*
> *aries, and the foundational idea of not glorifying fulfillment*
> *in terms of territory or resources.*
> (Teshome H. Gabriel, *"Thoughts on Nomadic Aesthetics and the*
> *Black Independent Cinema: Traces of a Journey"*)

NOMAD includes the effects of televisual and digital technologies on social
and cultural meaning. It is about the ability to be in at least two places at
once, to be in two or more moments of historical space and time, to be both
in and out of one's body. It explores the homogenizing tendencies of global
communications media in relation to local cultures. It concerns the influence
of these technologies over even those who appear to be outside the circuits;
over those who are otherwise perceived as marginal or who are willfully
peripheral.

NOMAD implicates persons forced to travel, those who choose to travel and
those who are cultural tourists (otherwise named as "voyeurs, flâneurs, mod-
ernists, appropriators"...)

NOMAD tries to foment radical imagination and instrumental media practice.
But where does NOMAD sit in reference to the "global village," corporate multiculturalism, "political correctness," free trade, or specific institutions?

> *When Western — even progressive — ideologies talk about*
> *decolonisation, it remains problematic for me, both in theory*
> *and practice. I am still expected to discuss my culture and*
> *explore my imagination through "their" language, in terms of the*
> *traditional versus the contemporary, where Native is still*
> *inscribed by the outsider's fixed values and practices... Should*
> *we not seek a scholarship of our own, articulated not simply by*
> *placing us as new participants in their discourse on art, but*
> *instead placing us on a path that moves on its own course,*
> *sometimes in their same direction, but just as often according*
> *to its own flux and flow?*
> (Loretta Todd, *"What More Do They Want?,"* <u>INDIGENA</u>)

LAURA: This proposal was at war with itself from the very beginning. I
appreciated your effort to question the flâneur's easy assumption of privilege, the ease of passage guaranteed to one whose position of centrality is
not in question — a center from which to appropriate, travel, or take the
still-unified perspective of the modernist. But this is a harsh denunciation!
Isn't it possible to be temporarily located at the center, to borrow the vantage point of the center from time to time?

A slightly ashamed Deleuze aficionado, I was excited that Banff was organizing a residency on the topic of "Nomad." Slightly ashamed, because this put me in the company of what I think of as air-guitar theorists who empty the politics out of Deleuze and Guattari's most provocative statements. But the proposal I sent you oozed with D+G-style language: "Deterritorialization, the subterranean process by which nomads redraw boundaries and undermine centers, is an important force for my work; so is the attendant notion of decolonization. My own writing and programming projects on are of a nomadic sort, in content and style. I work mainly on independent film and video production, as well as other media on the fringes of mass acceptance. Because they are marginal and contingent, these media have the power to make connections that cannot be made in the dominant culture. But they are not a ghetto; instead, as nomads do, they carve out spaces in the dominant culture and thus force it to reorient itself. I am also fascinated by decentralized technologies such as electronic mail, shareware art, and old-fashioned video bicycling." I also talked about how Deleuze's film theory helps explore hybrid cinema, or the film production of people who create new identities as a response to cultural dislocation.

The view of cultural movement as constant, productive flux is very optimistic, of course. What concerns me about the way some of us use D+G to talk about transnational movement is the valorization of flux for its own sake. The "shifting and constant movement that alters economic . . . and geographic categories," if not spiritual ones, sounds awfully like the flow of international capital (with which D+G identify it) — which relies increasingly upon fluidity, the mercurial ability of multinational corporations to pull up and put down roots at will; of maquiladoras and sweatshops to level labor forces the world over; of Marlboro and Matshushita to create markets from Yellow Knife to Hanoi. Are corporations the nomads of the 20th century? Does the mobility of individuals and populations, whether desired, forced, or both, imply a loss of identity (recognizing that NOMAD represents a step beyond the immobility of identity politics), a loss of the ability to connect meaningfully with others, until we are nothing but effects of the whim of capital?

I picture D+G's "nomadic" notion of deterritorialization as a map of territory whose boundaries are being eroded and redefined in different places by forces from outside and within, completely altering the form of the territory and moving its center so often that we can no longer speak of a center. Deterritorialization gives a model of how these authoritarian institutions might be undermined, not by Benetton-style managed multiculturalism but by giving the center over to cultural groups who might well radically redefine the institution's purpose — in arts funding, for example. Nevertheless, corporations seem to be the best deterritorializers.

SARA: I discovered NOMAD when I came to work at the Banff Centre. The residency idea originated with Muntadas, who to his credit was deeply generous in his willingness to initiate an idea and let it hybridize as new players and events appeared on the horizon. So it unwound. The first principle had to do with the constant movement of artists, their foraging for resources and material conditions with which to produce. Also of interest was the idea of the rhyzomatic, a figure which stood in for the ways that critical theory had emigrated to North America from France and other European *climes*. Here artists had appropriated concepts, matched them, grown them, and moved them into new constructs. Lorne Falk [then director of the visual arts program at Banff] mobilized this practice into Banff where he conceived NOMAD with a little Umberto Eco sprinkled in. Eco suggests the ways that histories move across time zones, allowing epochs to live side by side designated by the flotsam of past historical ideas. Marxist and structuralist historians have attached value to this parallel existence, suggesting that these remnants of the past in the present signify reaction and nostalgia but surely this notion requires disentangling from Western logocentrism. There is a problem with the reification of progress, after all, and NOMAD provided an opportunity to think about time in terms of density, not linearity.

This discussion poses the question, "who does NOMAD address?" Right from the beginning there was a tension between artists who work from the essential and those who work from the socially or culturally constructed. This tension dissolved into in-between spaces throughout moments of the residencies. Reading Deleuze and Guattari I was struck by the complex moves they make to create a new post-humanist world view, and, in doing so, in a return to the classic humanist gesture, they write the sources out of histor(ies). How can one engage in the French fantasy of the nomadic without discussing Algeria? Deleuze worked in solidarity with the Algerian revolution, as did many on the left in his generation. Say so! And where sits Fanon, in this latter discussion, whose work on the colonized imaginary suggests the ubiquity of the colonizer's roots?

NOMAD turned here. It began to consider the ways that populations do not move ideally or willfully, the sites where enforced diaspora meets tradition. This is a location where new cultural practices are born, where the speech of the immigrant can create nostalgia and a set of meanings valuable only in the new conditions. Diaspora and the colonialism that precedes it create not only content, but new forms, new structures. In NOMAD layers and textures of ruptures and creation would create new possibilities, for example in Thomas Allen Harris' *Heaven, Earth and Hell* which weaves between African, aboriginal and gay memories and imaginations. NOMAD paused to consider the interrupted movements of first peoples in the Americas and elsewhere. It included the violence and productivity of the African diaspora. Who are the stake holders in the nomadic stories? Who holds the privilege of description?

Opposite and below: stills from **Seams**, 1993, by **Karim Aïnouz**.

LAURA: I arrived at Banff when the residency had been going on for some time, and immediately saw that the issues I'd been interested in were no longer concerns for many of the artists/theorists there. The question of who needs to describe the nomad had been hashed over and almost discarded, because it seemed to veer close to the issues of appropriation we'd all learned to be suspicious of. But we kept returning to these questions of definition. It was only at the most superficial level that people were there because they were physically nomadic, i.e. that they traveled, whether to make and show their work or as cultural emigrants. Some were nomadic in that their intellectual universe was dispersed, as with the artists working on the Internet. Some felt the concern with nomadism was an attempt to appropriate aboriginal identity. Some felt our weekly discussions had devolved into circular arguments over who has the right to talk about nomadism, and hid out in their studios. So I came to view the tattered remains of the theoretical notions I held dear after they'd been taken for a drag over a lot of uncomfortable terrain.

SARA: We really goofed when we named what had been a collective and culture producing practice (nomadism) as singular, "the nomad." The objectification of the nomad, his or her production through discourse as a singular object outside of context plagued the residency, which too easily returned to the idea that artists are nomads because they move around a lot. This term eclipsed fundamental aspects of nomadic cultures, in which movement is not random but motivated, that cultural practice was not a separate zone but integral to producing meaning within the movement and where the nomad was only such as part of a larger social space.

The tension between a scholarship seeking to know and describe and a scholarship embedded in experience was the next question. The Orientalist eye also considered aboriginal cultures as "fixed practices." Is it only for the colonizer that "knowing" another culture is necessary in order to know one's own, or does cultural identity always operate through oppositions and then the next step, hybridities? To map the production of hybridity is to trace power. NOMAD emerges at a time when the international art (rat) world had raced over the *Magiciens de la Terre* exhibition of "third-world" art at the Centre Pompidou—celebrating the "magic" of reification, spectacle, denial of histories and contexts. On the other hand, in Canada, First Nations rights and claims for land and language would resonate as never before after [the golf course showdown at] Kanasatagwe (Oka). The project of many first peoples was not hybridity but reconstruction and reclaiming; culture was a form of ownership: land and language. NOMAD ultimately acknowledged that many movements are forced, many hybridities are a result of the violence of colonialism.

LAURA: First Nations media practice is evidence of a capacity for adaptation, change, and expression with new materials. So the notion of "tradition" for First Nations people includes change, to some degree, not a hardened attachment to certain forms. We debated this during NOMAD discussions. First Nations artists Joane Cardinal-Schubert and Faith Louis Adams, for example, argued that it is important to defend a place for traditional art forms that is protected from the modernist desire for incessant formal innovation, even if they do not choose to work in traditional forms.

At the same time, as Loretta Todd points out, First Nations artists may work on paths that have nothing to do with those of the mainstream art and media worlds. For us to be able to respect each other's work and defend its private space of development, therefore, I think it's important to defend the inaccessibility of cultures to each other. A "nomadic" practice is not in search of perfect intercultural communication and understanding — for we know how these can be a means of control — but of ways to coexist without seeking to make each other's practice transparent to us. Where our practices meet, it is like two eddies meeting and producing a stream that further changes the shape of the ter-

ritory... But we, especially we of the dominant culture, must not try to know everything about what others are doing, because knowing is the first step of colonizing.

The struggle not to be known, or the agreement to empathize without trying to understand, were at work in a lot of things produced at Banff during NOMAD: Gitanjali's tape *New View, New Eyes* about visiting her ancestral home in India and trying to accept her place as outsider to her traditional culture; Karim Aïnouz's *Paiaxão Nacional*, about the struggle between a Northern tourist whose "national passion" is the desire to know Brazil in the form of his Brazilian lover; Lyndal Jones's work in progress about Darwin in the Galapagos, where she contrasts the desire to classify living things with the love of undifferentiated life. And Helen Lee was working on the script for *You Taste Korean*, whose title is a sexy joke on the ability to know and classify cultural others.

SARA: So NOMAD flowed through D+G, Eco, through the opposing desires for instability (the West needing to refresh) and stability (the so-called margins, i.e., the majority, needing to reclaim, claim and create), and up against the transient image, whether simulacrum or hyperreality. NOMAD suggests the potential of technology while noting the implications of its exclusivity. Art works often used technology to mobilize the rational critical tradition of the left followed by direct emotional action and symbolic exchange. Was NOMAD a bid for reconciliation?

LAURA: It's interesting how you talk about NOMAD as an aggregate movement: it evokes a mass movement, like sheep grazing or molecules osmosing, more than a group of individuals. I like that sense that we participated in something whose movement we could not individually determine. Though, as well as the use of the singular, it being in all caps bugged me: it had the sinister connotation of a logo, or a corporate acronym.

But it was important to avoid a situation where we could all say "we're nomads here together," because that seems not only to appropriate nomad identity but also, more importantly, to misidentify the most important element of what we were doing, namely producing in a nomadic way. Nomadism, as a term that's useful for cultural producers in the late 20th century, describes a movement of deterritorialization rather than a "movement" in the modernist sense, namely the acts of aggregated individuals. In contrast, how can we claim nomadic movement as a condition that allows individuals to make meaningful connections? Part of the solution is to focus our attention on those points where flux is not homogenizing but produc-

Opposite: Stills from **Fast Trip, Long Drop**, 1993, by **Gregg Bordowitz**.

tive and transformative. I'm thinking of the intercultural exchange in Karim Aïnouz's *Seams* that allows him to read the lives of his Brazilian great-aunts through North American "queer" eyes, while allowing their lives to expand North American notions of sexual existence.

You note that hybridity is a violent movement, rather than the smooth, flowing movement that D+G's notion of Nomadism sometimes suggests. Intercultural movement is disjunctive, and it is the "ability to be in two

places at once," to recognize other places and times existing here in the present, that creates the uncanny shock that is so productive. So in *Fast Trip, Long Drop*, the history of his Jewish family's diaspora is intersected by Evel Knievel's flying motorbike, with profound effects of intercutting lost histories and mass-cultural tales so long repeated that they lose their historical credibility... Bordowitz takes license from his father's fatal and banal encounter with the legendary daredevil to make daredevils a model for his own daily confrontations with death.

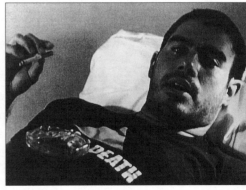

SARA: It was difficult to describe a nomadic artistic practice outside of the analytic terms of hybridity. What forms does nomadism take? D+G suggest relationships to space and mapping: the haptic. Discussions about the movement of space and time were the closest we got to defining a nomadic element in people's work at Banff.

Gregg Bordowitz in *Fast Trip Long Drop* provides constant tension between commitment to the moment and the need to reread and undermine its authority. He reconstructs AIDS activity footage and characters, Jewish history and his family through a series of devices which allow us to return to the original images without nostalgia. He also makes the unfashionable suggestion that there are parallels between historical moments and movements and the narcissism of our invention needs to be dispelled. This is the cardinal rule for NOMAD.

In *Time Line*, one of the aboriginal PSAs on self-government by Isabel Knockwood, Gary Farmer and Angie Campbell, time is evoked in linear accumulation from before and after conquest, but also as a constant layering of symbols and abstract concepts. Glyphs are imposed onto mountains which are post-carded onto other terrain, symbols fly across the screen and globes pasted with photo images move through space.

In *Good Grief* by Marjorie Beaucage the mourning of her brother's death accumulates through memories of both his death and their lives with him. Somehow, time stands still as a return to the moving images of the highway's centre line.

This relationship with personal memory, its writing into history and the loss of the remaking of culture is at the front of Leila Sujir's epic work, *The Dreams of the Night Cleaners*. In Sujir's video borders enunciate documentary and fantasy computer graphics interrupt classic narrative sequences. Sujir uses simultaneity to underline the need for many readings of one moment.

LAURA: D+G's "Treatise" valorizes constant flux as the origin of becoming. During NOMAD we witnessed production that expressed these values of fluidity, the ability to form new and contingent bonds, that are often the result of cultural displacement. We also witnessed it in terms of materials that are virtual, transmissible, eminently portable. One of the less-noted sections of the "Treatise on Nomadology" draws upon the model of metallurgy, as the art form of nomads per se (and as often with D+G, what looks at first like metaphor is actually startlingly literal). Metalwork is a portable art form, often small and intricate, thus able to express its makers' creativity and cultural character without being bulky like an altarpiece.

But D+G also talk about the virtues of metallurgy as a nomadic art form at the level of the material itself. Metals, they point out, are (generally) solids that nonetheless have a molecular structure like that of liquids. Remember from high-school chemistry, the astonishing fluidity, almost promiscuity, with which those molecules having four, or three, or five electrons in their outside shell could bond with each other, sometimes taking the positive (or "top?") position sometimes the negative, sometimes sharing electrons among several molecules until there are enough atoms for all to attain a temporary stasis? And due to the same quality of multivalency, they tended more easily to split off from each other and form bonds with the next molecule down, and the next... So that iron, gold, and glass actually have a mercurial nature, are actually more liquid than water, because of this ability to bond polymorphously.

Do portability and transmissibility make such an art form qualitatively different? How do these qualities compare to more or less virtual media like video, electronic imaging, and electronic communications?

I can't draw the causal connection between fluid materials, nomadic culture, and expression as confidently as D+G do. But, for example, the First Nations self-government PSAs produced at Banff, like the metallurgy D+G write about, are a nomadic medium, portable and transmissible. And they have a nomadic purpose: they will be used to organize governmental structures that will change the shape of Canada. Neither of these things is because they are made by and for First Nations people. The work people were doing on electronic networks — Wendy Kirkup and Pat Naldi of S.I.S., and the FastBreeder Collective, represented by Calum Selkirk—is also nomadic in both these ways, because it deterritorializes (that word again!) hierarchical information structures. I'm tempted, as you know, to look for formal signs of "nomadism": maybe there's a haptic form of vision that does not differentiate the world into separate, knowable, controllable objects, but understands the world in the more continuous terms of texture, of touch. And smell. There was haptic work going on during the residency: like Shawna Beharry's performances where she takes the products of her transcultural dislocations, saris and chappatis and incense, and dematerializes them until only ashes and fragrances remain. But these processes are terribly hard to figure in videotape, except when the tape itself is somehow against seeing — and Beharry's strategy, of course, is to destroy her tapes after a couple of viewings!

So I think for now it's best to look for what is nomadic in the way the medium works and in what sorts of cultural dislocations it creates. Not that it just documents the process of cultural dislocation, but that it carries that out itself: like Aïnouz's *Paiaxão Nacional*. His tape (shot on film) shows how complicated is the North-South flow of money and desire that defines tourism. It is organized around the gaze of a northern tourist and the voice of the Brazilian boy he is courting: their perceptions of the exchange are like two different world maps, each trying to impose its lines on the other.

PHOTO: CHERYL BELLOWS/THE BANFF CENTRE

On the set of **Time Line**, 1994, one of the aboriginal PSAs on self-government by **Isabel Knockwood**, **Gary Farmer** and **Angie Campbell**.

Sites of Struggle:

Exile and Migration in the
Cuban-exile Audiovisual Discourse

by Raul Ferrera-Balanquet

THE POLITICS OF LOCATION

The Caribbean as a region provides specific meanings to the formation of the self. The ocean, and the different movements created by the traveling ocean waves, along with the islands, the tropical elements such as the sun, the vegetation, and the fauna also contribute to the geopolitical construction of the self. It is in that geo-physical space where the individual self sees its reflection in the collective self. The collective self places the individual self into a socio-historical context where personal memories juxtapose with historical memory.

An immigrant who has experienced two or more geo-physical spaces has two or more different processes of self-collectivization, and two or more ways of relating to historical time. It is at this point where I affirm that the immigrant's audiovisual discourse has two or more voices, has two or more ways of focusing the subject matter, has two or more geographical sites of enunciation, as well as two or more historical and cultural positions.

EXTERNAL RUPTURE

Migration is a rupture which breaks, in the physical sense, the immigrant's notion of space. The space in which the immigrant newly lives is also fragmented due to the different socio-historical, sexual and cultural relations within that space, and with the subject. Here the immigrant has to confront linguistic differences, class status, cultural differences, as well as ethnical, sexual, and gender differences. When these spaces jump into, collide, overlap, juxtapose, and cross over, the formation of a system of fragmented images takes place.

Before the migration, the immigrant's concept of the non-experienced space is limited to his or her personal geo-physical experience. In the case of Cuba, the sea becomes the limits of the personal space. What exists beyond those limits could only be imagined by those that haven't seen it. In the

Caribbean, the information received from outside comes packaged in films, music, TV programs, magazines, newspapers, and rhetorical speeches. The radio from Florida, U.S. TV, and Hollywood films seen in Cuba, are the references used by the future immigrant/exile in the imaginary construction of the non-experienced space.

When migrating to the non-experienced space, the imaginary construction of the non-experienced space clashes with the "real space." The immigrant then, after the arrival, has to deconstruct the imaginary formation of the space. At the same time, the new factual experience from everyday life creates a new concept of that space.

It is at this moment where the juxtaposition, collision, fragmentation and rupture of the spaces take place. The architecture, the roads, the billboards, the automobiles, the way people dress, the food, the money, the language, the social, economic, ethnic, sexual, and cultural relations are different from the original space. Nevertheless, in order to understand the new space, the immigrant/exile has to take as a point of reference, the past space and the imaginary construction produced by the exported images. Chaos, disorder and collision take place in the psychological landscape of the immigrant/exile, much like the movements of the Caribbean sea.

The rupture/displacement created by the migratory process obligates the immigrant/artist/exile to reconstruct or re-map their notion of space. There lies what I call "the multiple visions of the geographical space." We are able to look from different sites, giving a more geometrical shape to our creative discourse. [1]

MIGRATION AND EXILE AS SITES OF ENUNCIATION

Donde yo nací, donde me crié,
como me formaron como vine aquí. [2] —PABLO MILANES

The Cuban exile, as well as other Latin American exiles, emerge from a colonial past that has conditioned the Cuban "nation" to be seen as a polarized culture. Although during colonial times there were different political currents for the exile, the Cuban's exile has always been seen as a binary condition dominated by the island government on the one hand, and the major economic force of exile on the other. The first discourse which placed me in exile is the patriarchal left nationalist ideology produced on the island. The second is an ultra right wing, upper class, male ideology that rejects the discourse of race, sexuality, ethnicity, and gender that is taking place in the U.S.

Nevertheless the Cuban exile is as diverse as the Latino diaspora. As Coco Fusco argues in her essay "Diario de Miranda," Cuban identity acquires different meanings according to the location from which it is enunciated. [3]

We cannot talk about Cuban culture as an homogeneous culture. The "Cuban" culture is a hybrid culture, a mestizo culture where African, Spanish, Arabs, Asians, Jews, and the little we had left of our indigenous population have mixed to created what we know today as Cuban culture. For years

the discussion on Cuban identity has been based in the notion that our culture is a product of a mestizaje between the Spanish colonizers and the African Slave. This attitude renders invisible the migrations that have taken place since colonial times and the importation of Asian slaves to work in the sugar cane fields. It also rejects Arabs and Jewish immigrants because of the Spaniards' latent xenophobia toward these two groups.

INTERNAL EXILE

Displaced in the "national" geopolitical space — outcast from my family by the patriarchal mentality of my Arab father who thought that to be a man you needed to have three wives, three families, and fight for the revolution because that was the macho thing to do — displaced from the educational system, because my sexuality was a "handicap," and even though I got good grades and was a student organizer, the system never rewarded me; displaced from my own adolescent years, I needed to grow so fast to survive that those years of transition happened in a matter of seconds. I was constantly silenced, not being able to articulate what was going on inside of me.

Internal exile has not ceased to exist in my life. It takes place in the United States everyday. As a Latino of African and Arab descent, I am forced into internal exile to experience the positionality of my mestizo culture. It wasn't until I became familiar with the concept of diaspora that I was able to recognize my Latino, African and Arab selves as part of my hybrid identity and travel within the three diasporas.

Needing to produce my Cuban identity, I couldn't position myself within the binary opposition that exists between Miami and Havana. Neither positions reflect my personal views and experiences as a Cuban exile. I am displaced from this discourse of Cubaness. For according to the island's hegemonic ideology I am a gusano, a worm, the enemy. And according to the exile's "dominant" ideology, I am a radical leftist, a sexual deviant who should be happy I was even accepted in the land of freedom — and be silent about racism, homophobia, classism and sexism.

It is fascinating to realize that my Cuban identity is not absolute and that it could be reinvented constantly. Here the questions of difference and "otherness" are used as tool within the space of my Cubanicity. As I discovered my position, I realized that I was traveling in a territory that was undefined by the political powers that want to force the notion of "Cubanicity." That movement led the self to a redefinition — a renovation process producing my diasporic/hybrid identities.

MAPPING THE MESTIZO SELF O ROMPIENDO LA IMAGEN AUTENTICA

When recognizing myself as Latino, another production of identity took place. I had to confront a history that took me back to territories outside the western culture right into Aztlan, the Mayan area, the Arab world, Africa, and the Caribbean. This identity also brought me back slowly to the present, pointing out the colonization of Las Americas — a point of interception with Cuban history, the occupation of the Southwest, and the civil rights movement. I learned the reason why a poor Cuban immigrant like me was able to study in this country was because the Chicanos and Puerto Ricans, along with the Jews and the African Americans, fought for the right for their children to be educated. This is a fight that the Cuban exiles never undertook because of their "ultra right classist patriarchal" position.

My place of origin is narrating itself at this moment as a geographical context that is larger than the island of Cuba. The recognition of the Caribbean as a Meta-archipelago where several islands connect themselves, interacting with the ocean, became a new metaphor for my traveling mestizo self. The Caribbean is a sinuous culture where time unfolds irregularly and resists being captured by the cycles of clocks and calendars. [4]

The complexity of the socio-cultural and historical process of the Caribbean presents itself as a chaotic entity where language, costume, rhythm and performance evoke multiple cultural selves. The ocean plays an important role in this complexity. Its movement repeats, reproduces, grows, decays, unfolds, spins, vibrates, collides, and seethes, always opening new systems of narration. As a meta concept, the Caribbean travels always to old and new locations, breaking its movement at a crossroad to create multiple movements that may never connect with its point of departure. The Caribbean then is an entity without center and limits. It is a meta concept which needs to be understood as a "chaotic" entity because it narrates a subjective self that

Opposite: still from **Caminamos Sobre Las Olas**, 1992.

49

defies the Aristotelian-Western European notion of the beginning, middle and end.

What made me leave Cuba was chaos, a crisis with its own internal movement. That crisis has intensified with the years. Today its velocity increases as I move back into my past. Simultaneously, my position in U.S. society is a struggle which moves forward with time.

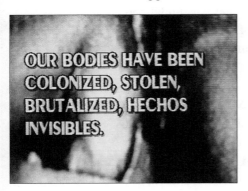

As I perceive movement, I am placed on a historical axis understanding the Latino migration to the United States as it is conditioned by the foreign policy of this country, and also by the military occupation of Mexican territories by the U.S. in 1848 and Puerto Rico in 1898. As an Arab descendent I have a socio-historical understanding of the conditions of the Palestinian living under occupied territory. It is the Arab/Palestinian situation which becomes a metaphor allowing me to understand what really happened to the southwest of this country, still occupied by the U.S. military. When I move on this historical axis, I see myself involved in an exile which is more than 150 years old, and which connects the Caribbean island where I was born with this country. It is through that connection that I also see my African self connected to a history of slavery and colonization.

MESTIZAIE AND THE MULTIPLE VISIONS

The obsessiveness with which Western culture engages in the notion of authenticity to maintain its colonial fantasy about the "other" has obligated me to confront exile and its relationship to colonialism and nationalism. According to the notion of authenticity, I am not an authentic Cuban. Exile has displaced me from the geographical territory called Cuba, and I am a Cuban living in the United States. From my position, the issue of nation intercepts with my exile to begin a critical discourse about my nationality.

The exile made me interrogate my whole identity. I discovered that I was not fixed in just one site, and neither were the audiovisual representations I produce. Then, as I was reinventing myself, re-constructing my history, I understood that my identity was a traveling

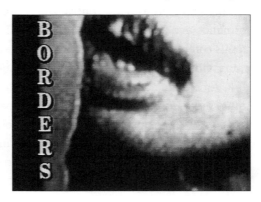

concept. The pluralities of my identities move me from being a Latino living in the United states to a Cuban in the exile, to a Carib-bean, to an Afro-Cuban, to an Arab descendent, to an Afro-Arab-Caribbean Latino Gay male, to an immigrant, to a working class Cuban in the exile, and so on. The shifting of my individual identities is always related to my plural identities and to the way my subjectivity travels across the territories where my diasporic selves intercept, clash, juxtapose, collide, super-impose and confront themselves breaking boundaries, rupturing territories, mapping new locations.

INTERNAL RUPTURE: MEMORY, NARRATIVE, MOVEMENT, LANGUAGE, SPACE, AND THE IMMIGRANT/EXILE SELF

Exile and migration forced me to remember and discover how my mind constructs a narrative around the image, the sound, the taste, or the smell that is remembered. The information stored in the subconscious is not complete. It does not have the same narrative qualities that an audiovisual text has. For me, the image I had in my mind is a signifier that needs to be associated with other images in order for me to understand the origin of the memory.

Is memory an artificial narrative construction that emerges as a product of my learnings? Within an audiovisual text, when two images are placed next to each other the framing of the image creates its borders. The space outside those borders is similar to the psychological space of the immigrant. Is this the dark space located just between the two images, or between the image and the viewer, or behind the viewer, or inside the viewer's head? And is this space similar, metaphorically, to the psychological space of the immigrant/ exile?

Opposite and above: stills from **Cities of Lust**, 1993.

My memory was displaced from its center by my political exile. In fact the sense of displacement I experienced after migrating to the United States was similar to the displacement I felt when I was outcast from my family. Then displacement became an important linguistic referent in my discourse. I continue to be displaced from the "center" of the U.S. society into its margins. But as I become aware of my displacement I move to the centers of my diasporas to decentralize the power that displaces me in the first place. Although I recognized my displacement, I do not like to be displaced because of my cultural identity, my skin color, my class background, or my sexual orientation. In fact the construction of this essay is a movement in opposition to the oppressive forces of the society. I do not want to displace that center, but I want my "marginal" position, my traveling mestizo culture and sexuality, to be recognized as the centers of my existence. I also do not want to move to the "center" because that will imply assimilation into the forces of the center, needing then to duplicate the center's oppressive forces.

As an exile/immigrant artist my work travels through an imaginary landscape where the diasporas I belong intercept. Understanding that the traveling is provoked by a forced exile, the production of my work constructs an imaginary history which brings the broken space, the rupture of the exile into a territory where I confront not only the exile, but also displacement, marginalization, and the activation of my diasporic self/selves.

THE HYBRID AUDIO-VISUAL DISCOURSE

I wanted to produce a history of my exile in a way in which it will seem "authentic," but in a fictitious way. How do you express hybridity through representation when the dominant discourse has already given static meaning to audio/visual images such as fiction and documentary? I was not going to be trapped, colonized by Western eurocentric linear and binary notions.

In this process I have produced three audio/visual texts that represent my personal investigation of these issues. *We Are Hablando(* 1991), *Ebbo For Elegua(* 1992), and *Cities of Lust(* 1993) create a trilogy that present my problematic as an exile/immigrant artist.

We Are Hablando was produced as a response to the historical moment in which I was living. The issues of censorship, that since 1989 were a heated debate in the art world, made me investigate the different aspects of censorship presented in the Latino diaspora. The video was made during the Gulf War, a period where my Arab self was activated also by this historical context. Deep Dish TV was organizing a series on censorship where I participated as a contributing producer in a program called *Vibrant Voices*.

When I talk about performance in *We Are Hablando*, I take into consideration the modes of addresses included in the text. The interviews, for example, were not pre-planned and took place after one or two conversations. The story, which appeared in the titles — white letters on black background — was constructed in the editing room as I was editing the tape. The TV footage I inserted in the piece was taken from the Spanish television which at the moment was constructing its own performance around the Gulf War.

The voice inscribed in the written story brings the oral tradition of the people of the Caribbean into a new form. Language is an interesting part of this story because the way in which it was produced presents a certain educational and class positions towards language. The immigrant/exile do not always speak and write perfect English. Here this narrative level focuses on this particular issue, reflecting back to the issue of censorship and the denial of a transformative language emerging from a socio-economic, cultural, and historical subject. A lot of times I have been censored for not speaking "proper" English.

When making *Ebbo For Elegua*, I began to research the Cuban exile. I ran across an article in *Areito* — a magazine published by the Antonio Maceo Brigade, about the Cuban children that were sent to the United States alone when they were seven and eight years old. In a conversation with Nereyda Garcia-Ferraz, I learn that the late Ana Mendieta and her sister were sent to an orphanage in Dubuque, Iowa when she was eight years old. Her parents didn't leave Cuba until she was fifteen. I have been displaced from my family for being gay since I was twelve. How could I put all these elements together into a video?

Still from **Ebbo For Elegua**, 1992.

I developed a character whose history was a mixing of my personal experience and the research I did. I found an actor that was able to understand the character, although he is a Chicano and not a Cuban. During the research I also started constructing my Caribbean identity. Working around the issue of exile has obligated me to deconstruct the notion of nationalism that was displacing me as a Cuban. In order to access the Cuban space, the Caribbean became a larger geographical context as my place of origin.

Since I started making films and videos I have developed a directing style which allows the actors to perform, not to "act" in my works. The script I wrote is used only as a point of departure for the formation of the character. Always taking into consideration the creative process of the actors, I had several meetings with the actor until I realized he knew the character. Then I interviewed him as if he were the real person. I finally broke that notion of fiction and documentary that was oppressing my creative process.

I intercut the interview with a performance where I paint my body, symbolizing the sites of my African identity. The video is divided in five parts: memory, internal exile, migration, family, and desire. The images were juxtaposed to emphasize the multiple visions of the Latino-African-Arab, the bilingual self, the pan-sexual self, and the diasporic cultural self. The production of my historical representation ends up being a myth where my plural identities become nomads.

Ebbo For Elegua was produced to question authenticity and to state that what we see cannot be taken as literal. The articulation of the audiovisual text takes place at different levels. The surface, the audiovisual image presented by the latino artist is a revolving mirror door which gives access to the symbolic, metaphoric, and poetical connections that take place on territories where I, as subject, enunciate the plurality of my identities.

When constructing *Cities of Lust (1993)* I found that already the notion of performance, inscribed in my earlier videos, was taking a more solid shape. At the beginning, I only knew that I wanted to make a video about my perception of male desire, but I didn't want to create a script. The notion of performance so intrinsic to the Caribbean identity took over the process since the beginning. I started viewing the present, my surroundings, and the males I contacted to access the narrative of the video. I found out that the men I ask to be in the video spoke about themselves and what they felt, which was not always specifically about what I asked them.

Still from
Resistencia,
1992.

In all the scenes the actors were aware of the presence of the camera. The majority of the images were constructed on the spot for the camera, while others were part of an experience that was taking place in which the camera was an accessory to the scene: scenes at the dinner table, and the airport. The interviews also fall in this latter category of performance. The interviewees became conscious that what was said was being performed for the camera.

Traveling is another way in which *Cities of Lust* unfolds as a Caribbean text. I shot in Havana, Los Angeles, San Francisco, Merida, Iowa City, and Chicago during a period of over a year. In all these places I found asymmetrical positions that at certain points were connecting to the narrative axis. My relationship with African American gay men in the United States has made me look at my long time Afro-Cuban friends through a new prism, taking our friendship to a new level. The notion of the diaspora allowed me to connect these two issues, nations and people, within the text, without explaining at the surface the underlying connection.

Time in *Cities of Lust* is a subjective time that never moves in one specific direction due to its own internal discourse. I didn't want to locate the audience in these specific cities during the viewing of the video because then the traveling would be too specific. These shots have elements that are paradoxical among themselves and take the narrative to another location.

As a displaced exile/immigrant Cuban, I attempt to reconstruct, in audiovisual terms, the underlying unity of my exile and my mestizo culture to provoke social transformation. I have resisted the notion of authenticity and chronological history. I have produced, and re-invented an organic experimental history that encompass the notion of territory where my plural identities travel trading metaphors and concepts, engaging in a subjective dialogue.

ACKNOWLEDGEMENTS:

The issue of representation in *Cities of Lust* as well as in the other two videos, is rendered by the communities to which I belong and the locations of these communities. My friendship with Cuban American artist Roly Chang Barrerro, Chicano videomaker Joe Castel, and Mexican American Film theoretician Roberto Rodriguez, was the underlying factor in the textual construction of *We Are Habalando*. It connected us with global issues such as censorship and war because, in our internal social dynamics, those were issues that were brought to our conversations during that historical period.

Cities of Lust was possible because of my communities. My friendships with Joe Castel, Thomas Allen Harris, Alfonzo Moret, Mauro Burgos, Karl Bruce Knaper, Jose Antonio Lozada, Domingo Montejo, and Orlando Diaz, were intrinsic in the rendering of the narrative. I have access to personal information because of the trust established within my communities and the long hours we have spent together doing our own internal processing.

Sharing equipment and material was also important in the production of this work. Joe Castel and Thomas Allen Harris provided images for my work and here the notion of authorship has transgressed its individualistic position, placing itself in the territories of my diasporas. Furthermore these video have been produced by the Latino Midwest Video Collective, a group formed in 1986 by various Latinos media artists living in the United States and Latin America.

This article was written with partial support from the Lyn Blumenthal Memorial Fund for Independent Video.

1. Gloria Anzaldua, *Borderlands: La Frontera*, San Fransisco, CA, aunt lute books, 1987.
2. *Donde yo nací, donde me crié,* song by Pablo Milanes
3. Coco Fusco, *Diario de Miranda*, London, *Third Text*, Fall, 1992
4. Antonio Benitez-Rojo, *La Isla Se Repite (The Repeating Island)*, Durham and London, Duke University Press, 1992.

The Sublime Object of Home

by Yau Ching

DEAREST YOU,

An exile's dream/trauma is that home is elsewhere. An artist-exile's dream is that her audience is elsewhere. There is always this "other" place to desire, to mirror your self-image, your fantasies, where you will "belong." Yet, one of the processes of colonization is to teach the colonized that they do not belong. The colonized deals with a perpetual embarrassment that she does not know what her nationality is (I never know how to fill those forms after some twenty years of existence). If the process of colonization constructs me, it also constructs "me" as an exile whose subjectivity compulsively tricks me into believing that home is elsewhere, while simultaneously being traumatized by the awareness that home is but an illusion.

We know that female subjectivity has to experience a double split in order to enter the Symbolic Order. The girl not only has to, like the boy, die a little in order to speak, that is, to enter the world of signifiers, but she also has to be in "drag," to claim the presence of a male voice in order to be heard. It may be true that once the subaltern speaks, she is not the subaltern any more. What I am more concerned about is: what are the processes involved in order to gain, or shall I say, construct that voice? What is being transformed when she moves from silence to speech, and what is forced to be lost in that transformation?

For a lesbian of color exiled in a straight-white-dominated society, for example, the experience of the fragmentation of subjectivity is multi-layered. In order for me to have a "voice," to realize a social presence, I not only have to be in drag as a man, but also have to be able to dress up for different occasions as white, as heterosexual, as Asian, as Oriental, as American (in Hong Kong where I grew up, I was very used to acting *as if* I was British), as the representative of the people of color, or a combination of any of the above.

Of course, the mere reflection of my presence in the faces of others would always remind that I am never, or never fully, any of the above. (The colonized's existential dilemma is to define her own image always in terms of the colonizer's but she is also forced to believe that she can never *really* be there. This is why mainstream representations of lesbians always foreground their mannishness but also constantly remind you that they are not *the real thing*.)

My voice, and more so, its flexibility, constantly embarrasses me. And you know, it is the realization of the gaps between the *you*'s you struggle to be, and the *you*'s you are being otherized as, that is unbearable. The more you fight to hide those gaps, to distance yourself from your otherness, the bigger the gaps and the pain. (You would say: "You have a British accent, but you are not *exactly* British." Worse still, I used to feel flattered by comments like this). But I cannot speak otherwise. Otherwise you won't hear me. (I am cute, therefore I am.) The (always already) westernized non-Western subject is a contradictory predicament to begin with. My subjectivity is necessarily as fragmented as my hard disk in order to be in working condition. (Now that I'm coming to terms with my multiplicity of selves by trying to articulate the processes of their construction, I am also negotiating the differences among them, and the pain. Does this cause further fragmentation? O well, you know this all will change in the next minute when I say something else. Will it really?)

Of course you know that even the he, the straight, the Brit, the white is bound to "perform" in order to enter the realm of discourse, and to project an illusion of consistent subjectivity. But the point is: the historical experiences of people from multiple margins produce the kinds of psychological upheavals different from the kinds of alienation experienced by the "center," which, as we know, struggles to hide its queerness. In other words, it is important to differentiate the queerness of the straight from the queerness of the queer (and accordingly, the queerness of the queer from that of the multiple queer, i.e. a subject split on multiple levels, not only in terms of sexuality and gender, but also race, skin color, language, class, physical conditions, and so on; a space where multiple margins converge), and to understand how that differentiation is constructed by historical determinants founded on negotiations, coercion, and often times slaughter. (The punishment for homosexuality in Mainland China as of 1994 is electroshock.) The theory of performativity has to take into account different levels, different kinds and different combinations of performativity in terms of different relations of power — and especially how they reinforce or counterbalance each other — in order to help us more fully understand the hegemony and violations of our histories.

While the colonizer conquers unknown vistas to expand his collections at home, or, travels afar just to confirm his civilization, he also robs the colonized the possibility of psychological stability, of "being home," and triggers within/among the colonized this unending process of home-searching. In other words, the colonizer's travels in the seven seas directly produce the colonized's apparently similar, but essentially reversed, travels in the seven seas. Diaspora, then, is a product as well as a reversal of colonialism.

The history of Euro-American imperialism has left us with a world where modernization means westernization. To critique the violations of imperialism and to decenter the West is not the same as to ignore the historical fact of global westernization, and fantasize the "native" and "uncontaminated" modes in non-western cultures, or non-western peoples living in western societies. In a recent exhibition at the New Museum of Contemporary Art in New York featuring two Chinese expatriate artists, the newspaper ashes in Chen Zhen's *The Field of Waste* are immediately read by Senior Curator France Morin (who organized the exhibition) as a signifier for *absolute* cultural difference:

> The work enshrines an ancient holistic view of reality in which matter and
> spirit, 'nature,' humankind, and manufactured objects exist in a constantly
> recycling continuum. Indeed, in Taoist thought, burning and the resultant ashes
> are not symbolic of death, as they are in the West, but of purification
> and transformation. (All quotations are from the programming essay on the
> exhibition flyer distributed in the Museum).

Where exactly in the work are these ideas of "recycling," "purification," and/or "transformation" suggested? How does the pile of ashes of *New York Times* and Chinese newspapers lead us to the above readings? Does the biographical data that the artist is from China (though currently living in Paris) neccessarily mean that he must know Dao, and not "western" signifiers, and must use Dao and not "western" signifiers to speak? Since the practice of the Daoist religion and the discourse of the Daoist philosophy have been politically banned, condemned as "pessimistic," useless thoughts, and were practically unavailable in China for some thirty years, what kind of a historical transgression is the migrant artist making if he is really foregrounding Daoist-Buddhist thinking in his works (as in another work by Chen Zhen called *"A world" in/out of the world*)? Why are ancient Chinese texts written more than 2000 years ago, such as *I Ching* and *Tao Te Ching*, mentioned all the time in the discussion of contemporary Chinese artists, without considering the historical specificities of either the texts or the artists?

The binary oppositions of "nature" versus "artifact," "tradition" versus "progress," form versus content, and intrinsically, the East versus the West underline the whole curatorial perspective. Morin says that the works were positioned "according to the principle of the Chinese chessboard." With the many different kinds of (Chinese) chess I have played (for example, the popular Game of the "Elephant/Minister", or the "National Essence" — the Game of "Surround," known in the West as the Game of "Go," not to mention other, more provincial kinds of chess or forms of playing that I do not know of), I am lost as to which she is speaking. She describes it as:

> Each of the two 'players' has his own long narrow space within the
> rectangular space of the Museum with the central space shared by both —
> opponents and collaborators in the same game, a game renowned for
> its use of strategy.

I am even more confused. Wouldn't this be appropriate to describe Western chess as well? In fact, the only Chinese chess I know that has a layout such as this would be the "Elephant/Minister" (the two words are pronounced similarly in Chinese, and they are used as interchangeable puns in the game), which looks and plays quite similarly to Western chess.

> In this particular chess game the visitors become the pieces. Going
> through the works they are positioned and strategically directed in a taolike
> path, the path one must follow to be in harmony with the natural order.

Apart from the fact that the positioning of the installations does not show any special characteristics of a so-called Chinese chess game, Morin also does not make an effort to explain how a Chinese chessboard can *naturally* lead to a "taoist path?" (Like all westerners who are renowned for their aggressiveness, when I play chess, whether it is Chinese or not, I only think of winning. How about you?) This so-called "path (that) one must follow to be in harmony with the natural order" is drawn *in spite of* the work. What kinds of qualities is the western curator presupposing and promoting in the (westernized) non-western artist's works, and what information and analysis are being systematically left out? (Would we **look for** the influence of Shakespeare in any of the contemporary British artists' works who happen to come our way? Or, should an Anglo artist cite the teachings of Plato as his most positive creative influence, what would you think of him?) How can a (westernized) non-western artist ever realize a voice of her own in the face of this kind of contextualization which claims to speak *for* her in the name of "tradition?" What is the unspoken assignment for the non-white artist in the current trends of "identity politics?" Like the subaltern who is spoken of before she can speak, the work of the non-white artist today is made before she makes it. Finally, what sort of space would this kind of judgment, criteria and paradigm of interpretation leave a non-western artist who chooses to be honest of her being "westernized" and decides to create **out of** that predicament? Isn't the exclusion of the westernized, ethnic subject exactly the foundation on which the West constructs its patterns of domination and hegemony?

I'm sure you will notice that the representational issues raised by a show like this is nothing new or special. In fact, cases like this create the day-to-day living conditions for the diasporic, ethnic subject in the West. (What is more horrible is that events like this push me to choose between silence, meaning complicity, and being the native informant, in which case perpetuating the role imposed on me to educate the westerner about "my native culture." In other words, acting as "the cultural broker." Here I go again...)

But once I suddenly had an idea about whether Mao had to go to the toilet or not.

Still from
Flow, 1993, by
Yau Ching.

Have you seen, for example, *The Little Buddha*? I saw it with two friends of mine, both of whom are immigrants from Hong Kong. Literally sitting close enough to, say, "confront" the screen, for two and a half hours we found ourselves in a ridiculously vulnerable, constantly frustrated, but ready-to-crack-up-any-minute kind of situation. The Eurocentric Western representation of Asian cultures again manifests itself as highly ironic to the ethnic spectator. How much is Bertolucci aware of the problematic of using an actor like Ying Ruo Cheng, a renowned theater director and lead actor of The Beijing People's Art Academy, to play the main character of a Tibeten Monk, Lama Norbu? It seems like Bertolucci is attempting to introduce Buddhism into "the Western world" and convey his vision that religion — in this case, Buddhism — can transcend cultural and biological differences. But it is exactly his presumption that cultural differences can be transcended before it is even understood and dealt with that makes his interpretation of Buddhism simplistic and naive.

Buddhists all over the world today, including Tibet, Hong Kong or New York, still insist in using Sanskrit, the ancient Indian language, or at least the sound of Sanskrit in chanting and praying at the expense of limiting the accessibility of the religion or running the risk of giving up the signifiability of language altogether in the belief that translation produces misrecognition. Representing a religion that fundamentally distrusts language, and its translatability, Bertulocci ironically translates every Sanskrit chant in the film into English, and at some point even has the monk chant in English on camera. (The chant "emptiness is form; form is emptiness" is a perfect example. In the original chant, the word "form," which tends to mean "appearances," is also a pun to "desires," which is lost in Bertolucci's translation.)

It is through avoiding the problematics of translation and cultural differences that the cinematic logic can give the white boy and his yuppie father *full* access to the Tibetan Buddhist world, that Jesse can play with the two other**ed** kids *without any problem*, and the white-identified audience following these two white males' footsteps would also have access to this world *without any problem*. While the film stresses the *absolute* difference of the West versus the East, of blue versus gold, of technology versus religion, it also provides an entirely unproblematized, and in fact very much **desired** (by the narrative and more importantly, by the "natives" themselves) intrusion of the Westerner into the Orient. The main plot of the film — however outrageous it may sound — is the Tibeten monks' desiring to host the white boy in their nativeland so as to adore him. How much have we really "progressed" from the age of Marco Polo? The Western Self fantasizes to be desired by the Other — the absolute different — and after invading and owning the Other, he, through his monopoly of the language, represents the Other's desire to justify his invasion.

HEY GIRL!

Sorry for the argument yesterday. I didn't mean to be mad at you. I hope it is clear that I, on the one hand, cannot accept current essentialist politics, which boringly fixate all of us, while on the other, reject the historical efforts of sinologists and their like of nativising non-Western subjects. It is a delicate balance to strike in our social climate. As far as making work and fundraising/survival are concerned, it is especially tempting to try to please either, or even better, both sides.

No matter what - STOP SAYING I'M AUTHENTIC!

Yes, I confess, one of the dilemmas facing an exiled artist is that she has too many audiences to please. (You're right — I'm just a goddamn opportunist!) It is like living in a room with mirrors from all sides. *Flow*, which was fabricated from the memories of a Chinese woman artist who grew up during the Cultural Revolution, was criticized in some screenings in North America and in Europe for not providing enough "historical facts," or INFORMATION on the period. I made the choice I made because part of the reason for making the tape was to give voice to some suppressed positionalities, and foreground the violence produced by the process of achieving historical hegemony in the context of contemporary Chinese and American history with which her life intersects. However, as a "native" in the Western world, I am expected to provide information about "my home," and not to offer a counter-discourse or metadiscourse on information available on my home and elsewhere. (I may not be a subaltern any more since I am priviliged enough to make a video, but I am still a subaltern in terms of what I am "designated" to say.)

I recently showed *Flow* to some friends of mine from Hong Kong. They were uncomfortable with the opening lion-dancing sequence and my use of a poem from *The Book of Poetry*. They said they found it exotic. I tried to point out that I was trying to use visual effects, sound effects and repetition in those scenes to introduce another kind of emotion and intervention into this worn-out symbol —yes — of our culture instead of just for the sake of providing visual pleasure (which was also abundant). They were not convinced... I began to doubt myself. Clearly it is very hard to de-exoticize traditional Orientalist symbols, and this is a burden that anyone who wants to produce representations of non-western worlds has to bear. The steps of an exile are harder to overcome because she is constantly torn between the western expectation of representing the "Other" worlds the way they have been represented in the West and the fellow-natives' demands of seeing their world as they see it themselves. This in-betweenness constitutes the impossibility of home, as well as the perpetual homesickness that cannot be fulfilled. Given the unavoidable fact that the tape speaks of where I am, lion-dancing is definitely a more important part of my life living on the edge of New York's Chinatown than living in Hong Kong.

Now we come to our favorite subject, our sweet, sweet home. I don't believe there can ever be one. Even in moments when I need a security blanket (O more than you know!), I would rather cling onto Andrei Codrescu's notion of exile, where an exile travels with this piece of something called exile, lives there and calls it his home. For someone like me who does not particularly believe in language, I do not mind calling diaspora my home, particularly because the contradiction is apparent enough. I know you hate the word. Me too. But what is more important is to stress the reality of our post-colonial, post-imperialist world where diaspora is a given-in-progress, where there is no home, and strategically speaking, there has never been. Then maybe we can use it as a tactic of political intervention to criticize both the western modernist notion of universality (WE ARE THE WORLD!) and the orientalist-essentialist fixation on authenticity. To say that there is a third world (or, more than one) within every first world is also to say that people in our world today are living in different degrees and forms of diaspora. That said, again, it is important to demarcate the kind of diaspora lived by a, say, fair-skinned Frenchman in New York, from that which is lived by someone like me, and that which is lived by someone in, say, China, where the representation (which we know, actively constructs identity) of diaspora is a political taboo. I hope we can then more fully understand our privilege *and* trauma of being westernized *and* in the West, as the compulsory spectator of the "Orient," in comparison to people who are doubly traumatized of being westernized and being our silenced spectacle in the Orient. To coin westernization as a trauma is not to glorify any pre-westernized pastoral fantasy, which only completes western hegemony. But let's leave it at that (when speaking of diaspora becomes a compulsive behavior).

You know, I too want to do "direct cinema," but how can I? How can I believe and then try to also lead the audience to believe that I can "convey" this woman's experiences to you without the mediation of my subjectivity? Doesn't the fact that it needs someone like me to be the essential mediator/translator tell you something about this woman's predicament? Don't you think the things I can/would translate and those I can't/wouldn't, the things I add into her stories, my (mis)appropriation of historical materials (for example, footage which does not correlate to the historical period narrated by the voiceover), and how much you can read all of the above, tell you something about "her," about "me," about "you," and most of all, about the relations of power among "us?" How can I tell you her stories without addressing these relations, when it is exactly these relations that define the possibilities of her histories? If one of the greatest achievements of the recent history of American documentary is its allignment with anti-hegemonic power (which I believe it is), then I think I am continuing that tradition. It is only that our views of how hegemony is constructed have changed. To represent (purely) a fetishized automaton called "the third world woman and her sufferings" is no longer an effective means of political intervention. We should now understand that representations on that level would only perpetuate the existing world order. (The fruitful development of American "experimental documentary" in the '80s and the '90s is obviously a historical neccessity rather than a coincidence or a "trend.")

Yes, my commitment to form, just like many other things, lends itself to different readings. You said it might have something to do with diaspora, but you were not sure how. Today, while I was trying to dig out some video stills in my extremely messy apartment, I formulated this theory: the positions available to a contemporary exile are very similar to those of a (dehistoricised) lover: *I am convinced that the well-constructed love story, with a beginning, an end, and a crisis in the middle, is the way society hopes to be reconciled with the language of the Other by constructing his own narrative, in which he plays a role. I feel that the unhappy lover is not even able to benefit from this reconciliation, and that he is not, paradoxically, within a love story; he is in something else that closely resembles madness... and the story is simply impossible from the lover's point of view.* (Yes, it is Barthes but I don't want you to look it up so that you can check how much I **mis**quoted it.)

I have tried hard to tell you stories in my letters, like those stories my mother used to tell me when I was small, weak in bed, and struggling to get my blood circulation going. Simple stories, like this one: there was a boy by the name of "Elephant," who kept a pet snake. Elephant was too poor to feed his mother, so Snake offered to cut some of his meat for them to make

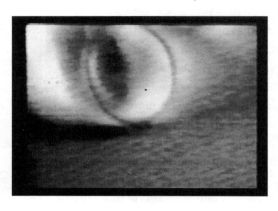

Still from **Video Letters**, 1993, by **Yau Ching**.

broth. Elephant accepted the idea but soon they ran out of food again. Snake offered them his gall. It made a delicious meal for Elephant's mother. But soon they ran out of food again. This time Elephant thought of Snake's heart. Snake found it out and swallowed Elephant instead. Then comes the Proverb: human heart knows not content; Snake swallows Elephant. (American stories need punchlines; Chinese stories need proverbs). This one is to preach against greediness. At the age of five, I was terrified by this narrative. Now I believe it was the first love story I heard. Notice how Snake breaks his heart because he cannot give up his heart. I too want to tell love stories. When you are on the road, and you do not have a lot of tools, it is very tempting to tell (tiny bits of) love stories, stories of desire — the deep desire to connect but never quite be there. That was how *Video Letters* came about (I think).

Yet, it just won't work. I cannot envision a story with a coherent plot and with *you* and you and me in it. (Rey Chow: "An obsession with the unification of China in *all* respects is what gives rise to the Chinese as an 'imagined community' in the twentieth century." This obsession with an however illusive unity and the violations it produces constitutes my obsession with digressions, fragmentation and independence.) Stories of desires are fragments of contradictions. When I say "desire" in my video, you know, it is desire and it is not. You desire whiteness and you do not. (Ian Rashid's book: *Black Markets, White Boyfriends*.) What else can I do besides embracing contradictions? Are videos, like what we like to believe, afterthoughts, or are they the surplus of thoughts? When I put myself in it, is it me or is it not? The only language of the self accessible to the self must be a split and incoherent one; one that is beside the self, and surpasses the self. (There is something very Zen about this, but I got it through some French post-structuralist, I think.)

If I ever understand art, I would have to say it is very much about losses. Art seeks transformations out of losses. But art is also the medium that creates losses. I cannot create signifiers except at the price of vast losses. When I put myself on screen, when I manipulated my image in jog, shuttle, or still, I felt I was dealing with a vulnerability that looked like a lover's position in our society today. (Not only that. She is also a dyke but does not tell coming out stories or have hot sex on screen, is colored but is not black, wears large specs, has a huge mole near her mouth and so on.) A position unclaimable. A position that won't get you into any film festivals, gay and lesbian ones, in particular. A marginal being that isn't even allowed within fashionable marginality.

Maybe that is why I have often used quotes in my videos and films. Maybe that is why I love special effects. (Here she goes again — intellectualizing her obsession with things pretty.) Visual manipulations and language protect the image. Why do I need so much protection anyway? It is true that I cannot stand seeing a bare self reflected back to me. It is also true that the comforts and linearity implicated in realism only make me more uncomfortable. I do not occupy a position stable and privileged enough to sit back and relax and pretend not to see form. For someone constantly experiencing flux, nothing, including form, can be taken for granted. Growing up in a colony means you are deprived of having a national cinema, a film genre or a television show (from Spaghetti Westerns to French New Wave to Star Trek) to grow emotionally akin to, to call it one's "tradition." The lack of nationhood translates into the quest for alternative narrativity.

When I chose to live in diaspora, I understood that I was also choosing a western privilege of reflexive mobility which is (becoming increasingly) impossible where I came from. I think a French gay writer once said, I love you so that I want to live in you. This affirmation of selfhood by giving up one's own body and inhabiting the other's is unimaginable in the historical context of Chinese totalitarianism. When there is no space for privately transgressive acts, art becomes impossible. While (Continued on page 325)

Spokesperson from Mainland China Lu Ping told Hong Kong People: "So?! Let me alienate you democrats!", *Comics from the Transitional Period '91-'92*, Hong Kong.

Family Secrets

A Dialogue between Sandi Dubowski (Tomboychik) and Mindy Faber (Delirium)

TRANSCRIPTION FROM PHONE CONVERSATION

SANDI: I think these two tapes work well with each other.

MINDY: Yeah I think they work well too. Many times there is this arrogance that film and videomakers have that you're the master of your material and you're in control, and controlling every bit of this information that you are presenting to people, and that the videomaker is the one with the intellectual capacity to read the subject. And what happened in *Delirium* was the power and authority of the director or, in this case, the daughter, is subverted in this one moment where the subject, my mom, demands the camera and turns the lens and the questions back on me. And in your tape you set that up from the very beginning. I think for many viewers it is very disarming for the director to announce from the beginning that he is willing to relinquish power and control and give the subject the power, even symbolically, to read or interpret her own life, even if that means shaky camera movements and low lit, unfocused shots. But for me this happened because my mom made it happen, and I in fact ended up asking for the camera back where you set up *Tomboychik* from the very beginning by giving your grandmother the camera. I wonder how conscious you were of this while you were making it because it seems to have this anti-polish or anti-mastered quality.

SANDI: It really just started out without me having very much technical training or equipment and being too impatient to wait to get it before I made a work. But I wasn't making a work. I was just making this home video with my grandmother. It just started out as this chronicle of my family history, but when that family history started surprising me, it became a video. Because I had no idea what was going to come out of my grandmother's mouth — we had the traditional grandchild/grandmother relationship. I never knew that she thought of her gender in that way.

MINDY: Oh you didn't?

SANDI: No, no idea.

MINDY: But, why were the wigs there?

SANDI: Well it seems like it was shot in a day — like it was just a trip to Grandma's. But it was shot over six months. So when she started telling me this history of her life and how she used to fight like a boy and push the boys into a puddle if they tried to get too fresh with her, it stirred my fantasies about having this completely queerified family — this gender-bending family. So, I started pushing it further by bringing the wigs and also playing with my own gender with her. I couldn't really come out and say it — the words 'gay man' had no meaning for her. The wigs were just a way for us to have the queerest relationship together. And she loved it because she was so performative.

MINDY: Yeah, I know what you're talking about. When you watch *Tomboy-chik* at the end there is a desire, at least on my part, for you to come out to her and to push it further. But I think you are coming out as who you are in a way that only makes sense within your particular relationship through the process of making that tape. I understand this because the ways in which I first started working with my mom developed as a way of communicating which I couldn't do unless the camera was on. There is something about family life that is so coded and pre-determined and the thought of actually talking to her about how I felt was impossible. But when the camera entered the picture and I took on the role of setting up scenes and she became the actress, then this whole other kind of dynamic was made possible that allowed for communication, collaboration and dialogue. And it wouldn't have happened necessarily if the camera wasn't on.

SANDI: Because it is so true with your mom that she is such a savvy performer. She is so camera sharp and my grandmother wasn't.

MINDY: Oh I don't know — I think she is camera sharp, actually. I think to you she is your grandmother, but to other people she's a charmer. And I think she is performing to a certain extent. Also remember that you may have worked six months with your grandmother but I started working with my mom in photographs and videos when I was a teenager, and she has gone from being inhibited in front of the camera to being very performative. This was a process, because the more we worked together the more she wanted to collaborate, and it shouldn't have surprised me that she would finally seize control of the camera after my constant probing about why she took everything out on me during my childhood. It was a logical step or a natural progression for her to do that. Because the fact is that she was being scrutinized by me armed with the camera, and her ability to finally break through that power relationship was born out of a

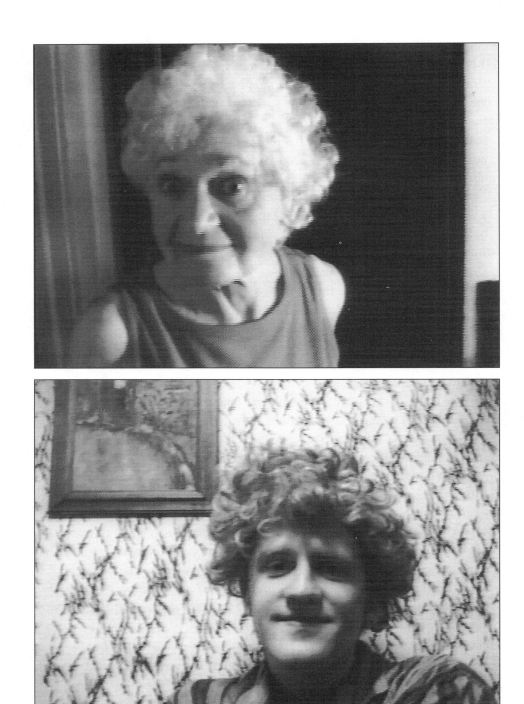

Stills from **Tomboychik**, 1993,
by **Sandi Dubowski**.

Stills from **Delirium**, 1993,
by **Mindy Faber.**

long process of becoming familiar and comfortable. But you do it so instantaneously.

SANDI: But I do it instantaneously in the editing, because I did have an agenda. I don't want this to be a portrait of a pathetic old woman. I wanted her to have power from the start.

MINDY: There is something else that is interesting to me — the fact that within the current field of media art and specifically within the area of queer media which has been very active for a long time now, *Tomboychik* still stands out as something very unique, because while there is a great deal of gay/lesbian work addressing the body and sexuality, there is very little work about family sexual history.

SANDI: For me the tape comes from living away from New York for four years and coming back to my neighborhood and my family now as a gay person. When I left four years before, I was straight. And upon my return I felt a need to queerify those institutions and those things that were rampantly hetereosexual. I'm so tired of the gay agenda these days and I just have no need for it.

MINDY: What is the gay agenda?

SANDI: Peter Friedman and I were speaking about the different generations in gay media. He felt that his generation was about creating a gay ghetto, while I felt the edge now is about leaving that gay ghetto and coming back to our communities and meshing our gay and lesbian sexuality with all the other identities that intersect it. My grandmother and I are Brooklyn boygirls, born and bred.

{A break in tape occurs here}

MINDY: Somehow I think that there are these very strict gender roles that our society defines as normal. And the more strict we are about these gender roles, the more false and unhealthy it is because people's needs are not really being served by these falsely constructed definitions. But I do think we need to understand the social and political context of people's lives in order to understand why they make the choices they do, rather than naming and blaming and risking further polarization.

SANDI: There is this part in *Delirium* where you talk about your social memory instead of personal memory and it's interesting how you take your localized family situation and talk about it in terms of madness, hysteria and how patriarchy defines that.

MINDY: Right, because from the very outset of the tape I announce my impetus for making the work was my frustration and anger at the fact that my mother blamed herself for her illness. But as a child growing up in that situation, it was so clear to me that this was a societal issue. And yet we live in a society that is so focused on the individual. And mental illness especially is always defined as an individualized problem right down to your DNA and genes. And the political structure is left off the hook. So it was very important to me to make this link, because in my mind personal memory and social memory were in the same camp.

SANDI: I wanted to explore — and I think this is why *Tomboychik* is really different from other gay tapes that explicitly state "this is who we are" — I wanted to explore the ambiguity about what happens when you wind up returning to your neighborhood where things just aren't clear cut. And I just think of my grandmother and how she had this 19th century view of sexuality in which you could be butch/femme, drag king/queen, but as long as you married and reproduced you were normal. My grandmother even told me that she didn't think she was a woman until she gave birth to my father. It was those little moments of undefinability of identity politics which were most interesting to me, and that's why I didn't want to include any theory or any text and just wanted to leave our footage raw.

MINDY: There is a certain way in which you don't need to introduce theory because your grandmother speaks the theory. There is something to be said for theory being formulated from art, events and communications rather than art replicating theory itself. I need to have a sense of discovery in video as a maker and as a viewer where the political agenda is not wholly decided from the onset. And that is something about *Tomboychik* that is really wonderful because you are right there discovering on par with you and it is not overdetermined where that discovery will lead you.

SANDI: With *Delirium* it's the playfulness that keeps your tape from being dogmatic.

MINDY: Primarly in my mind was this desire to strike a balance between emotion and theory and try to achieve this delicate tension between serious critique and playful humor. I was very conscious of audience and not really willing to relinquish any audience, I guess. I have always wanted to be able to show my work to people like my mom, and most audiences do respond whether they are initiated into the language of video or feminism or not. It's the subject that sustains interest.

JULY 1, 1994

The End (of Phone Conversation) . . . .

To: Mindy Faber
From: Sandi DuBowski

DEAR MINDY,

Here are a few things that I had scrawled notes about, but didn't talk about in our impromptu interview — which was really great. I hope it came out on tape. There are also a few things I can't remember if we discussed, so maybe when I look at the transcript I may add some more if that's OK. Also included are some excerpts of more prose-y writing I had done after coming back to NY from visiting Nana in the hospital. Let me know if any of this is worth including. There was a course, at school— *The Work of a Work of Art*. Is our essay *The Home of A Home Video*?

I made *Tomboychik* under my parent's roof, behind their back, with their camera, and with their mother.

It had its New York premiere at *MIX*, The New York Lesbian and Gay Experimental Film/Video Festival, which was held at The Kitchen. After the screening, this 60ish year-old lesbian came up to me and said in a big Brooklyn accent, "Hi! I'm Ronnie. I knew your grandmother. I run a pesticide business. Here's my card." She went back to our coastal Brooklyn neighborhood and told everybody. On Yom Kippur, the holiest day of the Jewish year, at Temple Beth El, Dottie Schiff's grandson approached my parents and inquired, "So I hear Sandi made a film about your mother." (She had died a month before.) "Oh," my parents said, surprised. "It played at The Kitchen." My parents looked at each other and asked, "Whose kitchen?"

I hadn't been home for a few days. There were piles of tapes around, some reviews, evidence of emergency trips to the post office, but unless my parents snuck behind my back, they still haven't seen the tape. Independent media is not their world. The closest they came was when my father yanked my mother out of the theater after 10 minutes of *My Own Private Idaho* (probably because he got turned on by the blowjob scene).

But when the New York State Council of the Arts awarded *Tomboychik* a Media Distribution Grant, things in the household changed. For my parents, The Government had legitimized this work. The Government had proclaimed its blessed authority with a fat check. Despite the gay movement's "Marketing Moment!" and Christian Right propaganda (those two-person childless households making over $75,000 a year!), my parents associated homosexuality with downward mobility if not outright poverty. But then, I heard my Mom on the phone brag to a relative, "You know these young people today have things they want to say, messages they want to tell society."

If anything, the message of *Tomboychik* is oblique, ambiguous. Rather than being an academic project of reclaiming lost family sexual history, it's a chronicle of how Nana and I fell madly, fiercely in love over six months before she died, in all its wacky drag-esque gender-blending ways. Our relationship in its intimacy is central. Its small and poignant moments build into an intergenerational, queer message, rather than a message that dictates our moments.

The studio at 594 Broadway was an alternative home. The Airwaves Project — ShuLea, Rea, Ela, David, and Kathy helped me visualize an active media community and provided me with the editing resources and advice which made making videos possible. Rea's friend was editing at the studio on the same system I had edited *Tomboychik*. I had just showed her *Tomboychik* the night before. She fell in love with my grandmother, her wink, the purse of her lips, the beret cocked over one eye. I called my answering machine and got two messages from my aunt, with a very shaky voice, "Sandi call me at Nana's. Something terrible has happened." No one was home. I called every hospital in Brooklyn. An hour later, my aunt arrived back after a long walk around the block. Nana had died. Five blocks away from my house, for five days, my aunt had watched her die, projectile vomiting on the wall, bleeding, unable to eat. She didn't call me because she wanted to protect me. I didn't get a chance to say goodbye. I was ensconced in my new home, one hour by D train away, with Nana trapped in a visual coffin. Eject, Rewind, Play. Eject, Rewind, Play. I'd avoided visiting for awhile. I was so busy editing, I said, but really I was scared of facing the truth of the hey hey girl's decline, and her eventual end. I was superstitious. I thought I caused her death by stealing her image and taking it into the borough she hadn't stepped foot into in 7 1/2 years. We had shot from September to January. In February, she had her first stroke, lost her memory and slurred her speech. In July, she died. Now I think *Tomboychik* is a living memorial and await the day when Nana and I will meet in some Jew heaven. She hasn't seen the entire tape, only the sections I showed her in the film, so I don't know if she'll press her lips to my neck for ten seconds and call me "loverboy," or call me a "good for nothing tramp."

I don't know why I grieve, bent over into the ground. It's not like she's there. For a time, I imagined she hid in my belly button, maybe curled in stray lint. On the day before the funeral my mother noticed a red spot on the ceiling in the family room. Aunt Miriam, Nana's sister, was lying on the couch, her position of the past 40 years, a schnorrer on a divan, expecting to be served. Mom got a sponge mop and I got a stepstool. But I claimed the spot was Nana clinging to the ceiling, the red of her blood refusing to leave the room. Mom snapped, "That's crazy," and Aunt Miriam just lay there weary for no reason. I climbed the stepstool to examine the mark and tried to fight Mom and the mop from wiping it away. I grabbed the handle and caused a smear of dirt, but at least prevented her total disappearance. Nan clung like a bug, or a bat, through the shiva period, watching her family gathered around her, even if she was 1/1000 of her original size.

Sandi

Nana, **Tomboychik**, 1993, by Sandi DuBowski

To: Sandi DuBowski
From: Mindy Faber, Video data Bank

DEAR SANDI:

I just finished your letter and the part about how when Nana died, and you thought you had caused her death through video. My mother didn't die, but she came as close as you can get. Within 12 hours of completing post-production on *Delirium*, I got word that mom was in the hospital barely surviving pulmonary edema and was being prepared for quadrupal by-pass surgery. I flew down to Kentucky immediately. I was unable to watch or show *Delirium* to anyone else until my mom was released from the hospital several weeks later. At that moment, I thought mom's heart attack was punishment for my self-ishness. But my mom assured me that it isn't the freezing of a person into a visual image that causes death. She told me as she lay in her hospital bed before surgery that the videos "we made together" freed her to die knowing that she was leaving something important behind "besides having kids." I was never quite sure until that moment how important these videos had become to her. I think it is also possible that your Nana was freed up to die by the making of *Tomboychik* and by the importance you placed on seeing her and hearing her stories. She must have known that — in you — she had a way to live on.

You also spoke of making a video behind your parents' backs with their camera and their mother. I, too, have always felt naughty when I made videos and photographs with and of my mom, because the process revealed family secrets and violated taboos of loyalty and privacy. But I also knew that I needed to show *Delirium* to every member of my family when I was done because even if it was painful, knowing they would see it would force me to stay honest. You asked me what scenes did my mom generate? In some ways this is like asking at what points did you as a videomaker, relinquish control or perhaps remain honest? This is somewhat difficult to answer. I have always worked with my mom in a fairly controlling way. I set up scenes and ask her, like an actress, to perform the roles. But I justified this by thinking of these scenes as way to initiate a dialogue with her although I was probably more interested in indoctrinating her with feminism than in really listening to her. So again with *Delirium* I had certain preconceived ideas which were informed by various feminist and psychoanalytic writings, and I began to script in my old familiar way based on these ideologies that I sought to illustrate. But my mom had become a video veteran by now and no longer contentedly and unquestioningly performed the script which I provided. She questioned the why's and how's of everything and continuously offered her suggestions throughout the taping process. The struggle to be honest and relinquish control for me was just that — a struggle.

- *I taped a three hour interview with my mom, but was dead set against using any of that footage until I realized I absolutely had to a week before my final edit session.*

- *When my mom asked for the camera during one of our last shooting sessions the*
  scene before she seized the camera was supposed to go like this:

  MOM: I'm simply incommensurable with the world.

  MINDY: But why did you take it out on me?

  MOM: Oh Mindy I just taught you the female role of submission like all mothers do.

But instead of saying this last line she demanded the camera and said as she pointed
the lens at me:

  MOM: *I never took anything out on you. Your'e a perfectly normal little child. I took*
          everything out on me.

I think this scene became one of the most powerful and critical moments in the tape
and her assertiveness at departing from the script forced a different structure for the
tape. The ending that I had already decided upon and did end up using actually falls flat
once I take the camera back because I reimpose this stubborn but simplistic conclusion
that her mental illness could be read as a rebellion against patriarchy. Her own reading
— that the only real pain suffered here was by her and any rebellion present was internally directed against herself — is a much more complex and painful expression than
the one I wanted to present.

With *Delirium* I felt like I began to learn to use video as a way of listening as much as
telling because the subject was my mom .

M i n d y

Mom and a dancing
woman from
Delirium, 1993,
by **Mindy Faber.**

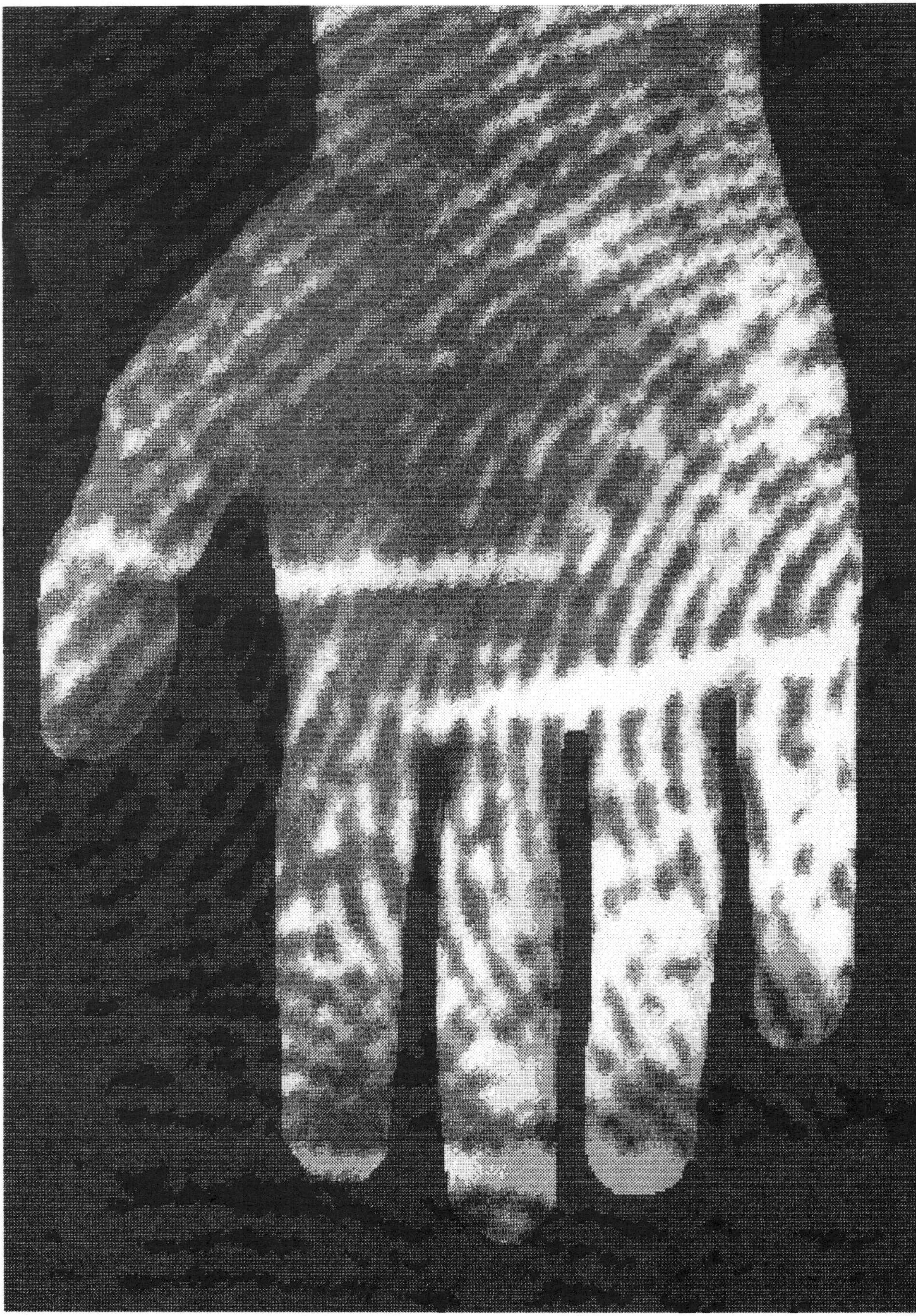

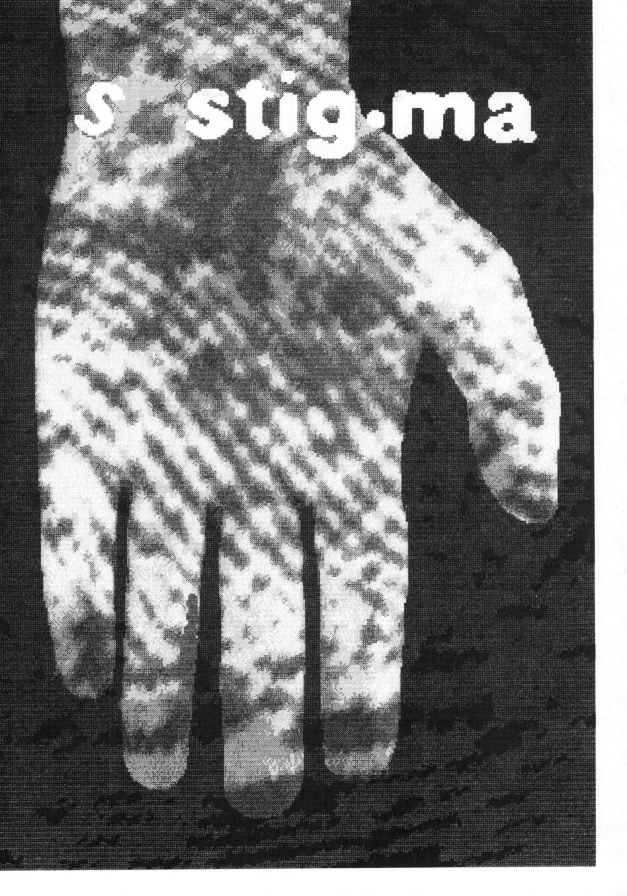

s   stig.ma

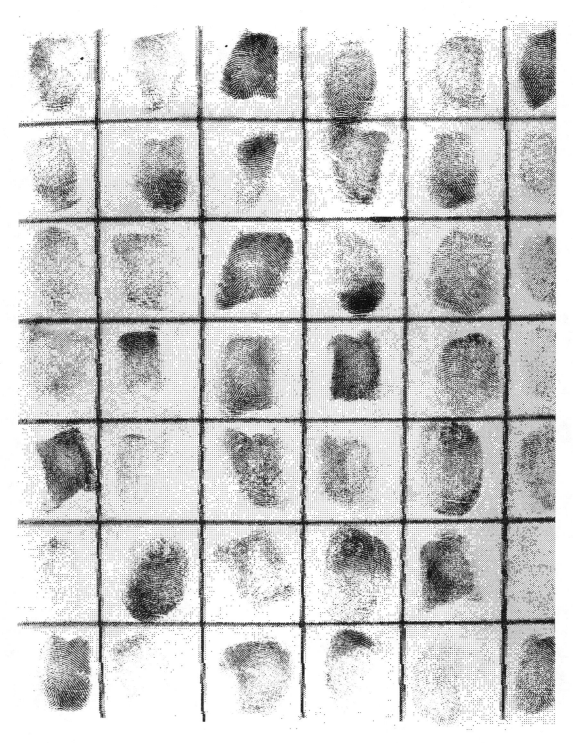

During 1993, the New York State Department of Social Services instituted pilot programs in two counties making computer finger imaging a requirement for receiving state welfare benefits.

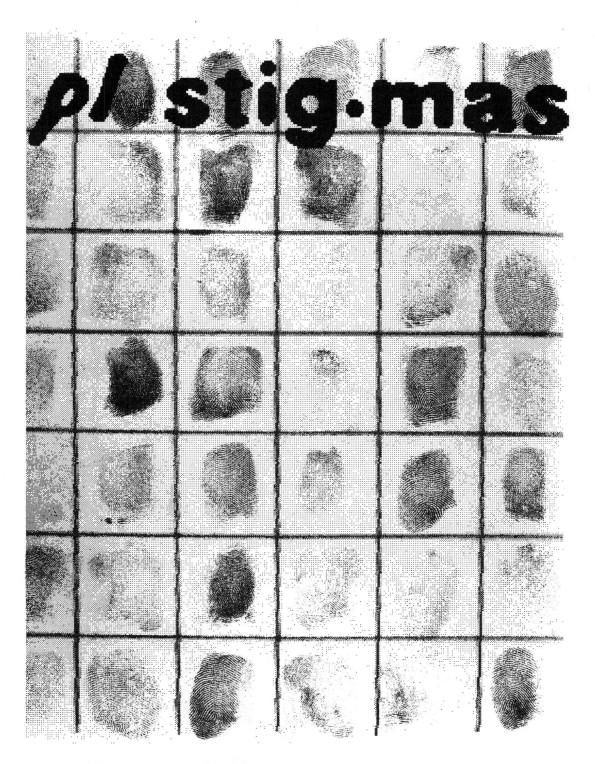

pl**stig·mas**

While the State claims the program is designed to catch people receiving multiple benefits, no such cases have been found. The program was recently expanded to twenty counties.

1. [斷袖]

SPEAK

西漢末期，哀帝與董賢間的關係，成為士大夫「分桃斷袖」用來描述同性愛的諺語。而他們兩人間的事，史書也有許多記載。

「斷袖」一詞，說法有二：一是董賢一次與哀帝同眠，但哀帝有事要起床，可是他的袖給董賢壓著。由於哀不相驚他，於是用劍將衣袖割斷，是謂斷袖。漢書本文：「帝曾畫寢，董賢偏藉帝衣袖而臥。帝欲起，賢未覺，不欲動賢，乃斷袖而起。」可見哀帝愛董賢纏綿細微若如此。故後世相欲好，良友斷袖，又曰割袖，恐驚其眠。

"This movement of the original is a wandering, an errance, a kind of permanenent exile if you wish, but it is not really an ex-ile, for there is no homeland, nothing from which one has been exiled"

Paul de Man in Con-clusions: Walter Benjamin's 'The Task of the Translater' in <u>The Resistance to Theory</u>, P. 92

In my translation, I chose to re-tell this story as a "myth of ori-gins" in a video that ex-plores ideas of com-monality and differences through the relations between speech, language, and desire - located in a gay Asian context - stories from Chinese and Japanese history, such as this one, are interpreted in a variety of contexts. My translation of the "cut sleeve" story brings out its homoeroticism by sparse narration I wrote in English, the intonation of the voice-over, and the video images of two (obvi-ously contem-porary) Asian men in an erotic encounter that I used to "illustrate" the story with. This juxtaposi-tion of dynastic history and contemporary image creates a resonance that is equal parts romantic pro-jection and political rec-lamation. It speaks to the longing for an identity and history our own, and the realization that cultural and sexual identities are articulated differently throughout history. It is at once a wistful and contradictory construct.

---

2. Cutting The Sleeve (1)

Emperor Oi was an emperor of the Western Han Dynasty. He did not care for women, but had a male favorite named Tung-Yen. A story about these two men is the origination of the term "cut sleeve", which came to be used as a signifier of male homosexuality in the Chinese court and literary traditions.

There are two versions of this story - one day, Emperor Oi and Tung-Yen were sleeping together. (perhaps they had just made love?) The Emperor had to get up, but Tung-Yen was still asleep, and he was lying on the Emperor's long sleeves. In order not to wake him up, the Emperor chose to cut of his sleeve instead. This was considered an act of great love and consideration for an emperor to ruin his clothing for a favorite.

In the other version of the story, Emperor Oi has ordered Tung-Yen to always wear the light clothes of the women, which had short sleeves, in their bed chambers, and forgo the elaborate costumes with long sleeves. It was because of Tung-Yen's ethereal appearance in such a cos-tume, which aroused the Emperor's desire. This has created a trend among the court re-tainers, who in their imitation of Tung-Yen's costume, hoped to win over the Emperor's favor.

(translated by Ming-Yuen S. Ma)

I. L'Emperereur Oi régna sur la Chine pendent la Dynastie des Han. Li ne s'intéressait pas au femmes, mais avait un favori qui s'appellait Tung-Yen. C'est une histoire que l'on raconte à propos de ces deux hommes qui a donné naissance à l'expression "manche coupée", qui finit par devenir un signifiant de l'homosexualité masculine dans la tradition courtoise et littéraire de la Chine ancienne. Il y a deux versions de cette histoire - un jour l'Empereur Oi et Tung -Yen dormaient ensemble (peut-être venaient-ils de faire l'amour?) L'Empereur devait se lever, mais Tung-Yen, qui dormait encore, reposait sur les longues manches de l'Empereur. Afin de ne pas le réveiller, l'Empereur préféra couper sa manche. On considéra que c'était une marque d'amour et d'égard considérable qu'un empereur abime son costume pour un favori. Dan la seconde version de l'histoire, l'Empereur Oi ordonna à Tung-Yen de toujours porter, quand il était dans leur chambre, des vêtements de femme, plus légers et aux manches courtes, et de reconcer au costume masculin, plus élaboré et aux manches longues. C'était par ce que l'apparence éthérée de Tung-Yen dans un tel costume éveillait le désir de l'Empereur. Cela créa une mode chez les serviteurs de la cour, qui, en imitant le costume de Tung-Yen, espérait s'attirer la faveur de l'Empereur.

Traduit du chinois en anglais par Ming-Yuen S. Ma, et de l'anglais en français par Bérénice Reynaud.

It was when I was in high school, I remember one time a bunch of us classmates went to the beach together. There everybody was staring at ___ ___ saying how this one has a great body, and that one ___ etty ___ would look with them, but somehow I did not feel ___ ut excited... But then saw these hot guys in swimsuits. They ___ ere ___ lly sexy and attractive to me. I was staring at them. I realized then that I was more attracted to men than to women. At that time I di ___ t know anything about homosexuality - but ___ started to wonder whether it is normal to like boys more than girls I was really afraid that someone might find out about this...

[transcribed and translated by Ming-Yuen S. Ma]
[Video still of Jack Lo from *Toc Storee*]

This passage is a transcription of an interview with Spencer Chan in Toc Storee, conducted in Cantonese. Primarily a vernacular language, Cantonese as it is now spoken in Hong Kong is constantly hybridized with slangs and other languages, much of its specific form is lost in the process of translation into written English. Therefore, I have chosen to include the original interview in the video, and have the English translation appear as subtitles. Spencer's story reminded me very much of my experience growing up in Hong Kong and realizing my own erotic attraction to other men. I chose his story to precede the "cut sleeve" sequence in Toc Storee both for its homoerotic content, which could be related to by all who have experienced such desires, and its culturally-specific articulation. In choosing to represent this story in a talking-heads interview format with its original language, Cantonese; and the historical "cut sleeve" story in an English translation overlaid with contemporary images, I want to set up a play between a fundamental realization of "gay desires" told in a culturally-specific format, and a cultural and historically-specific instance of same-sex love, reiterated in the language of a different culture. Visually, images that accompany these narratives re-present them again in a different context. Spencer's interview is accompanied by a visually reconstructed talking-head image of Martin Hiraga, another interviewee. Both visually and conceptually - in the splicing of Asian experience with Asian American image - Martin's image is out-of-sync with Spencer's narrative. This "badly" assembled image reveals both the mechanics of the interview format, and suggests a commonality between Asian and Asian American "gay" experiences while asserting their differences - thus adding on yet another layer of meaning, another translation.

MING-YUEN S. MA

Maya Nadkarni

Notes for **ROMANIAN HOLIDAY** (video project, 1994)

Mother and daughter, c. 1910

NOTHING YOU'VE

Sister, c. 1993

LEFT BEHIND

FITS THE HOLES

IN MY MEMORY

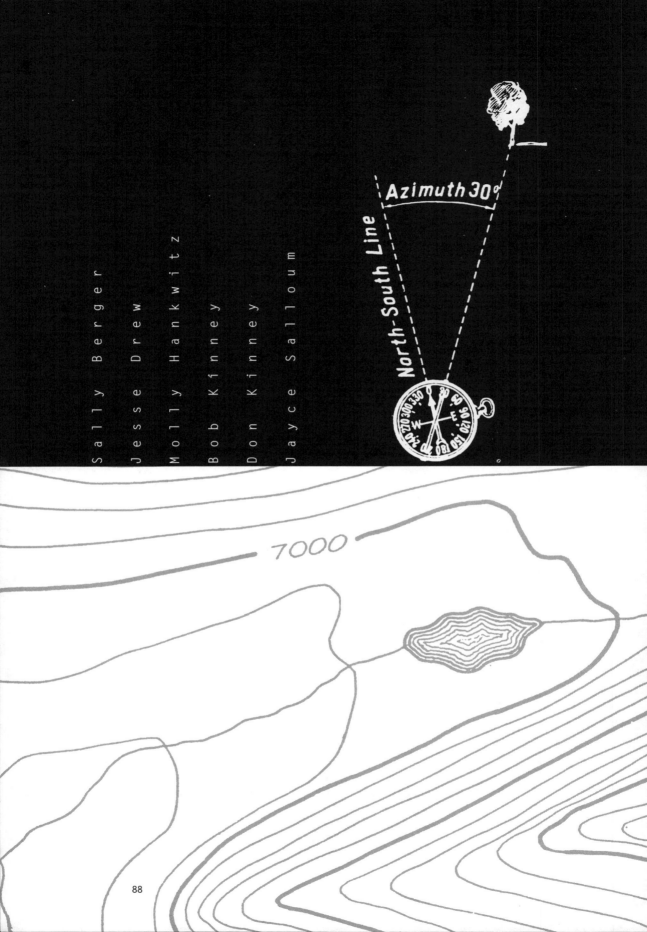

Sally Berger

Jesse Drew

Molly Hankwitz

Bob Kinney

Don Kinney

Jayce Salloum

Azimuth 30°

North-South Line

7000

SIGHT SPECIFIC

8000

8500

9000

LP: I think about bringing someone home to the place where I grew up. It's such a loaded proposition. Yet, I don't reserve this ritual for lovers or even for prospective lovers: I subject my friends to it. Partly this ritual is about revealing oneself in an obvious way: here is my mother who, as you can now see, I have already become. But the visit functions on more levels than that. Most likely, if I didn't have a car I wouldn't be so eager to make the trip. Because the hidden agenda is not about my friend listening to my mother waxing poetically about the tantrums of my youth. It is about getting that friend strapped into the passenger seat of my Pontiac. And it's really about the country roads. Not the ones of sappy poetry (Robert Frost), and not the ones of sappy lyricists (James Taylor), but the ones of sports utility vehicle ads. This is my terrain. Watch me hit the crest of the hill at just the right angle to catch a little air—butterflies in the stomach, right? In a big old American car with suspect suspension, this countryside reveals more miles of my history than I could ever speak. **KH/LP:** Even though we are becoming more "globalized," there are specific locations which have the potential to ground us, to carry a particular kind of weight. Perhaps it is the particularity and complexity of that place called home. The struggle to reconcile and locate a home—I think that is what this section is really all about. Over continents, cultures, and miles, trying to stabilize and make concrete that place, that concept, of home. Additionally, it's about the need to define, to somehow control—for one's self—where it is that we feel comfortable, where it is that we "belong." ¶ Often this quest involves a return to a site of struggle—over land, over representation, over identity—and efforts to demythologize and come to terms with a familiar landscape.

"Recent efforts at decentralization or separatism around

the world indicate how much place was repressed—like ethnicity or religion—in this notion of modern life. Technology reinforces the idea that local communities are archaic, even while making their image more available... In brief, as markets have been globalized, place has been diminished."

—*Landscapes of Power: From Detroit to Disney World*, by Sharon Zukin

¶ The horizon, depictions of the land, looking at the land, at movement and changing architectures—how does it affect us and our broader perceptions of the time and place? Has "place [really] been diminished?" KH: I have one friend who I walk with sometimes. She has a very different way of walking from me. I walk with a kind of bullying determination: I must get to my destination employing the most direct route. But she, on the other hand, is always stopping to look at the vegetation, the bushes, the flowers, the trees, so much so that at times I find myself half way down the block still conversing when I realize that she is way behind kneeling down to study a plant and name it. I move with a certain speed. I am fascinated with the pounding of my heels on the concrete, traversing an invisible map, an unswerving mental route straight from Point A to Point B. And I pride myself on the directness of the route. My friend, on the other hand, meanders and paints as she walks, the means being an end in itself, each step creating a new log of sites and smells. *For her, place has not been diminished.*

In the Face of Demons

by Robert and Donald Kinney

This article was originally produced, in part, as an oral presentation for the 1994 CAA Conference in New York City as part of the panel, "Now You See Me, Now You Don't: Lesbian and Gay Video," and the 1994 SPE Conference in Chicago for the panel, "Queer Collaborations."

MONOZYGOTE PRODUCTIONS is the incorporated identity of independent video artists Robert and Donald Kinney. As independent producers who focus on creating gay and lesbian representations, we are involved in a constantly developing process that draws on our identity as gay men and our relationship as twin brothers. We have (in common) experiences and desires that stretch back, literally, our entire lives. Though our past productions have played with the popular cultural myths about twins and their relationship to one another, it has never been our intention to mystify our own relationship, the manner in which we work, or the products of our collaborations. However, when talking about our work we have resisted the inevitable comparison and individuation that occurs when discussing our role as producers: who writes, who directs, who runs camera? At a certain point the separation of these tasks becomes both tedious and impossible given the dialogue that occurs both conceptually and practically within the collaborative effort. At the same time, re-absorbing two individuals back into what was for all intents and purposes a kind of tongue-in-cheek identity (Monozygote Productions) can be alienating to ourselves as well as the reader. So, with the understanding that alternating references to "Bobby" or "Donnie" forces a shifting focus that can be both unmanageable and confusing, we have decided to use the less interesting though more compact "we," "our" and, of course, "us."

Within our work, the fictions we create come to represent not concrete narratives about exceptional individuals, but broadly painted characters seated in sociocultural and economic circumstances that allow for a measure of discussion and dialogue. The characters stand as ideograms through which the discourse on gay and lesbian representation can be pursued. Each of the narrative constructs represents a myriad of ideas that intersect and surface as a collaborative effort. As the body of work develops, the videos are revealing similar characteristics that we, as producers, are trying to understand and sometimes can only brand as individually Monozygote-esque.

We grew up in the southeast corner of Iowa along the Mississippi River in the small, industrial city of Burlington. With a population of about 28,000, it is similar to a number of towns that dot the map in that area of the Midwest, while remaining a hub of residential, industrial and commercial activity within a specific rural location. During the 60s when we were in grade school, the town was economically very healthy. The main employer in town was the Iowa Army Ammunitions Plant (IAAP) which produced various kinds of military implements and munitions, most of which were being used in the war in Vietnam. War was good for Burlington, which meant it was good for the grocery stores, car dealerships, restaurants, day care centers, beauticians, waitresses and auto mechanics. It was also good for our father, who drove a truck in the area, and our mother, who worked on the production line at the IAAP manufacturing hand grenades. We lived in a cinder block apartment complex built during W.W.II to house the influx of workers for what was commonly known as "The Plant." Since then, the complex has devolved and been upgraded by commercial management into government subsidized housing.

During the 7's, when we were in high school, the town, like the rest of the country, went into a deep recession; the Vietnam war ended and "The Plant" all but shut down. Gas prices soared, industry moved out, beauticians' shops closed, and the unemployment rate in Burlington became part of some of the worst statistics in America. The trucking company our father worked for moved to Texas and he went to Greyhound to drive a bus cross-country. Like many women out of work in the area, our mother sought employment in one of the minimum wage "women's" factories producing wicker bathroom furnishings that ended up in the J.C. Penney catalog.

The two of us were privately sorting through the discombobulating though exciting discovery of our respective sexualities. This resulted in an endless round-robin from bathroom to bedroom; careful negotiations that

didn't go unnoticed. In the summer of '76, within days of our sister's death from leukemia, our family was evicted from the house we were renting. An aunt and uncle stepped in to help us move. Our mother, harried and self-conscious that so many of her belongings were being exposed and sorted through by her sister, found a private moment with us to ask if we had gotten rid of all the Kleenexes between our mattresses. We all blushed. The day had been hard on all of us.

While we both had part-time jobs through high school, classes were avoided at all opportunities (we each missed between 75-80 days in our Junior year alone). We hung out at the Country Kitchen, consuming a bottomless cup and a daily round of narcotics. Yet, we were absolutely estranged from each other regarding our sexualities. Our individual anxieties and fears separated us. Being our own worst mirror, we were content to be put into separate classrooms where the attraction to our similarities had less chance of drawing adverse attention. The verbal gay bashing on us as individuals and as twins was predictable, and much to our own consternation, true.

During our Senior year, our mother filled out financial aid papers with dubious information, and we received grants to attend the University of Iowa, representing the first generation in our family to receive more than a high school education. Iowa City was 90 minutes from home and too close to wrangle ourselves out of the web of family difficulties. Within a year we were forced to quit.

Upon leaving the university, neither of us wanted to return to Burlington. One of us bought a train ticket to New Jersey and the other a plane ticket to Japan. For nearly ten years we stayed away from the Midwest, from our family and each other. There was no reason to be part of the narrowness, the lack of choices, the homophobia, the racism, the misogyny, and the poverty. We left separately.

IN 1992, WE WERE TOGETHER AGAIN in San Diego producing a video entitled *Agora*, which was based in part on our experiences growing up in Middle America. During the final stages of that project, we received a generous grant from the Wexner Center in Columbus, Ohio. For the first time in 10 years, we were heading back to the Midwest. So with a great deal of nail-biting, we loaded up the car and headed east. Somewhere around Phoenix, we stopped at a roadside pay-phone and brought ourselves out of the family closet. As it turned out, coming out was a wonderful experience and we both felt as if we were, for the first time in many, many years, actually a part of the family. While our father hates to hear us use the word "queer", our mother is sure, we're convinced, that having two gay sons makes her inarguably middle class.

Our entire family attended the opening for *Agora* in Columbus, where they were surrounded by more queers than they had ever knowingly encountered. After the show, our father had an anxiety attack and forfeited the post-screening party for the relative calm of his room at the Holiday Inn. Our mother, who had just finished reading a bio on Rock Hudson, was anxious to attend her first homosexual party; a little fresh lipstick, a nervous readjustment of her shoulder pads, and she was in the car.

After *Agora*, we knew we wanted to produce another piece about the Midwest and decided to return to our home state to do so. This was a difficult decision to make. Returning to Iowa meant settling back into the place we had fled years before and confronting many of the monsters that still lingered, threatening to undo the strength and esteem we had spent years nurturing. At the time of this writing, after 1 1/2 years, we've managed to maintain our goals. *Demons* is now in the post-production phase. Working as data-entry operators, we've squeezed out of the premium rate of $5.50 an hour about $4,000.00 to produce the video and anticipate completing the project by early Summer.

THE FOLLOWING IS A BRIEF SYNOPSIS OF <u>DEMONS</u>

Demons is a dramatic horror story set in the rural Midwestern town of Sperry, Iowa, in 1961. The narrative focuses on Allie, a woman recently widowed and struggling to operate a small hog farm with the support of her teenage son, Dip. Allie's autonomy is repeatedly challenged as she staves off the vulturous opportunism of a corporate land prospector and the debts her husband left behind. In the midst of her difficulties arrives her brother-in-law, Gray, returning to the farm he fled years earlier. A suspect individual with rumors of mental illness in his past, Gray's attempts at incorporating himself back on the farm are repeatedly thwarted by Allie. Circumstances begin to knot as Gray pursues Dip, who reciprocates with the full passion of his burgeoning sexuality. In desperation, Allie devises a plan to circumvent the desire between Gray and Dip, an effort as much to maintain control of her son as to maintain control of the land she tenuously possesses. *Demons* is a story of three individuals caught in the struggle to survive, fighting for their own autonomy and the often competing strength of sexual desire. *Demons* was shot over a period of twenty days on Hi-8 video and is currently in post-production at the cable access station (PATV) in Iowa City, Iowa. Running time is approximately 70 minutes.

SPERRY, IOWA IS A SMALL farming community about fifteen minutes north of Burlington. Our younger sister, Angie, with her six children and boyfriend, Ted, live in Sperry where they operate a small hog farm. It was at this site that we shot the farm and house exterior images for *Demons*. Shooting on a weekend to weekend basis, amidst catastrophic flooding, June and July found our tiny production team negotiating a nearly impossible shooting schedule.

We had supplied Angie with a full script and storyboard of the intended production and stated clearly in our discussions that the piece dealt with gay issues. Our concerns were in part with the kids and the dramatized issues of sexuality that were going to be played out. Trusting our sensitivity to the issues, she asked that if material inappropriate for the kids was being shot we should ask them to leave the set. This we did on several occasions with the full cooperation of the children.

After the initial introductions between the performers, Angie, and her family, we began shooting. Everything was going well and production was a pleasure. We kept the gaggle of curious children occupied with small duties like holding up the clapboard and keeping the dogs from entering the camera field. Ursula, the actress playing Allie, became fast friends with Angie, while the other two performers were intent on exploring the farm. We ate lunch on the screened porch as the oldest boy delighted in introducing us to some of the gorier details of raising hogs, which involved an alarmingly sophisticated knowledge, for an eleven year old, of porcine sexuality.

For two or three weekends production went well. By the fourth, things began to go sour. The hour and a half to get to the farm from Iowa City was expensive and inconvenient. The heat and humidity were dreadful and the farm seemed to stink worse with every visit. The Midwest watched the Mississippi River rise to disastrous levels while the video project turned into a larger endeavor than the performers had anticipated. And as much as we tried NOT to interrupt the workings of the farm, we inevitably got in the way. Independent production seems to be about juggling and spreading out the inevitable financial strain, which means neglecting bills and meals for the sake of production. Time commitments became a problem as shooting started competing with other summer activities the performers and our single tech assistant wanted to attend.

Late Saturday night of the fourth weekend, we were shooting by the sow's pen. We were a two-man crew and Ursula was the only performer present. Monozygote Productions ran their four legs off trying to be everything the set needed. Ted and three of the kids were there too, partly help-

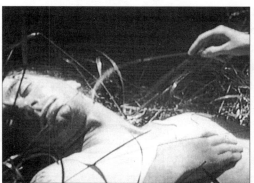

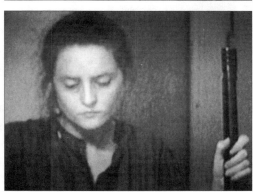

Stills from
Demons, 1994,
by **Robert &
Donald Kinney.**

ing out and partly being entertained by our clumsy efforts at lighting the night. The oldest boy and Ted dealt with the lights while Ursula kept the two little girls preoccupied and out of the way.

Now, apparently, this is what happened.

The two little girls wanted to know where the other two performers had gone. Ursula, in her usual generous and honest manner, told the girls they had gone to Chicago for the Gay and Lesbian Pride Parade. "What is a lesbian?" was their next question.

Ted and Nate apparently overheard the conversation. They both left the set immediately. All we knew was that suddenly and mysteriously two of our volunteers had disappeared. About 1:00 a.m. we wrapped up and headed back to Iowa City, exhausted.

The next Saturday we all arrived on the farm early and commenced shooting. By early afternoon the heat had gone into the high nineties while the humidity and bugs were almost unbearable. We had completed some work by the furrowing pen earlier in the morning and were setting up for a shoot in a field about a hundred yards from the house. To give the performers their call, one of us went to the small camper that was operating as both a dressing trailer and a set piece. Ursula was in the trailer, upset and crying. She was unwilling to discuss what had upset her, though later reports indicated that some angered exchange had occurred over lunch. Rather than allow the shoot to be interrupted, we decided to continue and deal with the problem later.

The scene was long and required a number of set-ups, which demanded a constant repetition of a difficult and emotional scene. The heat was draining everyone and the humidity was affecting the equipment. Tensions were high and one of the performers started to aggressively resist direction. The Radio Shack mic was proving to be nothing but a piece of shit. About that time, a large German Shepherd from a neighboring farm appeared on the path right next to the field where we were shooting. As suddenly as the appearance of the dog, Ted and the two older boys burst from the house with shot guns and

began firing over our heads at the trespasser. All of us hit the dirt.

The dog, needing no further prompting, fled the scene and we lifted ourselves off the ground and decided it was clear to resume shooting (the video). About this time, Angie walked onto the set with a pack of generic cigarettes in one hand and a lighter in the other. "Bobby and Donnie," she said, "we need to go and have a smoke."

Her complaints were serious and direct. Ted was concerned that we were interrupting his ability to chore the farm. We had to understand that they were as busy as we were and that there were certain things that had to be done. The farm was their livelihood and had to be given priority over our project.

Further, as we probably already knew, she had had words with Ursula and the other performers earlier in the day. She didn't feel it was appropriate that the children know that two of the performers on the set were gay. We had made certain choices about our lives, about who we were, but she didn't want that affecting her kids. They would go to school and invariably they would talk. She, Ted and the kids had to live in this community with a lot of people who weren't sympathetic to our concerns. They were people they had to socialize and do business with. Further, things were shaky enough for her already since she wasn't, and refused to be, married to Ted. It caused her to be a suspect individual amongst neighboring families, many of which were relatives as well.

The reason we've tortured you with this story of what could be considered a kind of pragmatic homophobia, is that the scene we were shooting that afternoon reflects the same issues our sister was addressing. On one level, the similarity of these two events, the confrontation with Angie and the performed fiction, is reassuring to us as producers in that the narrative we have contrived is suggestive of the circumstances around us. It is, at the same time, obviously difficult to confront these prejudices and their guarded parameters, especially when they are coming from someone you grew up with.

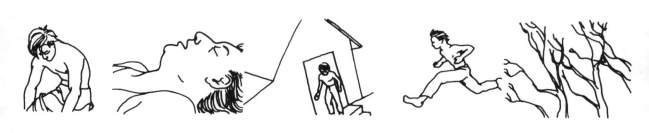

In the case of our sister's concerns and in the following segment from the production script, the issue of homosexuality exists within a knot of circumstances and issues that include gender, economic survival, knowledge and sexual desire. It is precisely this kind of complexity we have tried to bring to our narrative.

Day. Shot of ALLIE walking along a path. The camera follows her to GRAY's trailer. She goes up to the door, looks inside and walks away. Cut to overhead shot of GRAY lying in the grass, the camera pans up to see ALLIE walking toward him. She stops and ties a yellow scarf around her neck and unbuttons the top button of her dress.

ALLIE: Lazy ass. Gray. GRAY! Enjoying an afternoon nap?

GRAY: Only time to sleep.

ALLIE: How about sleeping with me?

GRAY: Aww, Allie! Yo don't want to sleep with me.

ALLIE: Don't tell me what I want or don't want.

GRAY: I'm goin' for a swim.

ALLIE: Wait! I understand what a man's needs are...

GRAY: Well, I'm needin' a swim.

ALLIE: Look. I'm no idiot. I've seen you. With your own nephew.

GRAY: He came to my place.

ALLIE: So what! You encouraged him. It's indecent. You're a growed up man.

GRAY: How old's the boy?

ALLIE: Not old enough to know what he's doin' is wrong.

GRAY: He knows what he's doin'. It ain't hurtin' nobody.

ALLIE: You're sick. You disgust me. Why don't you go away and leave us alone?

GRAY: This is my home, too.

ALLIE: Then leave the boy alone. He didn't know nothin' of the likes of your kind till you showed up.

GRAY: You're tryin' to keep the boy behind a fence. It'll drive 'em crazy.

ALLIE: Then stop encouragin' him!

GRAY: Can't expect us to be strangers.

ALLIE: What if somebody gets wind of this? You wantin' the law to come in here an' find out what's goin' on? If you're brother was alive... (GRAY goes to leave) You're gonna take him away from me aren't you?!

GRAY: We're just friends... havin' some fun.

ALLIE: Gray, please. I need the boy. Don't take him away from me. I can't take care of the hogs alone. If I lose the boy I lose the farm. I can't afford to hire

	nobody. I got no place to go. I'll starve. I can't just take off like you can.
GRAY:	I can't do nothin' about that.
ALLIE:	You no good louse. There's not a respectable bone in your body. You are crazy. I'll get you.
GRAY:	What'll you do?
ALLIE:	I'll turn you into the Sheriff. They'll lock you up again. Pervert.
GRAY:	That's not gonna keep the boy here. Besides, seems to me you're in no position to be askin' the Sheriff for favors. Why can't you just let things be. The boy's happy. I'm happy. An' you got your help.
ALLIE:	Come on, Gray. It can't be so different. Remember, I've been a married woman!
GRAY:	So find a marrying man. (He pushes her away)
ALLIE:	Shit. (She spits) I was a fool once.
GRAY:	I'm going for a swim.
ALLIE:	Pervert! Cocksucker!! QUEER!

END SCENE

Time Travelers

by Sally Berger

TWO YEARS AGO I WITNESSED the making of *Saputi (Fish Trap)*, one of a series of dramatic videotapes begun in 1986 to portray traditional life of the Inuit living in the area surrounding Igloolik, a small island and fishing port in northeastern Canada above the Arctic Circle in the Northwest Territories. These unique stories are not only created but lived by director Zacharias Kunuk and the Inuit families of the region who participate in them.

Saputi and the other videotapes by Igloolik Isuma Productions, co-founded by Kunuk (called Sak), Norman Cohn, and Paulossie Qulitalik, are made to enhance contemporary Inuit community life through the portrayal and revival of older Inuit customs. The Inuktitut word "isuma" means "thinking for oneself," and in accordance with its own directives, the company works closely with an Inuit cast and crew and is comprised of an active, majority Inuit board of directors. The actors, untrained non-professionals, often with other jobs in the community, gain experience by working with Isuma, and some have acted in other commercial film roles as well.

Board member Qulitalik is the principal actor and cultural advisor in *Saputi*. His wife Mary, who cooks for a local hotel, and their children regularly participate in the videotaped re-enactments. Along with others from the Igloolik community of 800 residents, such as David Amaqlinik who has held several leading roles, they are committed to working on each new production. Family and cross-generational participation is central to the making of the videotapes. Several families interact in each story as they would in everyday life. Details regarding performance, dialogue, and authenticity are discussed prior to videotaping each scene and decisions are made by consensus, "in response to the knowledge and experience of elders' advice."

The action is recorded by the patient and observant cinematographer Norman Cohn, an accomplished video artist who immigrated to Canada from New York in the 1970s. Cohn sought out Kunuk in 1985 after seeing one of Sak's first videotapes and finding similarities in their work styles. Cohn noticed that, as in his own approach, Kunuk lets the subject define the shape and substance of the material. Cohn and Kunuk share an interest in revealing the specialness of ordinary people and of the disenfranchised. A restless traveler prior to their collaboration, Cohn eventually settled in Igloolik to become a central figure in many phases of Igloolik Isuma Productions. Enigmatic like Kunuk, Cohn says that travel, "is not all about distance and airports," to describe the vision that he and Kunuk share.

Saputi (1993), which takes place in the fall, is the third of a trilogy of tapes loosely based in the 1930s and 1940s, revolving around seasonal hunting patterns. The winter tale *Qaggiq* (*Gathering Place*, 1989) begins the cycle, followed by *Nunaqpa* (*Going Inland*, 1991) about a summer caribou hunting trip. The premise for *Saputi* is the recreation of an abandoned traditional fishing method. The story was videotaped in August of 1992 on the land at Sanguinganiq, on the Melville Peninsula, a fishing and hunting area 40 miles "as the crow flies" to the west of Igloolik.

Saputi begins with a wide shot of the expansive tundra landscape, cutting to a slow pan of a river with a rock dam winding across it. All of these images are accompanied by the strains of a song. The saputi, or fish weir, is a type of rock dam that stretches across the mouth of a river to capture fish (in this instance Arctic char) as they swim upstream to fresh water for the winter. The recollections of elders who once lived a year-round nomadic life informed the process of videotaped historical recreation: the men provided information about how to position the rocks in the shape of a trap and to construct the kakivak and niksik tools used for spearing fish; women,

Young woman dreaming of meeting a young hunter.

103

knowledgeable about traditional sewing methods, scraped, pounded, then softened leather with their teeth and stitched the sealskin clothing — parkas, amatis (dresses with large hoods for women to carry their babies), and watertight kamiks (boots) — that were worn on the set. Throughout the six weeks of preparation and videotaping, teenagers, infants, and adults were completely immersed in the realities of a mid-20th century Inuit early fall hunting and fishing camp.

Being one of three people invited from outside the Inuit community to observe the shoot, I participated as a curator of contemporary video art interested in the methodology used to create these "living history" stories that bridge areas of drama, history, and culture. After a six-hour boat-trip in the freezing cold from the island of Igloolik, we arrived at a remote tent encampment for the crew and their families set up near the location site. The following evening Kunuk welcomed us, sweeping his hand across the vast, Arctic landscape of tundra, water, and sky exclaiming, "Welcome to the site of the next McDonald's Restaurant!"

Opposite and below: building the saputi, or fish weir, a rock dam across the mouth of the river to capture fish (Artic char) as they swim upstream for the winter.

Kunuk's irony is grounded in historical as well as contemporary realities. Over the past 400 years, a steady pattern of economic, scientific, religious and governmental incursions have taken place in the North: fur trapping, whaling, mining, geologic explorations, and religious missions were followed by Canadian government policies, law enforcement, schools, and the military. Contact with outsiders initially provided attractive resources to the original people who lived in the extreme and unpredictable environment of the Arctic, such as reliable food sources, ready-made hunting tools, fabricated clothing, and eventually snowmobiles, other land vehicles, convenience foods, and imported television shows. But the promise of ease introduced by other cultures undermined the independently resourceful Inuit lifestyle and religious practices so carefully adapted over thousands of years to support a complex human existence in the rugged Arctic environment. Foreign settlers brought

new and often fatal diseases and modern life introduced stresses and health issues reflected today in the cultural dislocation, boredom and depression felt by many young people. The speed and pervasiveness of damaging transitions which Kunuk has observed first-hand, as well as

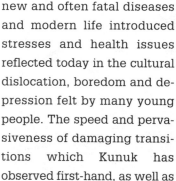

the time he lived on the land as a child, gives Kunuk a clarity of vision about the uniqueness and vulnerability of Inuit culture and prompts his questions about the edificacy of western societal values.

Television came to the Arctic North in the late 1960s with the advent of satellites which could downlink programs into people's homes. Radio, first introduced in the 1920s, and later television broadcasting demonstrated important modes of communication and entertainment for people separated by great distances. However, early programming in both radio and television followed similar exclusive patterns of development. Programs were directed at non-native northerners and made by outside producers in total disregard of the concerns of the native population. By the 1970s the capacity of media to alter Inuit culture, encouraging assimilation and asserting institutional control, was evident to northern Inuit organizations and researchers of media and culture. They observed that the radio and television broadcasts brought outside values, undermined the use of the Inuktitut language, created unrealistic desires and frustrations, and increased generation gaps between the young and the old.

The advent of the Anik satellite dramatically increased the English-speaking and foreign broadcasts into the region and native northerners responded by forming active, regionally-based organizations to intervene in the directives of the Canadian Broadcasting Corporation with the development of Inuit-initiated pilot projects. The people of the Igloolik area and northern Quebec resisted television until 1981 when the Inuit Broadcasting Corporation (IBC), the original television network mandated to produce Inuit culture and language programming, was formed. Centers in Iqualuit, Bakers Lake, and Igloolik surrounded Kunuk, raising his awareness of the political debates centered around media, and giving him access to the technology. He received training and worked as a senior producer on documentary programs in the Inuktitut language (*Walrus Hunter*, 1986) with the IBC from 1984 until 1990. Simultaneously, he used this time to develop his own artistic vision shooting footage of the Igloolik community with a video camera purchased from money earned selling his soapstone carvings. Kunuk's first independent video from an Inuk point of view was made during this period. His preferred working methods were dissimilar from the fast production required of weekly documentary news programs; his ideas required time for development. Additionally, the IBC which was controlled by Ottawa and hired managers from outside the north on a rotational basis, could not encompass his artistic nor ideological viewpoints. The process of remembering by doing, using the technology of television to dramatically and artistically re-envision, rather than journalistically document and record, has been the pivotal center of Kunuk's independent work since the mid-1980s.

Kunuk and Cohn recently received the Bell Canada Award in Video Art in 1994, four years after the founding of Igloolik Isuma Productions, for their first cycle of videotapes ending with *Saputi*. Following this recognition and monetary award, additional financial support came from Telefilm Canada and other contributors for the full completion of the non-profit company's long-envisioned 13-part series, *Nunavut* (*Our Land*). (Start-up funds came from the government of the Northwest Territories.) The *Nunavut* series is the first Inuit created and produced dramatic television series slated for the Northwest-Territories, as well as regions "south," with broadcast commitments in British Columbia, Saskatchewan, and Ontario. They plan to use this support to assist the growth of their community based, Tariagsuk Video Center to provide greater access and media training for local people. The Center has already begun to provide much needed meaningful and self-initiated employment for the Inuit of the region.

The first of the *Nunavut* series, with three half hour programs completed by 1994, *Qamaq* (*Stone House*), *Tugaliaq* (*Ice Blocks*), and *Angiraq* (*Home*), reflects a more defined and experienced approach to the deceptively simple historical recreations in the earlier tapes, including *Saputi*. These new works use the one half hour format and same process of dramatic reenactment as before. However, the *Nunavut* tapes, because of substantial financial support, are made with higher production values, at a faster pace, and with more directed and focused scenarios. The entire series is to be completed in 1995.

THE YEAR 1945, EXPLICITLY STATED by titles at the beginning of each segment in *Nunavut* , is the point of departure for each episode, the time when Canadian Federal government assimilation programs introduced residential and day schools and permanent settlements in the North. Historically, many families were separated as a result of these government initiatives. Kunuk's parents continued to live "on the land" in the traditional sense, and in 1965 at age nine Kunuk was placed with extended family members to attend school in what was then the relatively new settlement of Igloolik. English was taught as the primary language by teachers imported from metropolitan areas such as Montreal and Ottawa. Schedules, newly determined by the southern latitudes, were incongruent to the Inuit lifestyle that revolves around the Arctic North's long summer days and winter nights. After grade school, Kunuk was sent to the nearest high school, a boarding school in the city of Iqaluit, a two-and-a-half hour plane ride further away from family and friends and his rural homeland. Iqaluit, the area's governmental seat with equally large Inuit and non-Inuit populations and the poverty and excesses of a large city, is a stark contrast to the tranquil and pristine setting of Igloolik with its majority Inuit population. Kunuk stayed in Iqaluit a short time, but eventually dropped out (many of his friends never went) to return to the area of Igloolik and various jobs in carpentry and mining before becoming a video maker.

Because of its remote location, Igloolik is often cited as one of only several places where traditional Inuit culture has been preserved. At the same time, Canadian news media in southern metropolitan areas give alarming reports on the deterioration of the residents' health and lifestyle based on studies by social scientists decrying the overuse of processed foods and lack of exercise due to the increased availability of land vehicles. However, modern conveniences also facilitate hunting, travel, and communication and supplement the area's natural food sources. Kunuk is faced with these and other contradictions in contemporary Inuit daily life: in particular, his own children's fascination with television shows from other cultures. For many in the north, time spent in front of the television set intensifies during the long winter months. The Inuit Broadcasting Corporation prepares approximately five hours of Inuktitut programming per week offering a variety of children's shows, interviews with elders, documentaries and news programs about local personalities and events, and dramas. But popular television has had a larger impact on Isuma Productions, seen in the use of conversational dialogue and personal dramas. Kunuk is passionate about placing Inuit-made and based stories on television that are as compelling as the favorite soap operas and dramas from outside cultures. His stories reflect a radical approach towards change within his own culture as well as TV drama, and a driving vision for living now and in the future. The people who collaborate with him as well reach into their hearts and minds to pass on an Inuit legacy towards the future of their children.

Kunuk says as we watch the video shoot of the building of the saputi, "My argument is that there is another way of life and that other way is Inuit... It is important that we do it this way, in the sealskin clothes, like it was." Men and boys heave huge rocks in the icy waters, their hands covered with tiny black leaches. The younger people enjoy themselves, like the elders, but quaff at the stiff hoods and sharp edged sleeves of their sealskin jackets, and jokingly turn up their noses at the smelly sealskin tents. Two wet suits are shared by those working on the dam, worn underneath the sealskins to shield against the biting wind and cold water. The loose sleeves of the sealskin jackets are tied at the wrists in an ineffective attempt to stop the seepage of cold water up their arms. Clearly this is hard work for there are many

−The cooking's almost done.

sugar-laden tea and biscuit breaks inside a make-shift shelter to warm-up and restore energy.

The land and the history of the people who have lived in it for centuries informs every aspect of these videotapes. Inukshuks, stones piled into shapes that denote personal signatures, and other stone markers left from old caches, tent sites, and graves, dot the landscape. The earth, sea, and climate are the central life and death determining forces. In

Saputi, as well as in other videotapes, living in harmony with family and friends means learning from, and responding to, the environment. Decisions such as when and where to build the saputi are based on the temperature, rain, wind, tides, light, and animal migratory patterns. The soundtrack and specific visual elements evoke a physical experience of the natural environment: the sound of swift water rushing against the rocks of the saputi and the whisper of the wind is heard in the microphone; water drops form on the camera lens. The cold temperature, just above freezing even in August, is harder to convey, but can be observed through the camera's close attention to details such as Qulitalik's curled hands as he retreats from the icy waters of the river.

On the set everyone must be productive, and everyone develops large appetites. The most satisfying food is seal meat, because fat and protein are the best fuel for the body in the extreme cold. Carbohydrates don't last, but banik, a bread cooked in a frying pan over an open fire, is a special treat. People gather to eat and then spend long hours building the saputi, continuing into the twilight of the late evening, working hard, sleeping late, celebrating life. It is light for most of the hours around the clock during the summer months. Time is as expansive as the landscape. The sun comes up and goes down in the same direction, sweeping around the sky in a low arc. The slow rhythm of the character's actions, the silhouettes against the horizon of land and sky, the filtered light and grey skies which do not clearly reflect the passage of time, lend a timeless quality to the final edited version of *Saputi*.

As is often the case in the Arctic, natural events do not always happen as predicted. And everything happens in its own time. The final scene in the original treatment of *Saputi* written by Kunuk and Qulitalik reads: "Next morning the trap is full again and we see more fish like a long dream of fishing. Finally the head man says 'Taima' (It's enough), and they open the door so the fish can go upstream." But at the time of the videotaping the expected plenitude of fish and caribou were not to be found. The Arctic char had already run their course upstream and the caribou were foraging for food elsewhere. The story ends on a note of sadness with the families leaving their encampment without any fish or caribou.

But the process of making these videotapes provides the primary reason and meaning for their creation, not a pre-determined happy or tragic outcome. Each story contains elements of surprise stemming from learning to live in this environment and the relearning of old techniques. As the men prepare to start a fire from flint, Qulitalik's finger is burned by a spark. This is greeted with great mirth and the humor and enjoyment are contagious to the viewer. The recorded events do not idealize, but confront the impermanence, the very harshness of existence with acceptance. The ice porches will melt and sod houses deteriorate in *Tugaliak*, and fish traps will slowly collapse in *Saputi*, but the purpose of attempting these difficult tasks is to define what life is about for oneself. There is a moment in the final scenes of *Saputi* when the head man, Qulitalik, admonishes his cousin about being lazy. The moment is a poignant reminder of human interdependence, Inuit values, and the emotional pressures of an unpredictable natural environment.

All of Kunuk's videotapes reflect this subtle interplay between spontaneous exchanges and dramatically recreated aspects of Inuit life. The recreations are carefully planned and discussed, but there is no written script and the dialogue is mostly determined by what actually takes place during the recreation. The actors are often moved to strong emotion as events unfold, as in *Angirak*, when an elder woman inadvertently brings the parents to tears because she admonishes them about competition among the families and favoritism towards the children which pulls the

109

community apart. In *Quaggiq*, the engagement scene between a young man (played by David Amaqlinik), a young woman, and their parents was so real to the actors that you can see the astonishment on their faces and Amaqlinik's own nervousness.

THE VIDEOS DO NOT REFLECT life today in Igloolik where people live in clapboard houses, have telephones and fax machines, and wear manufactured clothing. They don't (as yet, although Kunuk has expressed an interest in some of these subjects) dwell upon the problems of poverty, alcohol, drug, and physical abuse, and teenage suicide. Their purpose is not to blatantly break down the misconceptions that people unfamiliar with the culture have about the Inuit living in a romanticized past or an unmodern present. Instead, they are about an historical, psychological, and philosophical process for those involved, each story evolving towards the next. A continuum is important as Mary Qulitalik explains serenely, "We seem to be doing a new story every year."

Three events that take place in *Saputi* reflect an exploration of Kunuk's own early memories and day dreams. They portend an interest in rediscovering Inuit cosmology, largely lost through the missionaries' zeal in averting traditional Inuit religious practices, as well as reveal the loss of youthful innocence and the vulnerability of the individual alone in the Arctic. These scenes, in which one boy hears strange noises on the tundra, another is spooked by a "rock" monster, and a young girl dreams of meeting a young hunter, are reminiscent of Sak's falling behind and becoming frightened on walks with his brothers and sisters. Shamanistic practises are broached more directly in the later *Tugaliaq* in a conversation among several characters that touches upon the mysteries of the Inuit religion that must have threatened not only the power, but the beliefs of the early missionaries. Significantly, 1945, the year in which the *Nunavut* series is set, is also the year when the government supplanted the role of the church as a major force in health and education. Anglican and Roman Catholic churches provide solace from the frightening aspects of shamanism for many Inuit and bring people together on a community level. On Sundays during the shoot for *Saputi*, families gathered in Qulitalik's tent to read passages from the Bible. The town of Igloolik is divided into two religious precincts and to Kunuk the church realistically and symbolically represents the destruction of oral traditions and therefore memory and history. This is related to the fact that Inuit language, Inuktitut, was first adapted into Cree syllabics in 1876 by an Anglican minister so he could teach the Bible.

Kunuk is drawn to video because he feels the medium bears a closer resemblance to the oral traditions the culture is based on than its written form. For centuries, Inuit culture has been handed down through speech and storytelling traditions. The dialogue in the videotapes is spoken in Inuktitut, which requires adaptation to keep out modern words that would not have existed previously. The soundtrack is punctuated by ajaja songs, poems put to music about significant events or feelings, sung by singers from the Igloolik community. The music and words of the ajajas have a repetitive, rhythmic pattern that evoke the moods felt when awaiting the return of an overdue hunting party or the coming of daylight after a long, cold winter night. Since the making of *Saputi*, subtitling in English of the ajajas has been added to explain the fullness of the narrative to non-Inunktituk speaking viewers.

Sak Kunuk's video works have added a new dimension to the meaning of history and culture and mark the development of an important new form in moving images that is neither documentary, docu-drama nor fiction, but a combination of lived and recreated experience. For me, the significance of this work became clarified in my final moments with the Inuit production team and families with whom I spent two full, but short weeks. When the majority of shoot was completed, everyone exited the camp late at night when the sea was the calmest in a fleet of outboard motors. Enveloped in the darkest of nights without lamps, we used cigarette lighters to signal each other until the stars appeared. The pilot on each boat searched for rocky islands looming out of the black sea. The sea sparkled in the boats' wakes mirroring the diamond-studded sky. In this intimate space between worlds and time we exchanged stories, huddled together for warmth, and drank tea. Mary Qulitalik noticed that my high-tech ski gloves did not warm my hands and lent me a pair of fleece-lined leather mitts. The teenagers suddenly spoke to me in fluent English about ice hockey, television shows, Arnold Schwartzenegger and other popular television personalities and film stars. They told me how ridiculous people sounded when they asked them if they still lived in igloos. Mary protested because she could no longer participate in the conversation — she speaks Inuktitut and it is difficult for her to understand fast conversational English. The

Silhouette of the departing hunters.

111

long boat ride transported us back to Igloolik and New York, other times and lives, and the contradictions of contemporary life that had been so briefly escaped.

Kunuk has said that he yearns to write his own ajaja song. These videos are his songs for his people, journeys back into time to reclaim the present. His stories visualize the oral history and recapture the ancestrage of the Inuit people of Igloolik, with an awareness of the fluctuating nature of history.

This work brings recognition to other ways of presenting television, with stories made by ordinary people about the extraordinary witnessed in the small details of existence. The natural landscape is at the forefront of Inuit life. It provides shape and meaning to the continuity of life, and requires the development of special skills to exist within it. The new media experience presented in these videotapes from the people of Igloolik is a gift for the present and the future for all people.

Sources for historical information in this article are:

Alootook Ipellie, "The Colonization of the Arctic," *Indigena: Contemporary Native Perspectives*. Canadian Museum of Civilization, 1992.

Lorna Roth and Gail Guthrie Valaskakis, "Aboriginal Broadcasting in Canada: A Case Study in Democratization," *Communication For and Against Democracy*. Black Rose Books, 1989.

Stephen Hendrick and Kathleen Fleming, "Zacharias Kunuk: Video Maker and Inuit Historian," *Inuit Quarterly*, VI:3, Summer 1991, pp. 24-28.

All stills from **Saputi**, 1993, directed by **Zacharias Kunuk.**

occupied territories; mapping the transgressions of cultural terrain

on the recent videotapes of Jayce Salloum

an interview/essay with Jayce Salloum and Molly Hankwitz

MOLLY HANKWITZ: I am responding to having been both moved and challenged by مقدمة لنهايات جدال (*Introduction to the End of an Argument*) *Speaking for oneself .../Speaking for others....,* (Jayce Salloum and Elia Suleiman, 45 minutes, 1990), when I saw it in 1990. Lately I have screened your earlier tapes and your most recent pair of tapes from Lebanon, طا لعين عا لجنو ب (*Talaeen a Junuub)/ Up to the South,* (Jayce Salloum and Walid Ra'ad, 60 minutes, 1993) and هذه ليست بيروت / كان يا ما كان (*This is Not Beirut)/ There was and there was not,* (Jayce Salloum, 49 min., 1994). This recent pair, with the addition of *(Introduction to the End...),* form a kind of trilogy dealing with the representation of Arabs, Palestinians and the conventions of myth-making in western media, the resistance to the Israeli occupation in South Lebanon, and the methodological queries you have had about the process of documentary. As a writer, it is one of my aims to take apart assumptions within discursive practices. This aim, I've discovered, is well directed at documentary. One asks: who looks at it, who it is made for,

Still from **(Introduction to the End of an Argument) Speaking for oneself.../ Speaking for others,** 1990, by **Jayce Salloum** and **Elia Suleiman.**

what the genre serves, how it has been conventionally exploited for ideological agendas, etc., what contextualizing critical discourse is doing. Perhaps we can point to some of the most meaningful processes in your collective practice and link them to queries of ethnographic recording in contemporary video.

Your tapes break new ground in media discourses on the Middle East. Visually and conceptually they're sophisticated. *...Up to the South* was produced in part for

the *Counterterror* series organized by Annie Goldson and Chris Bratton, "taking as its departure point how the 'term' terrorism has been used to obscure the historical roots of political conflict." This is another angle... the angle of the representation of terrorism, which is vastly important to our dismantling of the justification for our national "fears" of Arabs and instability in the Middle East. This is a crucial departure, it seems to me, when it comes to deconstructing arguments inherent in media rhetoric, such as, which forms of terror are acceptable and palatable and which are to be eschewed.

Your tapes have also been out long enough to have gained intellectual currency here and abroad. Likewise, the works seem to fit into an ensemble of *post-colonial* tapes which problematize conventional positionings, subjectivity, objectivity, etc. As an artist who actively participates in the redefinition of a specific genre, who would you like your videotapes to effect and why?

JAYCE SALLOUM: What we're really talking about here are seams and creases, or disjoints and fissures, if that. I'd love to think of cracks in the underbelly or an implosion of the stereotypes, the conventions, but that too may be wishful thinking. Redefinition may be possible on some scale at least within the work itself or the various discursive activities that take place around it. Maybe the most we can hope for is some type of lasting effect in our community, whatever community that is, and that in itself may take all of our energies.

I think of what I'm doing as rather obscure. It takes years to get a tape off the ground and out there, and takes such a toll that one has to be making it for oneself first, and then a small circle of friends and colleagues, expanding outward. Any *audience* beyond this is a rather amorphous object to predict, so I set up the work to be *read* on different levels by different viewers, at times in different languages (metaphorically & literally), and sometimes through the structure and familiarity of content, specific audiences would have access over others. I always try to construct an active audience, not providing easy answers or passive information, but often aiming to provoke, producing a productive frustration in the viewer. Here, the viewers are responsible for how they're perceiving, or at least there can be questions raised about the baggage they've brought to the work and the responses they have within a very particular/problematized *field* or set of inquiries. I'm not into this PBS style, knee-jerk game of show and tell. I don't think *understanding* is possible, or that the *subject* can ever be *known*, as far as the western viewer's understanding of the *other culture*. The most we can hope for is a kind of empathy, an awareness of the situation and some sense of the subjectivities at stake. This is both a visual/aural sense as well as a sense of the political/subjective positions.

I am still asked about balance and objectivity, as if there is a place where context is equivocal or there is a parity of voices and access to an audience. This question is not only naive, (often times the work isn't shown because of the overt politics of the tapes or because programmers can't find an opposing voice to *balance* it out), it also betrays a very narrow and simplistic understanding of media. There is no such thing as *objectivity* in this domain. You have to look to and through the subjective for whatever *truths* you find. Balance has to be looked at in a greater context than what you are seeing in one particular moment. We forget there is a whole history of misinformation, misrepresentation and blatant lies accepted as *truths* here in this county, and others like it, especially considering the history of the Middle East, and the more recent Israeli and other western aggressions there.

So there is no one privileged audience, but rather many corresponding or parallel audiences having various accesses to the work. Because the tapes are constructed in a manner that lends themselves to a discursive reading, referencing a ground, a history of social acts and re-construction, I am not worried that they could be taken out of context or de-materialized. Their arguments are self-contained. They're meant to be effective both conceptually and physically, at times actually working with the equilibrium, the visceral and emotional conditions of the viewer, though always with a direct connection to the perception, the reading of the representation, the history of that representation and the questions raised herein.

M H : I want to focus on *...Up to the South* because it is the most activist of your Middle East tapes. It's a self-conscious exploration of the issues on the ground in South Lebanon and of the visual means used in that exploration. This self-consciousness also makes it the most conventional of the three tapes. You have said of the tape,

> The story told/accounted for and revealed contains a particular
> subjecthood that one is at once close to but always kept distant from.
> Moving beyond naming and identifying, the experiences recorded
> trangress this imposition. In an attempt to make evident the machinery,
> the apparatus of documentary, the act of mediation is made obvious.
> Forefronting the cutting, the editing, the elimination and obsessions of
> the construction process, visual and audio segments are presented
> and received one after another. Basic blocks are linked conceptually
> over broken spaces, gestures are cut off, their weight collapsing
> them forward into a spiral of consecutive accounts that slice up, or

*sever the approach of documentary, the encroachment, the manipula-
tion that is the inevitable by-product of this history of scientific
and cultural imperialism. This is a mediating "language" of transposed
experience, a reluctant documentary.*

How were you aware of adapting, if at all, the nuances of this "mediating 'language'" as you went into Lebanon as a site of experience and documentary production? Did your methodology change, either by choice or necessity, when working
there?

JS: My methodology is constantly being re-invented, through the production and conceptualizing of each project I try to develop an approach specific to those sets of terms and experiences. Video does have certain constants,
though, like its mediating properties. These are often mixed up with the
properties of language. I mean, this term "language" has to be bracketed.
Video is not a language. It may have elements of language, but this substi-
tution is subject to misreading especially within the European video art
world. In Europe the two semantic vocabularies are constantly being confused and talked about in an overly simplified notion of "video as language."

In figuring the Lebanon project there was plenty of conceptual baggage
(not to mention over 1/2 ton of video equipment) that I was bringing along
for better or worse. Baggage that I had been working with/through in many
previous projects. There were also the tools of the process, the *syntax* structure or editing system and the critique inherent in it, the methodology of
research, the shooting mannerisms, the collecting of appropriated footage,
the intricate obsessive logging of it all, the refining and slicing up of the
material, the building of sequences, the re-joining, the deliberate weaving
and layering, the conceptual and physical shifting, the building of narrative
through recurrent images and metaphors, the spreading out of narrative, the
fragmenting of it into contin-
uous and discontinuous
threads, the use of disjunctive video and audio ele-
ments, the matching & mis-
matching and editing of
audio from material recorded and gathered, the use of
text in titles, sub-titles,
inter-titles & headlines, the
lack of easy monikers, the

use of visual and aural jokes, the use of laughter as a critical tool, the suspension of belief, the ending of information, the insistence on moments of pleasure and the production of frustration. These are all elements or "nuances" if you like, that I had been developing in my work in video and other media since 1978.

In *(Introduction to the End...)* I was able to direct these elements at a specific political situation regarding the construction of the *Arab* in the media and the representations of the Middle East produced by the West. Initially this project had started out as something very different from the way it ended up. In 1988 I went to the West Bank and the Gaza Strip and spent a few weeks recording Palestinian accounts of the occupation both inside and outside the *Green Line*, and was following around an NBC news crew to different locations. They were in the middle of this "eye witness" tour with educational and religious leaders from Houston, Texas. This was shortly after the beginning of the Intifada (Dec. 8, 1987).

After spending three weeks in Beirut, on my way back to California, I still was trying to figure out what to do with the forty plus hours I had recorded. I was adamant that I wanted to do something completely different than the works with appropriated TV footage that I had done before, partly because it was too labor intensive and partly because I thought that this type of material warranted a different approach. While I was mulling this over, I finished a short tape in California, *Once You've Shot the Gun You Can't Stop the Bullet, 8:00, 1988,* which combined footage from travels through sixteen different countries: from my former home in Kelowna, B.C.with my mother pointing to the Canadian map; to watching the *Cosby* show in Beirut. This tape tackled the idea of distance and alienation in moving through cultures and personal relationships... the space and separation that always remains. It turned out to be a blend of my older style of quick editing with some of the techniques we were to use subsequently in Lebanon when working with longer first person accounts. Right after finishing this tape, I moved to New York. I was thinking about what I wanted to do with the material collected in the Occupied Territories. I thought I would produce a piece which strung together stories of life under Israeli occupation. I started looking for someone to work with to do the translations and to help make sense out of the material, ideally someone both inside and outside of the culture.

After meeting with several Palestinians living in New York who were involved in the media community, I decided to work on *(Introduction to the End...)* with Elia Suleiman. After much discussion and negotiation, I agreed to turn this tape into a collaboration using my material as found footage,

Opposite: Still from **(Introduction to the End of an Argument) Speaking for oneself.../ Speaking for others**, 1990, by **Jayce Salloum** and **Elia Suleiman.** (Elvis Presley in "Harem Scarum.")

joined with appropriated footage ranging from Lumiere's depictions of Egypt, to Valentino, Elmer Fudd, *Exodus*, Elvis in *Harem Scarum,* etc., to *The Raiders of the Lost Arc* and *Nightline*. I dreaded the thought of once again coming face to face with volumes of television and movie material, but was reconciled to the fact that before one could make any more representations of/from the Middle East, we had to confront the representations that previously existed and formed the dominant images and stereotypes that we were up against. We had to carve out a space, arresting/deconstructing the imagery and ideology, decolonizing and recontextualizing it to provide a space for other voices and projects to emerge or exist. We mimicked the form of television, trying to subvert its methodology in an implosionary way. Basically we made a conceptual attack, an aggressive work, but conceptual nevertheless because realistically we couldn't hope to dent the mass of misrepresentation that existed and continues to exist.

The Lebanon project, including the tapes and year long workshops, both extended and provided alternatives to the positions adopted in *(Introduction to the End...).* Approaching Lebanon, I had to first *find* it, locate it, its history of representation, its consumption in the West, and its current situation. This is what *(This is Not Beirut)...* tries to deal with, this and the making of *...Up to the South. ...Up to the South* worked with the notion of accounting and re-counting experience. We (Walid Ra'ad and myself) had to devise a method to present these stories while still constructing a piece that would critique the documentary genre and its history of representing other cultures. This was done for the most part in the editing process, much after having been there. While there we gathered as much material as we could (over 150 hours of interviews and close to 50 hours of archival material), the methods we devised for this were more of a shooting plan, figuring out a schematic of representative subjects, then interviewing them and recording the moments in-between. So this was a new way of working for me. Instead of an all encompassing initial gathering of material, we focused on a group of people that we tried to locate and get close to. We had many discussions about what forms or levels of manipulation should/could be used when handling the interview material, what we had to *preserve*, remain *truthful* to, deciding whether scripting could be mixed into the *live* accounts, how to handle this material as opposed to the handling of the appropriated footage used in my earlier tapes. And what to do with this responsibility of representation, who and what it was responsible to: the subjects taped, or the object of the tape itself? We didn't rule out much in the gathering stage and figured the rest of it out as we went along. It's like this for each tape, though, trying to come up with the most appropriate methodology, usually stumbling along for quite a while without really knowing how things will look in the end.

M H : But this move from *(Introduction to the End...)* to *(This is not Beirut)...* is a dialogic development in which you disclose your process (and subjectivity) rather than focus on the logics of news media per se. I'm going to continue on *...Up to the South*, if you don't object, because for me the entire project provokes a certain amount of awe. I guess I connect some element of "danger" to the whole notion of "occupied territory," so your having traveled there and worked in this region of South Lebanon is disorienting. My media-induced western conceptions of "that (unfathomable) mess over there" has been exploded. Your experience is a fantasy that a lot of people probably would like to fulfill. Our curiosity is piqued by absence and what is seemingly forbidden. After all, the Middle East is usually represented *from the outside* looking in, as a place in which all the players are *historically* entangled, we have come to *think* that delving any further would reek disaster.

(This is not Beirut)..., if I understand it correctly, is a tape about the experience of being there, an "unwriting," if you will, of *...Up to the South* or of your positions being cast by the context of history while engaged in the production of knowledge about a place, this "site" of Lebanon.

Beginning with a provocative mini-history of orientalist images of Beirut, postcard fantasies and surrogate names for the city, such as JEWEL OF THE EAST or CROSSROADS OF CIVILIZATION, the first portion of the tape points to the eye of orientalism as it has rendered "exotic" this ancient city. The tape then elaborates upon Beirut using various mediations: a single take of a building, (one of the buildings vividly pictured in a glossy postcard you used earlier) which is framed for quite some time like a post-

Still from **This is Not Beirut**, 1994, by **Jayce Salloum**. (Place des Martyrs, Beirut)

card, archival footage, passages through landscape and buildings. But while viewing these takes, an effective contrast is made to the visual "ideal" depicted in the postcards — instead of an azure strand, or some luxurious rendition of Beirut as capital, we see vacant lots, destruction, weeds emerging from discarded objects, torn posters, beachfronts and mazes of dwellings, a poetry of reality. After some time you interrupt this urbanism with a handheld postcard, juxtaposed against its exact likeness (in reality) of a perfect blue sky. A relationship is drawn between the space of the viewer, what is being viewed and the interlocutor of the documenting process. A critical rupture occurs. After this, we are taken through Beirut from the vantage point of a moving vehicle which effectively exacts a relationship between the viewer, the person with the camera, and the world outside the car window. We glimpse Beirut as a composition of multiple landscapes, the imagery functions as a metaphor for the complex collagings, accumulations and layerings of your documentary process. They are notations which refer visually, without having '"to speak" it, to the complexity of Beirut.

Considering the range of your videotapes from, *"In the Absence of Heroes..."* *Warfare; A case for context, 105:00, 1984,* through to your most recent *(This is Not Beirut)...,* what links them conceptually into this area of "occupied territory" or the sense of a metaphorical and real landscape?

JS: One can't talk about *landscape* without talking about the politics of that land, both externally and internally. I mean to address both the *land* as concept and the land as physical substance, where *nation* crosses over into imagination and attachments are beyond the metaphorical. I see psychological demarcations as territorial as well. This is where conceptually as well as ideologically the work links up in its engagement or attempted trangressions of political domains. Starting with the earlier tapes where most of the footage was *appropriated* from television, this is pretty straightforward. I was moving into this space of a pedagogical device, this narrow transcription of information and emotion with an overwhelming influence in the political and personal realms of one's life. The trial here was to undercut the belly of the beast, its hegemonic status, using its own imagery, its own tools to expose its organs, its inner workings, so to speak. The danger was that people would read these incursions as formal collage and not see the other acts taking place between the seams, behind the various levels of production and destruction.

After this I went into other awkward areas of experience, *occupying* spaces or working with positions that wouldn't seem immediately or apparently mine to work with. I've heard *Episode 1: So. Cal, 33:00, 1988* called a "woman's tape" because of the obvious subjectivity of the speaking protagonist. It's more about moving between colliding or transferring cultures and the geo-political and social conditions of living in Southern California.

In *(Introduction to the End...)* this idea of spatial encroachment was further defined. There was the representation of the Occupied Territories (of Palestine) and that of the Arab subject. There was as well our own posi-

Opposite, top and bottom: stills from **Up to the South**, 1993, by **Jayce Salloum** and **Walid Ra'ad**.

tions and subjectivities claimed and denied within the collaborative process. The metaphorical aspect, so rich in the descriptive history of the Middle East, got carried into and reversed in the collaborative process: a westerner with Lebanese origins working with a Palestinian living in the West and trying to make sense of, or re-presenting, the triangulations involved.

Going into Lebanon we were familiar with the problematic *territories* (conceptually and physically) we were working within, and those we were trying to avoid. Lebanon had been used as a metaphor, as a *site*, serving the real and imaginary both for the inhabitants as well as the various *visitors,* throughout its history. It had been a ground for a history of claims, discursive texts and acts of *re-construction*, and had become an adjective for the nostalgia of our past and the fears of the future.

In the *West* we have come to understand so very little in spite of the massive amounts of *information* we received regarding Lebanon, the war and especially the situation in the south of the country. Just for one to even mention the name [Lebanon] brings all sorts of images to mind. What basis in which realities did these images have? Where in Lebanon were these realities situated? Who were we really talking about, *us* or *them*, or some other construction in-between? For it is *in-between* that a *documentor* in a culture or a landscape is caught.

Other issues we faced were, once again: the *West's* and our construction of knowledge *of* that area, and how the projects were going to be read; representing diverse subjectivities and positions of individuals and positions within particular groups; and the continuation of this string of *documentary productions* intricately tied up in the history of colonialism, post-colonialism and the mediation of images and this extenuated orientalism. What was our own position as image/video makers, "artists" etc.? We were placed, or

placed ourselves, somewhere between being family members, visitors, tourists, guides and unwilling orientalists: ...never occupying any one position for too long; fluctuating peripatetically between the act of re-producing and the deconstruction of such an act and its object;

121

setting out boundaries in the project and transgressing them; placing/situating our own subjectivities in relationship to the positions involved and to the instability of identity which exists within a diverse culture and the displacement between cultures.

In the Lebanon projects we also asked, what is the history and structure of the documentary genre specifically from the perspective of the subjects/culture viewed, and the practitioners practicing, especially in this West-East relationship? We stressed the imperative of local production and the need to be involved in the community at as much of a fundamental level as we could. In the tapes we made there is a heightened aggression towards the western viewer, a challenge to view the material for what it is: not positions of victimization, but of confrontation or at least an a non-acquiesced presence. I don't support a culturally chauvinist view. I'm more interested in the blurred aspects of a post-colonial condition, the non-essentialized positions, where hybridity is the norm and identity is a continual negotiation of sorts. I do champion and promote the position of the right to exclusive self-representation when that identity is being negated or trying to find its space. But I would draw the line where that claiming becomes exclusionary to the point where dogma takes over and the authority is not empowering anymore but reductively defining others' identity for them. That's the irony, when it's turned around and one's own identity, subjectivity, affinities or whatever you want to call them, are thus denied, and you are prevented from speaking. So, as is talked about in *...Up to the South* the point is more *how* one speaks, *how* the story is articulated and *how* references are made, on what level and at what point of contact are the issues expressed.

M H : *Thanks.*

Thanks to Craig Baldwin for his assistance. —**M H**

Newe Sogobia is not for sale!

by Jesse Drew

With the glittering gambling citadels of Reno in your rear view mirror, I-80 unfolds before you, stretching out upon the barren high plains of the State of Nevada. It cuts through towns like Lovelock and Mill City, Winnemucca and Battle Mountain — isolated outposts of gas stations and coffee shops perched precariously on the edge of an enormous expanse of dry rock, scrub brushes and sagebrush. The vast terrain of earth is only dwarfed by the endless open skies, a giant inverted blue bowl which meets the horizon's boundary as it undulates through hundreds of miles of rising heatwaves.

Somewhere past Battle Mountain and fifty miles short of Elko, a road cuts off to the right, jutting perpendicularly into the sagebrush. Passing few cars or dwellings, we continue travelling on this two-lane road for an hour. The vast expanse of open space and sagebrush seems unconquerable, as if we're riding on an enormous treadmill. Recognizable landmarks are 20 miles, 50 miles, and 100 miles away, so it's impossible to tell how much ground we're covering. After passing though a town with one general store and a post office, we see our destination — a clump of trees, nestled on the base of a dry, bald mountain, off in the distance.

As you head onto the dirt road which leads to the Dann's ranch, a sign greets you with:

WESTERN SHOSHONE NATIONAL SECURITY AREA:
BY SPECIAL ORDER OF THE WESTERN SHOSHONE NATION.

The Dann ranch is a several hundred acre spread of wooden structures, trailers, and cattle pens enclosed by fenceposts of gnarled branches. Tool sheds and workshops are scattered amidst old farming harrows and abandoned tractors and vehicles. The main house huddles under the sparse clump of trees, seeking the only respite from the blistering high desert sun. This tenacious homestead, rooted amidst the sage and shrubs of the Nevada desert, has been home to the Dann family since the quelling of open hostility between the Shoshone Nation and the U.S. Federal government around the time of the Civil War.

This area of Nevada high desert, known as the Great Basin, is the traditional land of Native American nations such as the Western Shoshone, the Paiute, and the Washoe. For centuries, the U.S. government saw these lands only as a miserable and punishing obstacle towards reaching the West. During the Civil War, the union government signed a treaty with the Western Shoshone which permitted the unobstructed passing of the railway. This

was critical for the shipment of silver from the Sierra Nevada to the East, which was used to fund the Union Army in its battle with the Confederacy. This treaty, known as the Treaty of Ruby Valley, did not cede ownership of the land to the U.S. Unlike many other treaty-based land deals, the U.S. Government did not think to acquire ownership as it never thought it would covet this particular land. To this day, the U.S. government has no legal claim to this land. The Dann's, like most of the other Shoshone, settled here and began to raise cattle when their previous nomadic life traversing and hunting in the Great Basin was coming to an end.

Still from **Newe Segobia is not for sale!**, 1993, by **Jesse Drew**.

For over a hundred years, the Dann family has lived on this homestead, nestled among the sagebrush, raising cattle and horses on land that has been home to their ancestors for centuries. They've been able to live in relative peace for most of these years, until recently, when the white man developed a renewed interest in this area they previously considered worthless. Renewed mineral exploitation (like gold mining) and the land's use as a testing ground for nuclear weapons has focused attention on who owns the land. The Bureau of Land Management, the arm of the U.S. State which ostensibly is designated "caretaker" of the land, has decided to step in and take over the traditional lands of the Western Shoshone. These "caretakers" of the land in the Federal interest, who have allowed 900 nuclear bombs to be detonated and have okayed some of the largest strip mining operations in the world, have decided that Western Shoshone cattle were eating too much grass and must be removed.

When the cattle rustling cowboys of the Bureau of Land Management (BLM) appeared on the horizon to round up Mary and Carrie Dann's cattle, they weren't prepared for the fight the Western Shoshone sisters would put up. After they erected a temporary corral and herded cattle into it, Mary Dann wrestled away from a Federal agent and jumped into the pen to protect her livestock. Adding to the unexpected resistance put up by Mary was the introduction of another factor — a video camcorder which was witnessing the event. Faced with the determination of Carrie Dann and the possible creation of another Rodney King video incident, the agents thought it best to let the fight continue another day, and the cattle were released.

This confrontation between Mary Dann and the Federal Agents was captured on an 8mm camcorder by a volunteer with no video experience. The camcorder had been bought recently to document how helicopters of the BLM had been causing stampedes of wild horses, causing them to run into barbed wire fences to a brutal and bloody death. After the confrontation, the tape was brought down to San Francisco where I edited a quick press release from the material which was then dubbed and shown to the press and Native American organizations. Condemnation of the brutality inflicted on these elderly Native women by our federal government was quick and furious. This confrontation in the remote high desert of Nevada has by now been replayed in thousands of dwellings, community centers, and offices via cable television and through the mass distribution of videocassettes by Native American groups and their supporters.

Producing *Newe Sogobia is not for sale!*, a half hour depiction of the struggle of the Dann's and the Western Shoshone, made me abandon many of the assumptions I had taken for granted about telling a story on videotape. Perhaps the most striking change was the way the geography altered my sense of time and space. Urban life, with its horizons obliterated by highrises, billboards, smog and apartment towers, causes one to focus

Western Shoshone territory in Great Basin area of Nevada.

Image of Western Shoshone woman, Carrie Dann's grand-mother.

inwards on the teeming rush of traffic and swells of peo-ple. The rapid pace of urban life tends to be reinforced by the closing in of open space and the compression of the visual landscape. The ubiq-uitous media environment joins in this spiral of speed as well, delivering the gratu-itous fast cuts of MTV and advertising. Video editors rarely challenge the notion that speed and rapid pace are the only way to grab an audience's minute attention-span amidst the visual cacophony of today's urban media environment.

It took a few days of wandering around the Dann homestead to adjust to the immensity of the landscape. It took me that long to adjust my field of vision to the great distances between visual objects on the horizon. From the base of the hill we were nestled on, I could see perhaps one hundred miles in an arc of 180 degrees. I could see when someone was turning off the main road by the post office by the plume of dust kicked up by their tires. As evening fell, I watched, from an old bathtub on the side of a hill, with hot mineral water cascading around me from an ancient hot spring, as a thunderstorm, far to the south, hurled bolts of lightning to the desert floor. The sky overhead was peaceful and sparkling with stars. Far off to the southeast, the sky flickered from the natural gas being vented and burned off from one of the largest gold mines in North America.

This sense of time and space became a natural part of the story of how the Dann's took on the most powerful state apparatus in the world. This expanded sense of time is evident from the minimal amount of editing and the prevalence of real time given to trying to relay the story from the Shoshone point of view. It is crucial to understanding what Carrie Dann is feeling to be able to witness with her while she is standing with her cattle in the holding pen. In the conversation between the police and the Shoshone, the spaces of silence and the minor comments and tone of voice are as important as the words in relaying the sense of the land and terrain. There is more meaning in the space of silence in the holding pen, with Mary pro-tecting her cattle and the sageland behind her, than in the actual confronta-tion itself. Mary's connection to the land is evident from her comfort and determination while she waits with her cattle.

Another concern of mine was to become as invisible as possible, because this story was that of the Shoshone's — not mine. Real life unfolds in real-time. As videomakers we sometimes rely too heavily on our own media construction, via heavy editing, effects and clever devices, which call more attention to the videomaker than the subject of the story.

While we witness a dramatic playing out of personal wills and interests, the battle is ultimately, over the land itself. The dramatic backdrop of the terrain serves as the silent, omnipotent witness as the original inhabitants and caretakers of the land struggle determinedly to keep it from being taken. For while the land is only another commodity to be carved up and sold to the U.S. agents, this land to the Shoshone nation is quite literally, their mother.

QUOTES:

Well, the way I look at it, the Western Shoshone people have been here since time immemorial. And so we refer to this land — all of us, as the Shoshone land. I look at this land from the basic point of our religious beliefs. This land is not just a land. This land is tied to us through our religious beliefs and it's also considered as a mother. It's mother to all life and not only to human life, but to all life. So, we look at this land from the basic point, not of individual owner-ship, but the basis that this land is mother to all things. So, it has a very significant meaning to us and we can in no way accept money for it, because it's like our grandmother told us a long time ago, this land is like a woman. A female. It provides for us all the necessities of life, from birth up the time we die and then we go back to the land.
— CARRIE DANN

Well, I was out checking on the cows. When I came back my brother said there was somebody waiting for me from the BLM office. So, I took

off my saddle and put my horse away and there
he was waiting for me in the house, and we
talked, and he says, "Do know you're trespass-
ing?" I told him I wasn't. I told him that
the only time I'd consider myself trespassing
is when I went over onto the Paiute land.
"Then I would be trespassing," I says. I'm in
our own territory, in our treaty. I told
him about the treaty and I showed him the map
and he told me, "well, that's a big territory."
And I told him, "Yes, and I said I'm still
within the boundary."

— MARY DANN

What happens when the mining companies get
done is whole mountains disappear or all this
gravel from the rocks underneath appears and
new mountains are created. And these new
mountains as far as I'm concerned, they have a
lot of cyanide in them. Maybe it's unfair
criticism as far as the mining companies are
concerned, but the open pit mines do destroy a
lot of land. Only that I understand that with
the new discoveries of ore where they have
to pump out a lot of water, they pump millions
of gallons of water a day, and I think from
looking at it from the points of being stewards
of the land, I don't know why they allow it;
I'm not what you call a hydrologist or
scientist or one of those people they work
with, but it's just basic sense that when you
take water out, your water table falls, and
when your water table falls I assume certain
mountains will become dry and the springs
will dry up, when this happens there'll be no
more life on it, the only life there'll be
is big equipment with men sitting on it and
destroying more land.

— CARRIE DANN

Still from **Newe Segobia is not for sale!**, 1993, by **Jesse Drew**.

The sun comes up in the east, sets in the west.
Water runs downhill. These are things that no
human being can change. Only the creator can
change this. So, Shoshone law as the creator
gave it to us is not like the law of the United
States where every year or almost every year
Congress sits in session and makes new laws and
does away with its old ones and so forth.
Shoshone law, once it's in place, that's it,
unless the creator makes the sun come up in the
west and sink in the east, then we would change
our law. As long as the natural law remains
as it is then Shoshone law is very simple, it
is based on the natural things that happen
in the land.

— RAYMOND YOWELL, CHIEF,
WESTERN SHOSHONE NATIONAL COUNCIL

*Je roulais lentement. C'était plein jour,
pleine lumière, chaud et sueur.*

I was driving slowly.
It was broad daylight, hot and sweat.

Adriene Jenik

*Je roule. J'hurle, gueul'e de rock, la bouche
pleine des paroles que je chante au même rythme
que la voix de femme qui fait éclater la radio.*

I'm driving. Howling, rock-jaw'd, mouth
full of lyrics I sing to the same beat
as the woman's voice exploding on the radio.

Ici dans le désert, la peur est précise.
Ici, il n'y a que du vent, des épines, des serpents,
des lycoses, des bêtes, des scelettes...

Here in the desert, fear is precise.
Here there are only wind, thorns, snakes,
wolf-spiders, beasts, skeletons...

Adriene Jenik

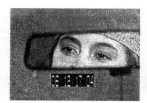

MAUVE DESERT is a film/video translation by Adriene Jenik
of Nicole Brossard's experimental novel of the same name.
Nicole Brossard is a celebrated Quebeçoise writer.

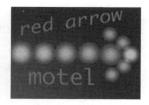

Mélanie is a fifteen year-old of the memory.
She steals her mother's Meteor every chance she gets and
drives away from her mother's lover Lorna and toward the dawn.

Maude Laures is the middle-aged academic who
stumbles upon Mélanie's life in a second-hand bookshop
and translates her into another tongue.

Adriene Jenik, a saturn-cycling video artist, brings the novel
from Montréal to the Southwest, from print to pyxel, from night
to day, and from one generation of women to another.

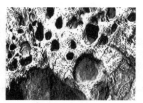

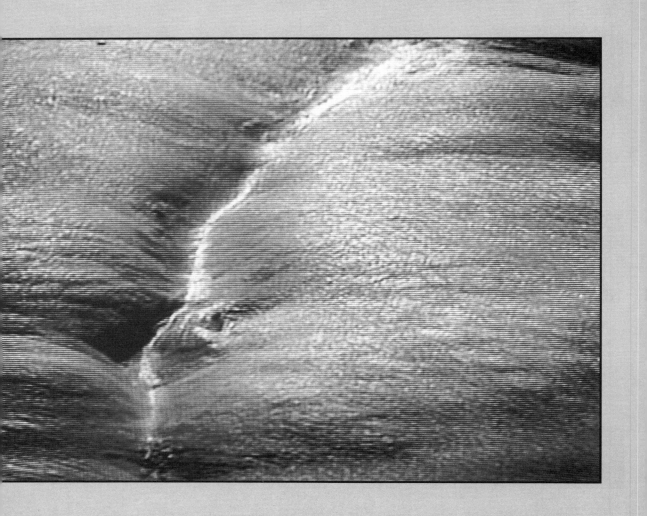

M A P S   O F   T I M E :

MOTHER

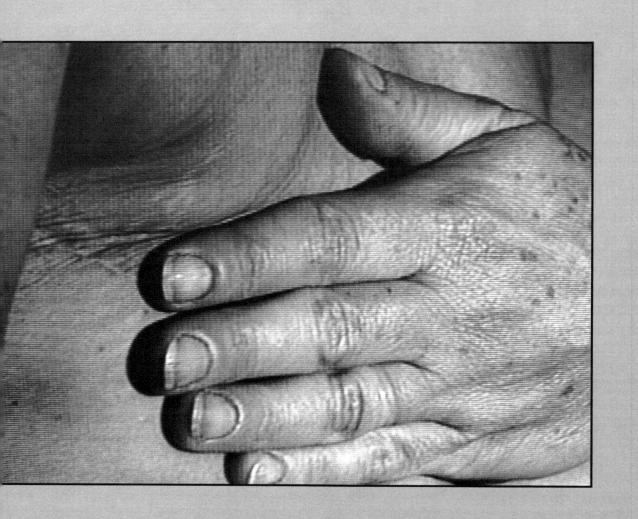

MAPS OF TIME:

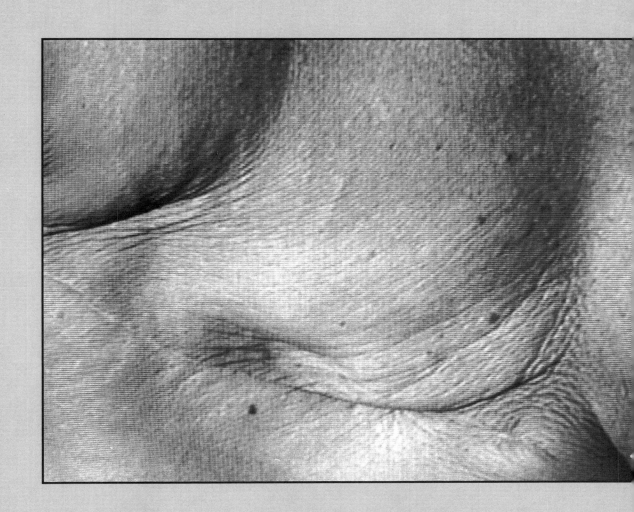

NANCY

Nanotechnology

Machines in the Microscopic Realm

AN EXHIBITION AT

THE MUSEUM OF JURASSIC TECHNOLOGY

October, 1993 – April, 1994

N A N O T E C H N O L O G Y is a term used to describe a number of new and emerging technologies. These technologies, however, can be divided into two basic groups: **molecular nanotechnology** — the process of building up or creating structures molecule by molecule; and **micromachining** — the activity of creating ever smaller machines through a variety of existing, if exotic, processes primarily revolving around silicon based techniques.

As the molecular nanotechnologist's constructions are increasing in size the micromachinist's devices are becoming smaller. Currently, micromachinist's measure their structures built one molecule at a time in nanometers (or billionths of a meter). While the techniques and procedures of the two disciplines are currently very distinct from one another, it appears that the two branches will inevitably meet at some microscopic place in the not too distant future.

While molecular nanotechnology appears to hold remarkable promise for the coming decades and has been called a revolution with potential impact comparable to the industrial revolution, this endeavor is nonetheless, in its infancy and, accordingly, the Museum of Jurassic Technology's exhibition concentrated on micromachines of nanotechnology in order to have tangible objects to display.

Research in micromaching is being done at a number of institutions around the country and in other countries as well. The applications typically mentioned in conversations on the future of this field include biomedical, robotics, communications, surveillance and transportation. While practical applications of this research are beginning to emerge, researchers in this field agree that the majority of applications for these astonishingly minute contrivances have yet to be imagined.

Opposite page:
fig. 01 MAGNETIC GENERATOR
Yu Chong Tai
California Institute of Technology

Right:
fig. 02 ATOMIC FORCE MICROSCOPE TIP
Yu Chong Tai
California Institute of Technology

Left:

fig. 03 WOBBLE MOTORS
Shuvo Roy and Mehran Mehregany
Case Western Reserve University

Below:

fig. 04 MICRO SPRING
Yu Chong Tai
California Institute of Technology

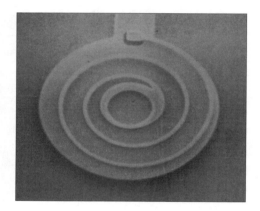

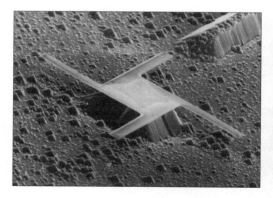

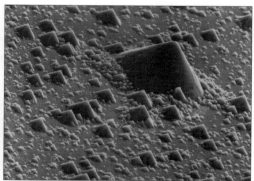

figs. 05 & 06 ETCHING OF MICRO-PYRAMIDS
Left: in process (2 micron "propeller" insures precise etch) and
Right: after completion.

fig. 07 PRESSURE SENSORS
ON THE TIP OF A PIN
Nova Sensor

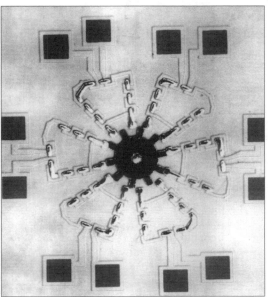

fig. 08 MAGNETIC MICROMOTOR
Chong H. Ahn and Mark G. Allen
Georgia Institute of Technology

THE MUSEUM OF JURASSIC TECHNOLOGY in Los Angeles,
California, is an educational institution dedicated to the advancement of knowledge and
the public appreciation of the Lower Jurassic.

Like a coat to two colors, the Museum serves dual functions. On the one hand,
the Museum provides the academic community with a specialized repository of relics and
artifacts from the Lower Jurassic, with an emphasis on those that demonstrate unusual
or curious technological qualities. On the other hand, the Museum serves the general public
by providing the visitor a hands-on experience of "life in the Jurassic."

THE MUSEUM OF JURASSIC TECHNOLOGY

9341 Venice Boulevard, Culver City, CA 90232-2621 (310) 836-6131, Tel.

I dream of a city where I live. There, there are many others like me. They are all different and they are all the same. They are from everywhere else, ending up here to begin again, bringing their trunks and suitcases full of clothes, books, trinkets, souvenirs, rituals, riches of different types and varying degrees, dreams, memories, filters of thousands of people and pages of interpretations and re-interpretations, faiths, values and reasons, looking for some space to unpack, carving out space where there is none, pocket islands, nations next to nations, cultures within cultures, side by side, they come and settle, entering old habits, forcing them to change, stirring a dormant strain of xenophobia embedded in the skins of inhabitants accustomed to notions of their own superiority, they scream: "go back home you filthy foreigners", even though they probably know that we have indeed "come" home, "back" is meaningless in the vocabulary of immigration. Living side by side with no borders, boundaries that do not need papers to cross them, like they were a long time ago.

Now, still under a system devised and implemented by western colonial powers centuries ago, the world fools itself into believing colonialism a thing of the past, that the history of mankind is one of conquering and war, colonialism being but a footnote in that history, that now a state of independence exists in independent states, 'responsibility' is a dirty, outmoded word, that now everyone is a victim and per-

I live in a city that is not my city. The city where I live is not the city I live in. My city exists both within and without the city where I live. You want me to tell you about my city yet I have never lived there. I want to tell you about the city where I live but you say it is not mine to tell about.

In the city where I live the terrain is constantly shifting. Yet the maps don't have to be re-drawn, they just have to be read differently from the last time. It is easy to get around. Many people, however, find themselves lost. Or, in constant motion, they remain in one place. There are many circles in this city.

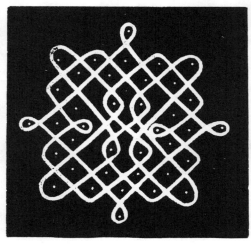

In some parts of the city the past is embedded in every step you take. In others the future takes place before a present emerges out of the past. Memories get mixed up with dreams.

It is painful to walk in some parts of this city. The streets are paved with thorns sharp enough to pierce you shoes, walls are abrasive and it sometimes rains stones. However the unturned corner is always compelling. Promise keeps most people keeping on in this city.

The city where I live has many habits, hard to break. Yet, amnesia is an ingredient of the atmosphere, and pervades the growth of this city. Thus the city is always surging ahead, unshackled by the past, its growth swift and inventive. But it cannot remember, its structure carries no wisdom and this may be its downfall.

Text by Meena Nanji
Design concept: Meena and Ameeta Nanji

petrator of some injustice, that colonial residue is non-existant or at least inconsequential for the present's complicated times.

But we are still embedded in that system. Colonial nation states. Land compartmentalized without regard to evolved divisions. Not only was land torn up, but psyches too. Complexes of white superiority built to cover up the mess, the torn down scapes of people and place. With amazing resilience these still stand almost unscathed in 'independent' nations. Yet how can we function in a state that is our very tearing apart? Only in fragments.

So fragmented they move, pearls of mercury un-forming and re-forming into ever more minute globules, slipping and sliding across lands and customs until they gather up again, once more a unified stream, in the cities of the west. Ironically it is here that they are finding our prior cohesion, strength, voice. So now, slowly, peacefully, familiar with the city's codes that were first imposed and later mimicked in their own, they are taking over the western city. Reclaiming land and ideas, not in accordance with old colonial paradigms, but with an unconscious, organic wisdom, they are relocating not only in new land but in the new loci of power. Gaining access to places never before dreamed of.

Access to recovery: recovering a memory, values of who they were before they were de-valued, before the desire to be someone else was instilled in them. covering their old ideas, they are forming and gaining access to new ones. Access to education, to technology, to knowledge. Losing their languages, they are becoming fluent in the languages never uttered, that slip through fibreoptic cables and wires, nonsensisical numbers which carry communiques of power across the globe in seconds, abstractions that can destroy people and nations while causing no damage to the inanimate.

I live in a city that lives in me. This city encompasses the whole world yet it is as cozy as a living room.

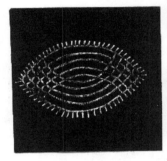

There are many routes to the same destination. If arriving is your point then the shortest route would be best. But these are always subject to heavy traffic. If you enjoy the ride you may take a longer route. Then, however, your destination may change location according to your mood. Its' name, however, will remain the same.

There is no fear of the unknown in this city. Strangers are welcome. We are all different and we are all the same. Always changing, this city is secure in transition.

I know some of the streets well yet there are still many places to discover. I can go to one part and smell the smells of my childhood. I can walk to another and new scents, never before experienced will hit my nostrils. Sometimes they intermingle, the old and the new, and this is when I am the happiest.

Dark passageways, silent alleys. Sometimes I am afraid in this city. There are places I do not venture to visit for fear of encountering a memory on those dark streets that may throw me off my way.

Their growing numbers wreak havoc with the denominations of power, as they are counted and recounted, perpetual churnings of statistical evidence supporting their lesser value be it academic or gastronomic, but these numbers cannot keep up with their own that keep growing and growing, along with their demands of a different Way, their demands that they be recognized in the states they are in, be they rich

or poor, educated or not, their demand that the "equally opportunistic" gives way to equal opportunity, they are waving their hands in the air disrupting those carefully encoded messages emitted across the airwaves, permeating the atmosphere, that keep them out of their control.

Together in place but not yet in meaning, they are alone, with individual visons of utopia, yet something is emerging out of this combination of unlikely elements. The common experience of sharing the indignities of immigration, the bizarre juxtapositions and strange contradictions have given rise to a radical transfromation already in the works, emerging from the raw need to survive as whole, unfragmented people. States of natinhood are being destroyed amongst and within them as they force the western city to be the site of their true liberation.

PROBING INTO SCIENCE
DIANE BERTOLO

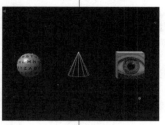

Elements shown here for illustration purposes only.

CLICK

CLICK

CLICK
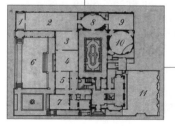

Library, Laboratory, Museum

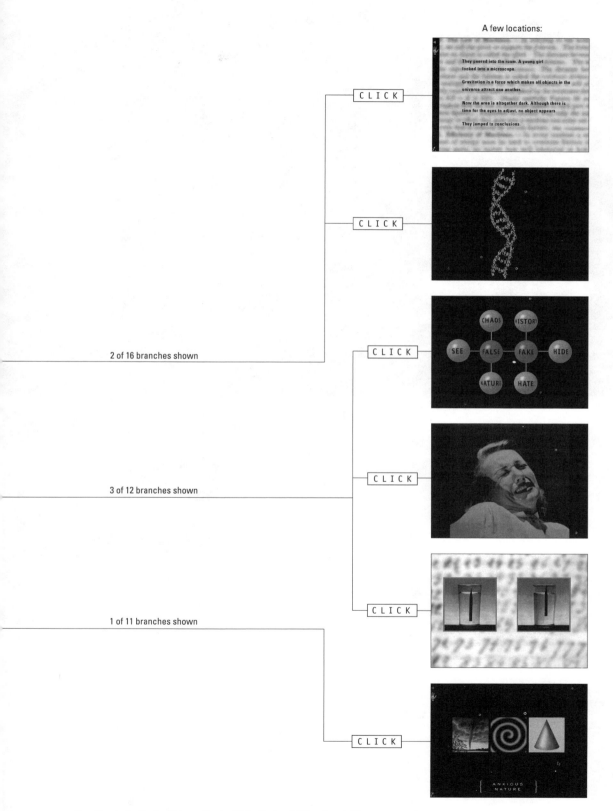

A few locations:

They peered into the room. A young girl
looked into a microscope.

Gravitation is a force which makes all objects in the
universe attract one another.

Now the area is altogether dark. Although there is
time for the eyes to adjust, no object appears.

They jumped to conclusions.

CLICK

CLICK

CLICK

CHAOS   HISTORY

SEE   FALSE   FAKE   HIDE

NATURE   HATE

CLICK

CLICK

CLICK

ANXIOUS
NATURE

2 of 16 branches shown

3 of 12 branches shown

1 of 11 branches shown

Kaucyila Brooke

Jane Cottis

Frances Salomé España

Harry Gamboa, Jr.

Victor Masayesva, Jr.

Merata Mita

Alberto Muenela

Chris Ortiz

Michelle Valladares

980

980

1000

1020

1020

Boundary Line

COMMON
GROUND

KH: I asked a friend of mine if she would ever consider living in another country. My "new country" in which to live was filled with romantic notions of a better life, a simpler life, and ideas of escaping what I know as the American self-confident attitude that we can fix *anything* and save *anything*. I was dreaming of opposition and action based on fleeing. ¶ But her answer surprised me. She suggested, "If that country wants us, I would consider living there." ¶ "If that country wants us." This concept sent me reeling. Suddenly in that small sentence I realized how very far I had to go to escape what I considered colonizing and dominant about the U.S., because I, too, had internalized it. And I also realized that I was making assumptions about the communities there, that they could easily be my own, without really understanding their common ground. **LP:** I've always been rather skeptical about identity politics, afraid I would too easily get subsumed under someone else's agenda. I always felt that privileging one dichotomy—like queer as opposed to straight—ran the risk of obscuring other points of commonality or difference amongst queers. And all evidence seemed to support this. ¶ In graduate school there were 4 dykes in a department of 32 graduate students. A one to eight ratio, if I may. But the word on the street was that the department was overrun with lesbians who ran the place. We were perceived as a unified, undifferentiated front: all the descriptions that ever trickled back to me sounded like some flanking platoon on midnight maneuvers. ¶ On the one hand, this conflation of our identities as "Amazon Lesbo Feminists" annoyed me. In terms of personality, politics and policy, the four of us were actually nothing alike and this eradication of our difference was belittling and disrespectful, especially in an environment where finding an "individual voice" is the party line. ¶ But, ironically, it was the perception that we had consolidated a lot of power in our "group" that actually gave us more power than we would have otherwise had. We hadn't planned on creating a unified front, and in fact we didn't see ourselves in this way. But others did. And they found it daunting. They respected us, in a perverse and sort of fearful way, as something which was bigger than the sum total of the parts. And this presence did have an impact on the department, and the people in it. This experience helped me to recognize the usefulness of strategic unity, and understand that, while I may have an attachment to my "individuality" (ha!), coming together and sharing common ground can have political efficacy. ¶ I see this section as a map for the politics of carving out a space where people come together and build coalitions based on affinities. KH: And what is a map if not a way to identify the relationships in a specific area, the relationships one ground has to anoth-

er? Maps also chart how a region is con *within* itself, its own orientation, its own particular character and "natural resources." ¶ As landscapes of living pictures, such as groups of peoples, are identified, they illustrate (out of necessity) the process of un-conventional representation, needing to be flexible, authentic and unprecedented. Such mapping is a reflection of the needs of the group, not one imposed from an outside charter, posing an external image of embodiment. There is a mandate to draw one's own map, chart one's own ground, plot and define one's own heartland.

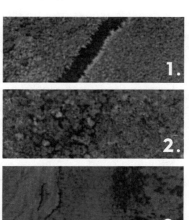

1.

2.

3.

Imagining Indians

A Native American Film and Video Festival

Introduction by Michelle Valladares
Essays by Merata Mita, Alberto Muenala
and Victor Masayesva, Jr.

Introduction

by Michelle Valladares

For two years I traveled from Indian conference to festival to powwow as production manager of Victor Masayesva's last film *Imagining Indians*. At some point in each event, over drinks, or a meal, or in a panel an inevitable conversation would arise around the following question: "Who has the right to film the Native American's story?" On the most obvious level this sets up a discussion of the indigenous producer vs. Hollywood, independent documentarians and ethnographic filmmakers. While the rights of each can be rationalized back and forth, the more demanding issues are those that we outsiders must confront. We who travel back and forth between the non-Indian and the Indian worlds, who have made these various communities the subjects of our work and the focus of our interests, must now examine the nature of our system of beliefs which give us the privilege and funding to fulfill our curiosity. This occurs when many of our colleagues in those same communities feel they are denied similar funding for a variety of reasons including a lack of a funding history, academic credentials or experience.

A consciousness around issues of representation has been created by filmmakers, writers and political activists, who have brought attention to the histories and stories of indigenous communities. But still it is a fact that in 1992, during the Columbus Quincentenary which was protested/celebrated across the United States, approximately a dozen dramatic feature films with Indian subjects were released and not one was produced or directed by a Native American filmmaker.

Within indigenous communities, the non-Native's involvement is debated. Some support it. Some are against it. Some have mixed feelings. The consequences vary from individual to community, to clan, to tribe. One is clear-

"Prayers For a New World"c   Designed by Victor Masayesva

IMAGINING INDIANS
A NATIVE AMERICAN FILM & VIDEO FESTIVAL
SCOTTSDALE CENTER FOR THE ARTS
JUNE 2 - 5, 1994

Poster for the **Imagining Indians** festival.

ly visible and that is the proliferation of indigenous film/media organiza-
tions, festivals and events that are linking together native communities
worldwide for information, resources and empowerment. Navajo, Yu'pik,
Quichua , Cheyenne, Mohawk, Ponca, Choctaw, Chippewa, Maori, Cree,
Aboriginal, Hopi, Arapaho and the members of many other groups gathered
together to dialogue and screen work amongst themselves at the *IMAGINING
INDIANS A Native American Film and Video Festival*, held at the Scottsdale
Center for the Arts in Scottsdale, Arizona from June 2–5, 1994. What differ-
entiated this festival from many of the previous I had attended was the fact

151

that it had been entirely programmed and presented by two Native American groups; ATLATL, National Service Organization for Native American Arts and the Native American Producers Alliance.

Before I left for Arizona I was struck by the media coverage of the Zapatista Rebellion in Chiapas, Mexico. The Zapatistas, who articulated an eloquent and urgent platform for the political and human rights violations of the nine million indigenous peoples of Mexico, utilized the media to effectively communicate their demands. Many of these same demands and hopes were expressed through stories from Mohawk to Santa Clara Pueblo to Northern Cheyenne to Choctaw in the screenings at the festival. Although the audience at the Imagining Indians Festival was mixed it was clear in the presentations that the agenda was about Native peoples talking to each other about issues of representation in media. There was a sense at this event that indigenous artists were powerfully taking their own stories and using their own voices to direct the discussion.

In this spirit, the following essays by Merata Mita, Victor Masayesva and Alberto Muenela articulate some of the positions presented at this festival and at other occasions. The list of films and videos screened over the four days is not comprehensive but provides a rich sample of the work available from various indigenous communities. For more information on the films, videos or artists please contact Ava Hamilton of the Native Producers Alliance at 303-494-8308. The work is out there and I urge you to fund, program and write about it.

Opening Comments

by Merata Mita

Given the corrupt world of film and television that assails us daily, we as indigenous filmmakers, recorders and programmers have a moral and spiritual responsibility to share our work with our own communities and to present it to the rest of the world.

Many of us have been given the knowledge and the stories of our old people and have succeeded in harnessing some of the skills and technology of the modern world. With the combined teachings of the old and the new, we are uniquely placed to show our people how we can manage the new ways and yet remain true to ourselves. We can use the new knowledge our way and make it more effective for us, by infusing it with the ancient wisdom of the old ones.

On a political front, it is absolutely necessary to present our films and videos to the mainstream. If only to remind the majority cultures that we are still here, and that we have something to offer that is not sterile, manipulative, commercially motivated or intellectually shallow. For when it comes to the management of natural resources and care for our Mother the Earth, they have nothing to teach us and much to gain by learning from us.

Our films and videos come out of cultures that have survived plunder, appropriation, and commodification over hundreds of years. Yet much of what we have retained speaks to a value system of indestructible qualities, like the people themselves, and produces work of proven aesthetic value.

Also challenging, on a political level, is the subject of cultural and spiritual copyright, as well as legal copyright. The question is one of control and why we are continuously disempowered in the process of film/video making, in the studio or television station. These are potent issues which are also matters concerning the basic human rights of indigenous peoples, who still live and practice their own cultures, albeit with reduced means, often in hostile environments.

Imagery and symbols are representations of the collective consciousness. They come out of specific histories, cultures and experience. But too often the desire of the dominant culture to define, categorize, and control, stifles the flowering of a different or unique aesthetic. Whole areas of ethnic and indigenous art and expression need to be liberated from the straitjacket of institutional control and definition.

What is held to be sacred by indigenous people is made profane: layers and levels of meaning are reduced to one dimensional, hip lines. The multilayered complexity of indigenous art forms is discarded in favor of the Adman's simplistic renditions. Indigenous motifs are discarded along with the people as soon as their capacity to make money has ceased. The richness of our imagery, symbols and icons is sacrificed to the banality of the white boy hero westerns, souvenir shops and tourism. This creates a destructive state of tension which could be made constructive, if funding and resources were shared more equitably, and more respect and recognition was given to our nations, histories and cultures.

There have been very deliberate attempts to deny our spirituality, as well as concerted efforts to intimidate, assimilate and integrate our art forms into the mainstream by people with neither care nor respect for what we create. In effect, we are being coerced or seduced into debasing our cultural icons and devaluing ourselves as people.

Much of what we revere is in recognition of the ascendancy of the universe, the ancestors, and the principles on which our belief and value systems were founded. Our arts always had a celebratory aspect as well: they functioned as a means of passing on knowledge and history; they showed a respect of living things, and acknowledged the significance and insignificance of our place on this earth.

There is no better reason to be a painter, a potter, a filmmaker, a video recordist, a screen printer, and to produce, to direct, to photograph, to sculpt or to create in any medium. And with this comes a responsibility to our people, past, present, and as yet unborn, to uplift, to uphold, to realise the visions which will nurture and sustain us into the future, wherever and in whatever forum we find ourselves.

We must fight for our independence, for our right to have our own production companies and studios, and to decolonize the screen. We must tell our own stories. Stories for us, about us, and by us, and in so doing, indigenise and humanize the world around us, making it a better place for our children. We must pressure the power for self determination in the production of film and video on a community level, and on a larger scale. I see this festival as a step on the road to empowerment, and I am honored to be a part of it.

Cinema as an Instrument for Indigenous Peoples Identity

by Alberto Muenala

Our culture, through time and space, has experienced different changes. These transformations are the result of our peoples living as well as being exposed to the dialectics of different times. We have appropriated and infused certain elements and symbols with intimate meanings and values; this love for things that surround us is what makes us different. For example: our mother tongue that we speak in most indigenous towns; our relation to the Pacha Mama that we belong to; the garments we wear everyday; and all forms of our spiritual strength fashion and maintain our identity as we come to terms with circumstances and struggles across time.

In Equador, our spirit of indigenous identity maintained by communities and peoples of diverse nationalities has not been broken, despite certain repressive politics, indigenous integration to the western system, and of a uniformed making of the proletarian peasant class. Therein lies the importance of indigenous organizations and structures that work with a politics of common action.

The arts, including cinematography, come to terms with the needs the organizations are creating. Generally speaking, Native peoples are a cinematograhic people. I utilize this term in so far as we are a people in constant movement and development.

The time has come to change the ideology regarding our peoples. There are those who think we are "natural" peoples given that we cohabitate with nature, yet they are openly critical towards us if we leave our huts and change our garments. In our culture all the arts develop, perhaps richer than in other ones, because we live the everyday. In ritual and celebration, for a marriage, for a new house, for the death of a child, the very same family members are the ones who create music, who dance, who perform...

We were condemned to silence yet we were never silenced. Today our voices arrive and are heard in court-houses, as in the case of Texaco vs. Cofanes vs. The State. Our cultures have been studied as folklore; they claim we speak dialects instead of languages; they claim we make crafts instead of art; they have considered us second class citizens solely for being indigenous. The use of a new cinematographic language can rectify these and other errors.

If through cinema we can counteract and transform a part of a whole ideology structured in the very sources of control and power, we will be contributing to a necessary, useful and just cause in these times of war of communications.

Paternalism and the absences of commitment to truth, in most cases, have been negative factors in the development of a new cinema. Year after year, indigenous media has been exploited in cinema as images of misery, confusing our traditional culture. A few years ago indigenous concerns and issues were only a social phenomenon, camouflaged here and there. Today the Indigenous Movement has a political presence. Through the years, it has been managing and struggling to reach concrete goals that conform to a "political project" from grass-root organizations. Cinema about Indigenous peoples must chart a new route, one that shatters the established language of Indians as objects. The new cinema treats us as subjects, as protagonists and producers of our own histories. This task will not be an easy one if indigenous nations are at the margins of a traditional political process and if a Cinema legislation for development of Equadorian cinema and video is not recognized.

We suffer a colonization that has not allowed the development of a cinematographic language. Only through a rupture with colonizing messages, assuming our own identity, will we transform and develop new imagery. Filmmakers must place themselves at the service of the just and noble causes of our times; they must achieve through art the maximum possible expression, art is universal and for all peoples.

I invite all my colleagues and comrades that work in film and video, professionals and amateurs, to participate in current and future debates on film and indigenous peoples. We must build a movement of one's own cinema, we have many roads to traverse and many paths to re-discover.

This essay was translated by Victor Zamudio Taylor.

The Emerging Native American Aesthetics in Film and Video

by V i c t o r   M a s a y e s v a ,   J r .

The current crop of commercial films and television programs on Indians purportedly from the Native American's perspective is a half-lie — for in essence, they were produced by and for Whitemen. The half-truth comes from employable Indians in responsible positions along with the usual Indian consultants. How then can such media goodwill produce such illwill from the affected communities unless it were compared to the U.S. government offering to manage our lands and natural resources? This is the conundrum.

If film is about imagined space and time it is conceived from the imagination of people who have constructed those times and spaces differently. Spaces have been determined on this continent by the indigenous peoples as cliff dwellings, teepees, longhouses, mountain passes, river crossings, great plains and dry plateaus, and time by seasonal movements through these spaces. I have seen many uncomfortable white people in our public plazas, uneasy in unfamiliar spaces. Whereas, I feel comfortable in the narrow passages where I might pass a young girl going for water, or where a mother might be preparing food. And certainly I feel the sacredness of the ancient kivas that are at the ancient ruins of Chaco, Canyon, Mesa Verde, Betatakin, and certainly our ancestral ruin Kawestima (Keet Seel) to name one. Then why are we continuously left out of imagining these spaces and times on film?

Indigenous people around the globe are feeling indignant from compromising every day, every hour, every sentiment, about how they should fit into outsider's films. This indignation is countered by the outsiders with a glib: do audiences want to spend their money and spend their time watching films by Aborigine, Apache, Hopi, Maori, Zulu, Zuni directors? Judiciously, they conclude all the public wants to see is a good film. Unfortunately in America the radical and incendiary premise of film saturated with color, race and difference as conceived by indigenous producers and directors is demeaned with this improbable conclusion for a good film is being described by accountants and not by a multi-racial, film-going public.

We have contributed our share of cliches in our short run as film and video producers, certainly those tired cliches that we disparage when seen in outsider's films. As my Blackfeet friend Darrell Kipp has stated humorously, for a film or video to be Native American it must have three elements: a buffalo, an eagle, and flute music.

If we indigenous filmmakers were to show our difference, we would infuse film with the same reverence which we have for our oral and performing traditions. By expressing our distinct tribal voices we truly would be expounding and espousing the indigenous aesthetic.

I, as a Hopi, would ask: does "larger-than-life" occur within indigenous cultures? Do adults involve themselves in serious make-believe or is this inquiry blasphemous? What is the closest approximation in our cultural experiences to film? In what situation do we totally immerse ourselves and accept all of the occasion's permutations, the logical and the illogical together? In my experience it is our oral traditions and "Tikiveh," which is dance, song, ritual, ceremony and worship.

What is our understanding of oral traditions and the Tikiveh? First it is performance. It is the old one for whom every expressive wrinkle and fold radiates humor and imminent, barely contained revelation, similar to the suspense created by an overblown balloon, suggesting a derivation for the Hopi expression "tsikyaknani," or to break as to break an egg. To tell a new story or sing a new song is to break an egg. Needless to say this original breaking is always delivered in the mother tongue, and the song forms are repetitive, serving memorization, stability and repetition like the mnemonic designs of computers, tape recorders and computer chips.

Second, they are socially redemptive for stories and Tikiveh always have a socially redeeming function. The stories inevitably conclude with yanhakam or yantakkkat ovi, meaning this is how or this is why. It is both admonishment and encouragement. That is why it is redeeming. Tikiveh involves cleansing and reaffirmation of the good life: family and community.

Native Americans have nourished this intimate relationship with "larger-than-life," sometimes explained as spirituality, so we can reflect on our own ceremonies and rituals and understand how crucial that relationship is. When we can stretch our tolerance to include film experience as a conduit for the same experience then we have the right to demand compassion and human caring from the film experience.

Respectful of tribal spirituality and out of a strong faith in the possibilities of film, Native American filmmakers will develop not only their own stories but their own style and techniques based on a critical understanding of Hollywood films as the blueprint not to duplicate. Consciously and willingly, Native Americans will pursue an aesthetic which revels in film's possibilities to express human redemption. Alternatives to cuts, only as indoctrinated in us by all the Hollywood films, and special optics instead of prime lens, are only a minute indication of how we will express our difference which will also encompass special computer and digital creations. Native language would be essential to this expression of the Native American experience as well as some of the following: in dealing with motivation, Native American directors would reveal their understanding about their world; how we use a 360 degree pan to tell a story, rather than to show facility in a physically complicated move; where we begin and end a sequence again without drawing attention to complicated dolly track configurations, but to exploring why motion must follow a certain order; how we look at motion itself and the transitions between events, expressed not as cliched shots of moving cars to reach the new set or situation, but transitional shots which express the rhythms of a unique order. For example these transitions might be falling rain, a new born foal, mature grasslands, or a personal object or item infused with ancient meaning. A new film logic driving the Native American aesthetic which permeates all the ins and outs of technique, style, dramatic continuity, how narrative is begun, ended, cut, extended without didacticism — all this begins with a Native American director. The mishandling of a sacred bundle might be a simple primitive screen event for an outsider but for a Native American director and audience this would be paramount in all the surrounding action.

Some would argue for the primacy of the scriptwriter. In the Native American tribes there are at least as many scripts as there are tribes, which number around 500. But beyond the tribal entities themselves are the great number of stories with which we grew up. This is the legendary story pool which I know Disney dipped into in the 60s for the Hopi story: The Boy and The Eagle. So, there is no lack of scripts. This returns us to the scriptwriter's precedence and the question is raised: who is the author if the material is derived from an identifiable communal base? In fact, if a Native American screenwriter were to demand the same privileges as Esterzhas he would be run out of the community. So, the screenwriter has a different position in the world of Native American filmmaking with the inclusion of tribal stories as intellectual properties.

Contradicting my exposition of an indigenous aesthetic are some of my

Native American Producers Alliance colleagues who claim there is no Native American aesthetic, only a personal vision. However, in forming an alliance, we agree there is a common process and it is becoming clearer with more NAPA films. And before we let go of our present strong sense of clan and tribal identity, I believe deep searching and questioning of our indigenous creative expressions and languages is critical to defining our commonality, despite our distinct tribal roots.

In the year 2000, I see that language and the songs made from these languages will not be used profoundly. The created words that are so delightful and so appropriate for a new moment or the songs — when we heard them expressed for the first time they touched our deepest emotions. Our Native American languages will no longer have this effect as our languages fall into disuse in the dominant culture and as we drift away from inspirational roots. Rains songs for corn fields will not be heard by the clouds.

I see a pan-Indian culture which celebrates a modest, temperate reunion of feelings among tribes and hides fierce, independent, loyal tribal identities. Time will come to be perceived in a biological framework so that change will be understood in one person's lifetime similar to leaves falling, antlers dropping, and snakeskin shedding in a year's heartbeat, rather than in the impersonal spin and gravity of a slow, slow, slow universe.

Facing this daunting future, the current group of Native American filmmakers have run out of the luxury of access to the creative oldtimers for whom language and song was the ultimate human creation, particularly when it was woven into ritual, ceremony and performance or worship. Sadly, fewer filmmakers knowledgeable about tribal aesthetics continue to create the songs that are sung and danced to by our community. At this late hour the indigenous aesthetic has become faint and it is critical we recognize and accept this situation and begin the changes which will stimulate profound and exciting films, originating from an indigenous aesthetic.

Then it may be we are forcing original experience into an unsympathetic form. Maybe film is the inappropriate conveyance, the wrong medium. Maybe the Native American aesthetic will mature in film-based-theatres, which are especially constructed for virtual reality conceits, dynamic motion venues and hyper-reality experiences. Maybe this, and yet undeveloped venues, are the future of Native American film in which the experience will fully reveal the profundity of the original experience — when the original experience is no longer possible, when the priests are no longer living to provide the conduits into larger-than-life experiences. The crucial question becomes: What is it that is so important that it must be shared? What are the risks that tribal people are willing to take to make this available? Indeed, what risks are Native American filmmakers willing to take and make?

In her concluding remarks
following the festival, Merata Mita
observed the following:

IMAGINING INDIANS was a unique and important festival which left an indelible imprint on those who participated.

There are many reasons for this. For me the most important one was having our indigenity, our nativeness, be the basis of our gathering as film makers, recorders and artists.

We were the raison d'etre, not the "other."

Occasions like this are rare for us. Not many gatherings outside the tribal one have such a distinct First Nations' philosophy and no other festival I have attended has celebrated native works in such an unabashed and uncompromising manner. We all succumbed to the feeling of affirmation which pervaded the atmosphere.

Many difficulties are encountered when tribal people make liaisons with other bedfellows in order to have access to public venues and forums. It was obvious that a lot of hard work and diplomacy was going on in the background and to everyone's credit there was little negativeimpact. We were extremely happy and more that appreciative of the efforts being made on our behalf by the Native American Producers Alliance, ATLATL and the Scottsdale Arts Centre.

The subjects under scrutiny in the panel discussions and entertainment sectors were many things to all people—or all things to many people—involving, interesting, topical, challenging, at times difficult, at times emotive and emotional, but in our lives, this talk we talk, or this walk we walk, is an exposition on survival past and present; and the articulation of our visions and hopes for the future. And so it is with the songs we sing, the dances we dance, and the experiences we share.

We are never far from our ancestors and our unborn children, and this festival re-affirmed that.

The only jarring note came from non-coloured, non-indigenous people who came with their excess emotional baggage. They have to understand that we have right to say what has to be said, without our having to deal with their reactionary, colonial regression being played out in our gatherings. Our anger honestly and openly expressed is healthier than our anger repressed. That some non-coloured, non-indigenous persons construe our honest feelings and freedom of expression as a personal threat and attack is indicative of the distance that they have to travel to meet us on equal ground. The alternative is always open to them: to leave if they do not like what is being said. Some chose to interrupt or disrupt valid debate and discussion with their plaintive whining and moaning about their perceived images of themselves as victims!

We are not naive, and the tolerance and righteousness that the christian world preaches gains respect in our eyes from the action rather than the word.

The screenings were exciting to me. There on the screen was the blossoming of an aesthetic, imagined onto the screen through all the imaginings. As yet undefined, symbols and imagery unlocking, decoding and encoding, a quickening of the memory, molecular memory, memory of the mind, the heart, the spirit, the soul. And oh so familiar, and yet very different ways of seeing, of being, of communicating — secret messages, secret hearts, secret minds, laid bare.

Crying is an integral part of healing.

My wish is that this is only the first of many such festivals. It was an honour to have taken part, a rare privilege to have met the wonderful and talented people that I met. The Native American Producer's Alliance deserves to be congratulated for recognising the need, having the courage and taking the initiative.

A version of the essay by Victor Masayesvs, Jr. was first published in *The Independent Film & Video Monthly* and was funded in part by the Center for the Arts Criticism in St. Paul, MN.

The City That Never Weeps

Excerpts from preliminary script

By Kaucyila Brooke and Jane Cottis

NARRATION

The motion picture you are about to see is called *The City That Never Weeps*. My name is Jane Cottis, and I must tell you frankly it's a bit different from most moving picture shows you've ever seen.

As you can see, we're flying over a city, a particular city. This is a friendly city, one of America's Finest, and it welcomes us into its hungry harbor. This is a story of people and a story of the city itself. It was not videotaped in a studio; to the contrary, our stars, Dan Wasil and Maria Kosmetatos, and the other actors, Joyan Saunders, Kaucyila Brooke, Roberto Bedoya, Mary Jo Hart and others played out their roles on the streets, in the houses, and in the rooms of the city itself. This is the city as it is, pavements littered with

rubbish, highways stacked with cars, buildings in their naked steel, and people without stage makeup.

Our camera looks around and gorges itself with the surplus of details. We cast its eye right onto the streets, meeting up with the tourist, the road worker, the street walker, the homeless, and the lesbian. Our City is like a stage where all kinds of characters unfold and the plot thickens and sometimes it even thins. But this metropolis doesn't just provide the arena for our story; it too is a character in the intricate stories in which we see ourselves portrayed.

This neighborhood is called Golden Hill. A single father is waking up to his four year old's fun gutter games, and one of those noisy grass-trimmers is the alarm clock for the rest of the neighbors. On the next street, everyone seems to be already up and running, the school bus ferries the city's children to the learning shores and over-head, in the sky's highway, an airplane transports it's passengers to an unknown destination.

Behind the scenes of the Big Kitchen everything is usual. Onions are chopped for those delicious home fried potatoes that go with breakfast in this fancy diner. The dishes are stacked and washed to make sure there is no shortage when the morning horde arrives.

Finally we enter the most intimate city, the house itself. Like the television screen you are now watching, the home is best suited for interpersonal stories. Unlike the exterior action and plot,the home embodies our histories and memories. Passed from room to room, they lie deep in the living room furniture, they echo through the bathroom plumbing and are packed into the grout surrounding the kitchen sink. The home is the mouth of all stories. And in one house, one unique house, there is a familiar room where you don't have to look out but can take time to look within. The lesbian Crying Room is on Grove Street in Golden Hill, San Diego. A rather normal building on an ordinary street. Here, rather quietly, lesbians go to cry.

MARIA: Well, the way I think the lesbian Crying Room came about was that, you know these gay men have a lot of things out there for them. Lots of gay men kind of things.

DAN: Here we go.

MARIA *continues:* Men kind of stuff, gay men kind of stuff. But there really isn't very much for lesbians.

DAN: By which she means gay white men.

MARIA: I didn't say that.

DAN: No, but you meant it.

MARIA: You said that. I didn't say that.

DAN: Okay, you go ahead.

MARIA: So I think what happened was there had been a fairly large uprising here in San Diego. People don't know this but San Diego has become a major enclave for lesbians. (They) come from all over the world. Just like San Francisco used to be an attraction for gay men, San Diego is becoming the drawing place for lesbians.

DAN: That's true.

MARIA: And so we needed to respond to that demand. And being as we are kinda central here in San Diego, there was this uprising at that bar nearby. The lesbian bar.

DAN *agrees:* Umm hmm.

MARIA *continues:* Because the men kept wanting to come to the lesbian bar and they were outraged, just outraged, and literally crying. Crying, just bawling, crying.

DAN: Weeping because they no longer had a place to call their own.

MARIA: And I think that they were looking for a place to cry. The crying kinda struck me as I was watching it on the news.

DAN: That's true, I remember that night we were going to go and then there was that big discussion about whether I should go and I ended up not going because...

MARIA: Men were not welcome.

DAN: Men were not welcome and I shouldn't go and I should try and be supportive of women having a space of their own...

MARIA *interrupts before he finishes his sentence:* Especially tall white men.

DAN: Well, yeah, I would have stood out so bad.

MARIA: So anyway, umm... we had some friends who frequently come to our house and it just kind of evolved into that mode. And we recognized the need for women, especially lesbians, to be able to come and cry and we had this extra room...

DAN: Yes, it certainly wasn't anything we sought out per se. There was an evolution, a response that we had to community events that were larger than anything that we had anticipated. It was just a place to invite our friends to come stay but then the demand grew and we found ourselves in the midst of it.

MARIA: Much as the demand grew at one time in San Diego for the Navy. Navy men started coming here from all over the world and so we built housing for Navy people and they took all that marine stuff and it became a big Navy town. Now we need to respond to the influx of lesbians and we have just one-one very small part of what's needed.

DAN: Right.

MARIA: The demand that, you know, we're experiencing here. But we decided we were best suited to have the Lesbian Crying Room.

Narrator VO: Do you have any mottos for the lesbian Crying Room?

DAN AND MARIA *in unison:* It's never your fault.

MARIA: That's a good one. It's never your fault.

DAN: It really isn't.

Cut to Kaucyila in Crying Room.

KAUCYILA: (And) Dan and Maria were very worried but gracious. They were concerned about me without being prejudice against you. It's quite a talent but they never said, 'What did you do? Wasn't it your fault?' Because, of course, it wasn't my fault. It was your fault.

Cut Back to Dan and Maria on couch.

DAN: It's been our experience that that's true. All the lesbians that have stayed in our room- it's not been their fault.

MARIA: It's nothing they've done. They're always right. You're always right.

DAN: I think history will bear us out on that.

Cut to Joyan in Crying Room.

JOYAN: I did feel in fact that something horrible had been done to me. I felt affirmed in that by being here, in this place, not to wallow in it, but just to acknowledge that a wrong had been done, and to give that whatever time it needed and then to get on with things.

Our lives are not ordered like maps. The events don't have street names, but change with each glance backwards. Imagine walking on a hot summer's afternoon through the abandoned streets of San Diego. You find yourself in surroundings whose character is of a nature unknown to you. A few blocks ago, you knew each of the building's tiny details. Like a well thumbed book you could have read the story of each structure with your eyes closed. Now, derelict warehouses surround you. The dusty pavements that used to listen to your footsteps trip you with their dirt-filled crevices. You hasten to leave the unfamiliar territory at the next turning, but after having wandered about for a time you suddenly find yourself back on the same street where you feel cast out, alone and apprehensive. You hurry away once more, only to arrive, by another detour, at the same place yet a third time.

Cut to Kaucyila in the Crying Room.

KAUCYILA: Well, you really pissed me off because you were ignoring me and you weren't coming home and so I left. I thought well, you weren't going to come home and I won't be there when you do get home. So I called up Dan and Maria and said, 'I'm having an argument with Jane. Can I come over and spend the night?' And they said 'Yes, sure.' or something like that. 'Of course,' they said. 'Whatever you need dear because we have this room and we'd love to have you stay in it. Is everything okay?' And I said, 'Well ultimately, probably everything is okay or maybe it's not.'

JANE *interrupts:* I thought you said that you said that it might be the end of the relationship?

KAUCYILA: I thought it might have been the end of the relationship.

DAN: You were very upset.

Cut to Dan and Maria on living room couch.

DAN: Honey, do you remember how we got started with the Lesbian Crying Room?

MARIA: No, you mean who was the first person in the Lesbian Crying Room?

DAN: Yes, I know we had set aside — we had wanted the extra bedroom for when friends visited but do you remember when we really got... yeah, I think Kaucyila was the first visitor.

MARIA: Umm hmm, two years, three years...

DAN: Might have been three years ago.

MARIA: Four years...

DAN: She was having an argument with Jane at the time, I'm not sure what it was...

MARIA: That's what I mean. What was it about?

Cut to Kaucyila in Crying Room.

KAUCYILA:Okay, the reason I came to the lesbian Crying Room, I think this is it. I was applying for a lot of jobs and I was waiting to hear and I'd sent all these applications out and I was waking up in the early hours of the morning, like five o'clock and I would just be anxiety racked. And I would sit on the back porch and I would just weep and you would sleep, you would sleep through the whole thing. I mean, the porch is just inches away from our bed and I would be out there weeping on the back porch and would you wake up? No — because it wasn't bothering you, was it? And besides it was too much pressure really to have someone who was upset about their job search around the house. You'd just sleep through it all and so I'd had enough and I was waiting for you and you were trying to get away from me. So I thought, well, I'll just leave and go and stay at Dan and Maria's.

Cut to Dan and Maria on couch.

DAN: Might have been four years ago. Might have been fifty years ago.

MARIA: No, four years ago. Yes, It was very late at night the first time...

DAN: We were in bed, ready to go to sleep...

MARIA: Awakened from bed.

DAN: You answered the phone.

MARIA: No. She just came to the door. No. No. You're right she called.

DAN: She called.

MARIA: And said something like, ' I have no where to go'.

Dan: Right, very distraught.

MARIA: 'Can I come to your house?'

Cut to Kaucyila in the Crying Room.

KAUCYILA:Well, I can't really remember why I came to the lesbian Crying Room. It was years ago, it must have been three or four years ago — mybe it was ten years ago.

JANE interruprts: We haven't been together ten years.

KAUCYILA: Listen, who came to the Crying Room?

Cut back to Dan and Maria on the couch.

DAN: We had to get up, put some clothes on.

MARIA: And let her in and you didn't really know what to say.

DAN: I didn't. We opened a bottle of wine as I recall .

Cut to Dan offering Champagne

MARIA: I thought you offered her a gin and tonic.

Cut to Dan offering gin and tonic

DAN: It might have been a gin and tonic. Memory fades doesn't it. But I
         remember that she came, we had something to drink, talked for about an
         hour or so. We gave her the room and told her she could stay as long
         as she wanted.

MARIA: Do you remember why she came?

Cut to Kaucyila in the Crying Room.

JANE: Well there are two sides to the story.

KAUCYILA: No there isn't. I'm sorry. Don't you understand the idea of the Crying
         Room? There's only one side of the story in the Crying Room.

Cut to Joyan in Crying Room.

JOYAN: I had a dream actually one night before we
         — I think it was probably the day before
         she told me what was going on. I had a
         dream that night and in the dream there
         was some kind of a natural disaster that
         occurred and L and I and you, Kaucyila,
         were in flight from whatever this disaster
         was and we were taking refuge in a big
         cathedral kind of building and the three of
us entered it together and L was heading in one direction. She was heading to the left and I went to follow her and you said, 'No, don't go that
way,' and you took me to the right and you led me up a flight of stairs so I
separated from her at that point. And I got up in the morning and I told L
about this dream and I really believed in the prophecy of this dream
which was to me at the time, umm, about either being able to take care of
myself or find other people to facilitate that.

   She came home, I'll call this she 'L' for lesbian, anyway she came home from school and sat down and said she had something to tell me and she said that, she said, 'I've been seeing someone else.' I asked her who this person was and I asked her how long it had been going on and she wouldn't tell me either of those things and those were crucial bits of information for me to orient myself amidst this catastrophe. So without telling me either of those things she left, she left immediately, within probably oh, a good fifteen minutes, twenty minutes, a half an hour of having told me these things and she went to be with her roommate who was meeting her somewhere for coffee "to support her"— in her words. And I was left there on my own without anyone to call up and ask to be with me. She also didn't want me there that night. She told me that she didn't want me to stay there at the house, at our house, in our bed anymore. She wanted me to leave the house, to leave town and to get out of the state all in one fell swoop. So she didn't want me there when she came back and that's when I made a long distance call to my friend in Chicago who referred me to the Crying Room.

While I stayed here, I didn't sleep very much. I couldn't sleep. I would sleep for a couple of hours and then wake up and then start making phone calls, you know as soon as it was a halfway respectable time in the midwest which was where I wanted to call mostly.

Cut to Dan giving instructions on using the phone.

JOYAN: I didn't eat. The only thing I could eat was a banana smoothie — a banana and a glass of milk. That's all I could eat and that wasn't really eating that was just swallowing. I couldn't chew.

Cut to Dan offering fruit.

JOYAN: I couldn't stomach anything that had to be chewed. I cried a lot. I don't think I've ever cried that much in my life and I don't know why that is. I don't know why it was easier to cry this time than it had been at other times in the past. I've never felt so completely betrayed because I've never, I had never trusted anyone, prior to trusting this person who betrayed me and I suppose I felt more clean and pure in my grief than I ever had before. I really felt that I hadn't done anything to precipitate this, you know. Nothing other than the ordinary day-to-day bullshit. If I had it to do over again perhaps I would have treated her better than I had, but I certainly treated her better than I had treated anyone ever previously and yet I think I was betrayed more badly by her than anyone ever. But I had loved her, I had trusted her and there was something about that. There wasn't much regret or recrimination of my part. The grief was easier to get to. So I cried and cried and cried. I talked a lot while I was here. I talked on the phone a lot. I talked a lot to Dan when he would come home at the end of the day. So I cried and I talked. I suppose that's mostly what I did, and I cried while I was talking.

Cut to Dan sitting on front porch.
DAN *speaking to camera:* For four days.

Narrator's voice over:
The city takes us into it's bosom like a selfless lover. In an osmotic exchange we flow in capillaries that carry and surround our indelicate catastrophes. We travel in its arms, its fingers point in the right direction. It gives us its tongue to exchange communication kisses. Its backbone offers emotional support. Its membranes flood into streets of desire. We gush into its swollen veins until eventually, reaching it's clogged heart we burst into hysteria, in its inevitable present. We overflow into its waste, the bowels of the city, betrayed by the city, our lover. Desperate for its passionate embrace, it leaves us nowhere to go but cul de sacs and blind alleys.

It's 4 o'clock in the afternoon and this is the city and these are the streets. A lesbian walks up the steps now. Tomorrow a new story will hit the head-lines. But today someone, somewhere will take care of this lesbian. She won't be forgotten, not entirely, not altogether.

These stories will not end with the credits. Our characters' lives will continue in a disorderly fashion. You could be the next person to enter their lives. Out in the city? Or in the Crying Room? Perhaps you will begin as a simple subplot, an extra, then co-star. You may work your way into controlling the narrative, then leave them for a better story (or for your side of the story). This has been *The City That Never Weeps*. There are over 8 million stories in the city and the stories are endless.

THE END

All stills from
The City That Never Weeps
(work-in-progress), by
Kaucyila Brooke and **Jane Cottis**.

Ni de aquí, ni de allá

Latinos/as in the Imagination
of Southern California

Introduction by Christopher Ortiz
Essays by Frances Salomé España
and Harry Gamboa, Jr.

Introduction

by Christopher Ortiz

Ramona (1910) is one of the first films D.W. Griffith directed in California after film production began to shift from the East Coast to Hollywood. Unwittingly, or not, Griffith began what we may say are venerable Hollywood traditions, many of which continue until our day: choose a big name star for your film, give the white star a juicy role playing someone non-white, and take that role from a best-selling novel. Instant box office success!

Griffith's film takes its title from Helen Hunt Jackson's novel (1884) about the tragic love of Ramona, a half-Spanish and half-Indian girl (a mestiza), and Alessandro, a full-blooded Indian. Wandering around California on assignment to write stories about the Missions for her East Coast magazine, Helen Hunt Jackson became enamored of Southern California and decided to write a novel combining her new found love of the region with her previous defense of Indian rights. Thus, Ramona was born: a mestiza used as the vehicle for a well-meaning liberal, political and social agenda. Instead of achieving its intended agenda, the novel ushered in the first big real estate boom in Southern California, encouraged more East Coast (im)migration, and established tourism as a viable industry (tours of Ramona's hacienda and of Mrs. Jackson's original itinerary became immensely popular). Mrs. Jackson's Ramona is one of Southern California's earliest victims of commodification (the Indian rights aspect of the novel forgotten in short order) and a fictional character whose romanticized and tragic emplotment subsituted for the long and complex history of a Spanish-speaking presence in California.

From the rise of the Western novel in the 19th century to the great sucking sound of Ross Perot, the image of the Latino/a in the United States has veered between two poles: the noble and tragic Spanish señorita or mestiza and the lustful and violent spitfire; the good and humble servant or the devious and unscrupulous bandit; the romantic and sad inhabitant of the past and tradition or the backward and corrupt obstacle to progress and modernity. Within the history of the United States and its border relations, the image mobilized has always been tied to political expediency.

In the official history of Southern California and the Southwest envisioned by Helen Hunt Jackson and her successors, Latinos/as have been neither here nor there. (At the present moment, we are "illegal" aliens.) As an alternative vision to Hollywood's stereotypes and Washington's rhetoric, Chicano and Chicana artists have been creating images that explore and celebrate the complex histories and experiences of Latinos/as in the United States. [1]

San Francisco based Chicana artist Yolanda López has a well-known piece of poster art (1981) in which an Aztec figure holds in one hand a newspaper with the headline "Immigration Plans" and, pointing with the other hand, poses the question, "Who's the illegal alien, PILGRIM?" From the Mexican-American War in the mid-nineteenth century to the present, the historical and political presence of Latinos/as in the now United States has always been interwined with the issue of territoriality.

From *Ramona* on and through a series of greaser films in the Teens and Twenties, Hollywood tried to come to terms symbolically with issues of land rights, cultural difference and territoriality that arose after the Mexican-American war. The greaser films were early precursors of the Western genre and a continuation of the Western novel. More often than not, the issue of land rights and cultural conflict took place in a rural landscape and the expanding frontier, although the latter was a misnomer as there had been Spanish/Mexican settlements in the Southwest from the Seventeenth century. The Mexican was the bandido, the decadent aristocrat, the loose woman, the interloper, the Other in these representations.

Although the presence of Latinos in the countryside has been a historic constant in the Southwest, the other experience often overlooked has been the long history of Latinos in urban settings. Even before the arrival of the Pilgrims at Plymouth rock, Mexico City was a major metropolis by the end of the Sixteenth century and the main administrative center of the Spanish Empire in Latin America. Alburquerque, Santa Fe, Los Angeles, and San Franciso are just a few of the historical indications of the Spanish and Mexican impulse to found cities and pueblos. However, the urban history of Latinos in the United States is often reduced to a picturesque tourist attraction such as Olivera Street in downtown Los Angeles. And in the contemporary scene, our urban presence is reduced to the mean streets of gang wars and stereotyped inner-city barrios.

At the same time, to speak of territoriality runs the risk of a creating a Latino/a counter myth to that which was created in the Western and in literature of the frontier. The Spanish/Mexican settlement of the Southwest also carries with it a legacy of imperialism and colonialism which cannot be glossed over. The northward march of settlers from Mexico also meant genocide and enslavement for the indigenous populations of the region. Let us not forget Fray Junipero Serra. And counter myths obscure the rich and complex histories of the many populations which found their way to California. The work of many Chicano/a artists is not about establishing a counter myth or reclaiming geographic territory now lost, but is rather about creating a cultural and spiritual territory in which the place of Latinos/as in the contemporary United States can be explored and in which new cultural and political identities can be created with an acknowledgement of the past and with an awareness of the problems and issues we face in the present.

As members of a generation of Latino/a artists who began to work during the struggle for Chicano/a civil rights in the 60s and 70s, Harry Gamboa and Frances Salomé España have been important figures, among others, in the vibrant and alive Chicano/a art scene in Los Angeles. For both of them, Los Angeles is their geographic, historic and spiritual territory, the place which shapes and influences their work. And the medium they have used to give image to their respective visions is that of video. Their use of video has been one which has profoundly explored the aesthetic and narrative possibilities of this art form. Both artists could be termed experimental in their use of video; however, their styles and aesthetic projects are distinct.

Frances Salomé España has defined as one of the main projects of her work the search for a Chicana aesthetic. Using experimental and abstract images and non-linear narrative, Salomé España draws from a wide variety of sources — indigenous myths and stories related to women, performance art and her own personal history, among others. For example, in *El Espejo/The Mirror* (1991, 5 minutes), Salomé España narrates a complex story of identity while sitting in her parents' kitchen in East LA. As she narrates, images of her foot reflected in a mirror under her feet are intercut with her image speaking and with scenes of the garden outside the kitchen. The narrative is non-linear and several viewings are necessary in order to understand the complex work. The piece deals with fetishism, women's voice and history, and the place of territory, both imaginary and real, in the constitution of identity.

In *Anima* (1991, 3 minutes), Salomé España has female figures sitting in a kitchen. As the video unfolds, the women are transformed from fully fleshed to skeletal images that are an important part of the Day of the Dead celebrations. Stripping women of their flesh, Salomé España defetishizes women. By reducing women to skeletons and placing them in a kitchen, she critiques and foregrounds the various ways in which women have been culturally constructed: as both life and death, as sensual objects and sources of decay, as mothers and figures of male fantasy. Salomé España's work is a theoretical and artistic exploration of Chicana women's representation.

In the 1970s Harry Gamboa helped to found ASCO, a Chicano/a artists' collective. One of the group's projects was to explore the way in which art could be used as a means of political expression. Now working independently, Gamboa explores the family, the individual and the freeway as artistic and theoretical concerns. Gamboa explores the narrative possibilities of the freeway, not only because it is an omnipresent part of our landscape as Angelenos, but also because the freeway has had a historical, cultural and economic impact on specific communities such as East LA which was geographically divided from downtown and partly demolished during the construction of various freeways in the region. And as a concrete fact, the freeway continues to influence the way urban design and space are conceptualized.

Against this backdrop, Gamboa examines the family and other personal inter-relationships. In *Vaporz* (1990, 7 minutes), he uses the format of the telenovela or Spanish-language soap operas to take a look at the relationship between two lovers as they go from fast food restaurant to fast food restaurant in an effort to mask their ennui and mutual dislike for each other. Sex and food take on a different and surprising meaning in this piece.

Just as in *Baby Kake* (1984), *L.A. Familia* (1993, 37 minutes) takes as its subject a dysfunctional family. Using a great economy of means in his video, Gamboa critiques and explores the complexity of the Latino family, a critique which goes beyond the often simplistic stereotype of the Latino family as more united and close than non-Latino families. With humor, some pathos, and drawing from a wide range of cultural and artistic practices such as the telenovela and performance art, he analyzes the various stresses and pressures which the urban scene places upon these families. Utilizing video in a variety of narrative and technical ways, Gamboa gives voice to the interesting and untold stories that unfold in the overlooked cotidian aspects of people's lives.

Because Latinos/as have been positioned as neither here nor there, the question of cultural and historical identity has been an important theme for a number of artists. Profoundly political and tracing a part of its origins to the struggles of the Chicano/a and civil rights movements, this work of creating images has its own history that is intimately related to Hollywood and independent of it. Most importantly, these artists demonstrate that within the history of independent and experimental film and video in Southern California, Latinos/as have had and continue to have an important presence. [2]

Notes

The present essay is an expansion of my program notes for an exhibition of the same title that I curated for "Scratching the Belly of the Beast: Cutting Edge Media in Los Angeles," a film and video festival organized by Film Forum of Los Angeles in March of 1994. Both the work of Harry Gamboa and Frances Salomé España was featured in the exhibition.

1. For a collection of interesting essays on Latinos/as in representation, see Chon Noriega, ed., *Chicano Cinema* (University of Minnesota Press, 1993) and Chon Noriega and Ana López, eds., *The Ethnic Eye* (University of Minnesota Press, forthcoming). Also see, Rosa Linda Fregoso, *The Bronze Goddess* (University of Minnesota Press, 1993).

2. I have included here the work that was programmed for the Film Forum festival of video and film. The listed films and videos are only a small portion of the work that has been produced by Latino/a film and video artists in Southern California. The Griffith film was included as a point of historical reference.

   Ramona   D. W. Griffith 1910 (silent 10 minutes, film)
   D.W. Griffith's film recounts the tragic love of the mestiza Ramona and the Indian Allesandro in early California. Based on the best-selling novel by Helen Hunt Jackson and starring Mary Pickford, Griffith's film was a box office hit at the time of its release.

   Ramona: Birth of a Miscegenation   David Avalos and Deborah Small 1992 (22 minutes, video)
   With humor and irony, this video explores the way in which Hollywood has constructed interracial relationships within a system of formulaic and cliched arguments.

   Mi Casa   Edgar Bravo 1989 (12 minutes, film)
   For many Angelenos, dayworkers standing on street corners are a familiar and often ignored sight. Edgar Bravo's beautifully photographed film takes us beyond the street corner and into one of these men's homes.

   Chicana   Sylvia Morales 1979 (15 minutes, film)
   Chicana focuses on the image of the Mexican/Chicana woman from pre-Columbian times to the present. An important text in the Chicano/a movement, Morales' film acts as an affirmation of Chicanas and a critique of the male centeredness in other films of the movement.

   El espjeo/ The Mirror   1991 Frances Salome España (5 minutes, video)
   In this experimental video, Frances Salome España explores the construction of her image and identity as a Chicana artist, an image which is intimately linked to the history of her family in East LA.

Marisela Norte: Portrait of a Los Angeles Poet Sophie Rachmuhl 1991 (5 minutes, video)
Sophie Rachmul provides an intimate portrait of the poet, Marisela Norte. Although not Latina, Rachmul presents a brief portrait an important and well-known Chicana artist.

Baby Kake Harry Gamboa 1984 (9 minutes, video)
Made with the collaboration of members of ASCO and starring Gronk and Barbara Carrasco, this dadaesque video tape explores a dysfunctional family.

Crónica de un ser Sandra Peña 1990 (7 minutes, video)
Taking as her point of departure greaser films from the early silent period of Hollywood, Sandra Peña explores media stereotypes, gender issues and her own identity as a Latina.

Jezebel Spirit Melody Ramirez 1991 (3 minutes, video)
Using found footage, Melody Ramirez presents images of women set to the soundtrack of a preacher ranting against the quintessential bad woman, Jezebel.

Agueda Martinez: Our People, Our Country Esperanza Valdez 1977
(16 minutes, film)
Nominated for an academy award, Valdez's documentary provides a glimpse into the life of a seventy-seven-year-old woman whose name provides part of the title. Agueda Martinez's remarkable story follows the cycles of life and comes to represent the historical presence of Latinas in the Southwest. The film will be presented in its original Spanish version without the English voiceover.

NEPANTLA'd Out

by Frances Salomé España

> *The discovery of the ways by which a cultural identity can be strengthened is vital in order to face dangers and make room for changes and interactions that truly benefit one's own being. The salvaging of values, symbols and meanings with an awareness of cultural self-determination will, in turn, permit participation and collaboration within broader contexts, not in a forced manner, but rather through the pursuit of common goals.[1]*

Nepantla is taken from the Mexican Nahuati language and refers to the place between, in the middle of something, or in transition. At its worst it suggests being neither here nor there, in confusion. At its best it is the notion of transition and movement, at least with an understanding of one's self rela-

tive to time and place. It is a word the native
people used to describe their reality after
the conquest. In the context of territory, the
architecture of boundaries, borders, and
space, and particularly in relationship to how
I define my own voice and my own terrain for
creating art, I've appro-priated its use to
make fire about process, Chicano Art, Chicano aesthetics, y más.

As a woman, and particularly as a Chicano
artist, the challenge to articulate perception
has hardly ever fallen easily upon me.
Making fire is making fire. I seek new
parameters within film and electronic
media because those that do exist
have posed severe creative limitations, borne of a different mood and
world view. Trial and disgust in the
editing room over industry codes and

film capital standards forced me to give it up and speak in my own tongue.
The challenge to reposition, begin transition, return the spirit to the tribe
embraced additional dimensions: adapting film language so that it more
accurately articulates my vision — experimenting with approach until the
artist's tools interpret form and style in ways more applicable to my own
experience, in ways more relevant to me.

Those aesthetic principals particular to Chicano art are evident in our literature, as well as in our visual and theater arts. Film and electronic media
art translations, particularly within the conceptual form, are less apparent
and relatively recent contributions to Chicano art.

How does Chicano art articulate its vision? In Los Angeles the dialogue
addresses an aesthetic movement intrinsically linked to sensibility and reality; where aesthetic concerns are not held separate from those dynamics
which frame our lives north of México, in the environments which have
inspired us. It addresses a sensibility which forces new perception, and
forges a vision which is rich, creative, far-reaching, indigenous and whose
time is now.

Chicano aesthetics do not speak to formula. Our community speaks in
many voices. And in fact it is our diversity which brings the work its
strength. I cannot provide a neat definition. I cannot define the concept in

Top still from
Anima, 1991,
and bottom still
from **El
Espejo/The
Mirror**, 1991, by
**Frances Salomé
España.**

eurocentric terms. I will say that these principles speak to history (past and current) and destiny, and challenge the artist to move beyond borders (nepantla) — to address the world with that sensibility intact. The conviction is in defining ourselves on our own terms, even redefining the whole notion of what American art is thought to be.

> In an attempt to escape Nepantlism, even while
> amid the dangers that continue to threaten its onset,
> the Chicanos' response and their aim are to define
> their identity as a base from which to orient
> their actions and their interactions, and thus to
> make their demands heard. [2]

Chicano art addresses the artist's experience and reality within a context. Chicana/o artists are creating art within a historical context or environment that deals with certain historical realities which cannot be denied.

As an imagemaker I am seeking innovation in all aspects of the work, exploring film and electronic media as an art form, particularly within the context of work which reflects or evokes personal interpretations or aspects of Chicano experience. I am experimenting with the formal ways of dealing with meaning, addressing aesthetic principles particular to Chicano art which suggest I have faith in my own vision of things, and in myself — no matter what.

> Historians and anthropologists, who study their own
> and others' universes of culture, must perceive the
> increasingly urgent need of endangered societies
> to deepen from within their knowledge of themselves.
> In this way they might succeed in surpassing the
> threats of Nepantlism, by recovering their own
> values, symbols, and meanings. They might even be
> able to enrich their awareness of their own identity,
> opposing it to images that others have forged. The
> opinions of others, elaborated from outside, will
> then be the object of a more critical appraisal and
> only with difficulty will they serve as vehicle for
> subtle types of induced acculturation. [3]

1–3. Miguel Leon-Portilla, *Endangered Cultures*

Losing Sight In One "I"

by Harry Gamboa, Jr.

I recently walked into a small liquor store to buy some emergency junk food for a 100 mile trip that would take me across several freeways in order to do a few daily errands in L.A. As I was about to pay for the chips, candy, Twinkies, and losing lottery tickets, it occurred to me that the several other customers who seemed to be hypnotized in front of the cashier were completely engrossed by the static shot of the rear of our heads which appeared on the small closed-circuit video monitor that was sitting on the shelf next to the sign which read, "You break it, you pay with your life." I waited several minutes in anticipation of a horrible crime which would be captured on tape and screened at a mass funeral, but no one moved as the discolored video image continued to document a critical moment of perceptual decay. I tossed a $10.00 bill on the counter and exited in the hope that my disappearing cameo role would not disturb their collective trance.

As I was about to approach the on-ramp of the 605 freeway, I instinctively turned into the drive-through lane of a recently abandoned *McDonald's* which had been transformed into a *Natural Fry* post-modern reconstituted soy burger joint. I wanted a Big Mac but was trapped in line between a customized '66 Impala lowrider in front of me and a brand new Mercedes with gold plated rims and trim to my rear. As I slowly approached the electronic menu board, I was surprised to see my license plate number superimposed on a still-frame close-up shot of my face on a full-color video monitor. The words "Coke" and "Big Fries" were typed across my eyes and mouth as I declined to place my order. I was troubled by the extent of the surveillance efforts of the business community and wondered if anonymity was a right or a privilege. As I drove past the window, I accepted the fries and coke. I paid my bill in pennies and explained to the young part-time worker, "A burger is a burger, no matter who you have to murder." [1]

The 605 freeway cuts across many freeways which point toward every corner of L.A. County. The selection as to which direction I might take was a logistical nightmare because the traffic was jammed to a crawl in all directions. I wanted to get to my destination via the emergency lane but numerous stalled cars blocked my way. I was stuck in an underpass as several small tremors shook the fries out of the paper bag and caused them to dance across the molded plastic dashboard. I was uneasy about the concrete overpass above me and was uncertain if I was performing as a proper motorist who was within range of the traffic controller's video cameras which scanned the area from strategically subtle locations above and beside the freeway. I had a strange sensation that I should be "acting," or at the very least, that I should have memorized a script before leaving home. The camera was pointed at me. It would have been much easier to endure if the director's voice could have been broadcast through public speakers to tell us what to do in such a jam.

HERITAGE IN HYSTERICS

During the month of December, 1991, I was commissioned to produce an interpretive/documentary video on the personal and cultural experiences related to the preparation or consumption of chiles. The video was to be presented before the National Science Foundation in conjunction with a lecture by internationally acclaimed Phytochemist and researcher, Dr. Eloy Rodriguez, of the University of California, Irvine. The completed video is titled, *Fire Medicine*. The video includes various vignettes of people eating chiles: a mother attempting to force-feed her 11 year old son to eat a raw jalapeño chile; my mother and her two best friends creating a batch of salsa using 15 types of chiles with dangerously large knives; and several individuals who provided testimony of their relationship to chiles. The following is a transcript of Roberto Bedoya's videotaped testimony:

BEDOYA: (He is holding a green jalapeño in one hand and gesticulating with chopping motions with his other hand.) My friends were having a meal. I'm not much of a cook and they said, go ahead and chop this pepper up. So, I'm sitting there, standing there at this table, kind of chopping away and doing my part for this meal, and I rub my eye because it starts to hurt. It starts to feel weird. My eyes feel stingy. But nevertheless, in that process, I kind of got a seed underneath my eyelid and it was the worst thing that ever happened to me, and I just started to yell and scream. And I couldn't even articulate what was going on. I was crying, you know, and my friends rushed over and they kind of figured out what was going on, and they took me to the sink, put me underneath the faucet and flushed out my eyes. And the seed came out and I was just crying for a long period of time. And that's my memory of peppers and basically, I don't really like them. 2

Opposite:
Stills from
L.A. Familia,
1993, by **Harry Gamboa, Jr.**.

DESERTED URBAN DESERT

The sustained automatic gunfire has kept the streets and alleys vacant for several hours. The heat continues to build as it approaches noon when the temperature should reach 100°F. Several of the mortally wounded victims are sprawled on the sidewalks and on the front lawns of the California style bungalows. The dead on the street have guessed the riddle of the bullet. The survivors watch TV at home. The nameless people who will continue to live are the ones who have mastered the ability to become true chameleons, and there are a few who select to fight back with crude handmade weapons or shiny imported firearms. It is a typical weekday, holiday, in which everyone has time to kill in the urban desert.

ZERO DEFINITION

There is no video cassette inserted into the camera. The battery has been fully discharged. The camera is switched to the "off" position. Everything which will not be recorded is not for the record. I carry the camera with me wherever I go for two weeks and point it toward everyone I encounter during that period. On several occasions I mount it on a tripod so that I can be in front of the camera as I engage in dialogue and transactions with unidentified strangers. Certain people are either intimidated or empowered by the presence of the camera. Some people quickly assume the role of a "star" while others  immediately revert to "suspect" status. At the end of two weeks there is nothing to review or edit. Nothing is documented or memorized. There is only a blank cassette on the shelf and blurred static in my mind's eye.

TRIGGERINQ A NUCLEAR FAMILY IMPLOSION

The concept and reality of the average American family is extinct. Parents and children are diffused entities that have no model of "home" when there is no "house." The living room is in a vacated alley, the kitchen is spread along an endless stretch of asphalt, and the master bedroom is any public space with concrete pillows. White picket fences are reinforced with razor wire. Opportunity never knocks when there isn't a door to slam shut at the end of the day. The slice of the pie is rotting in the gutter. Every member of the family is lost in a picture imperfect urbanscape of dead ends, skewed horizons, and artificial social turf.

L.A. Familia is a conceptual documentary video which examines the

meltdown of a Chicano nuclear family amidst the environment of an abandoned, visually distorted, and anonymously populated contemporary Los
Angeles. ³ MOM (portrayed by Barbara Carrasco) and SON (portrayed by
Diego Gamboa) are struggling to cope with poverty, mutual hostility, displaced memories, misdirected logic, and fateful phrases that are echoed
against graffiti splattered walls. The video fades in from black with an elevated panoramic view of the city from a vantage point atop the Hollywood
Hills as MOM and SON argue:

MOM: I've tried everything to keep you in line. Nothing seems to work.
SON: Yes it does.
MOM: I've tried that tough love shit but that doesn't work. Nothing works.
SON: Money works.
MOM: Money spoils.

Mom and Son continue their argument as it becomes clear that their
ambivalent relationship is doomed to separation. Mom is frantic and bitter.
Son is 14 years old, jaded, and intent on surviving despite the overwhelming
odds.

DAD (portrayed by Humberto Sandoval) emerges from L.A. County Jail
after an earthquake has rattled the computers into releasing him from
imprisonment a year earlier than expected. He walks along the street in his
boxer shorts and leather shoes. He limbers up to freedom by doing push-ups
on the sidewalk. His initial monologue and behavior provide hints to an attitude that is selfdestructive, absurdist, and confrontational. His first impulse
is to locate Mom and Son.

L.A. Familia chronicles the half-lives of the family members as they
respectively experience isolation, alienation, arguments, aborted reunions,
dysfunctional confessions, and an ongoing sense that everything is crashing
inward. An extended period of time transpires on screen reflecting the
social and physical realities of the sporadic 24-month shooting schedule.
Dad undergoes various transformations as he appears as a hardened ex-con-
vict, a schizophrenically confused street person, a repentant father, and an
urban outcast. Mom is presented in a cyclical pattern of being strong-willed,
emotionally paralyzed, reprimandingly moralistic, and existentially erased.
Son literally grows up but there is a sadness which is permanently attached
to his acquired survival skills for life on ground zero. The nuclear family
implosion is imminent when Dad, Mom, and Son finally meet for the first
time on a pedestrian bridge that is enclosed with chain link fencing and is

suspended over the opposing 8 lanes of a busy freeway:

DAD: Son.
SON: You're not my father. I don't have a father.
MOM: What are you doing here?
DAD: What's in the bag? Who have you been fucking?

The elemental structure of the family unit becomes unstable and collapses as innuendo quickly leads to harsh accusatory arguments, which then escalates to outright aggression as Dad produces a Heckler & Koch 9mm semiautomatic pistol as he threatens to kill Mom and Son. They are terrified and run for their lives as Dad shoots off several live rounds. Dad catches up to Mom and Son as a collective compulsive/convulsive attack of religion/fear brings the family to an uncertain but conclusive fate.

My Eyes Unseen

My vision is impaired by intrusive images:

1. Cops shooting rubber bullets at Mexicans/Chicanos for crowd control.
2. Blind followers in large numbers.
3. Children mimicking strangers on TV.
4. Synthetic sympathy from any devil's advocate.
5. "English Only" signs.
6. Blank faces in familiar places.
7. Tattooed graffiti.
8. Open sores which read like an open book.
9. Flesh and bone on pavement.
10. The unrecognizable phantom in the mirror.

1. From the vignette, *Fast Lane*, in the video *Vis-aVid* (1991, 13 minutes) which was awarded the Premio Mesquite for Best Experimental Video at the San Antonio CineFestival, 1992. *Vis-a-Vid* is included in the MacArthur Foundation Library Video Project. Written and directed by Harry Gamboa, Jr.
2. *Fire Medicine* (1992, 14 minutes). Executive producer, Dr. Eloy Rodriguez. Director, Harry Gamboa, Jr.
3. *L.A. Familia* (1993, 37 minutes) was included in the exhibition, *Identity and Home* (November 18, 1993 - January 9, 1994), at The Museum of Modern Art, New York, NY. Performance. Text by Humberto Sandoval, Barbara Carrasco, and Diego Gamboa. Director, Harry Gamboa, Jr.

seoungho cho

Images from I BLINKED THREE TIMES, a videotape by Seoungho Cho
and THE ISLAND WITH STRIPED SKY, a videotape by Seoungho Cho
and Sang-Wook Cho.

Obstructed texts from:
The Poetics of Space by Gaston Bachelard,
Silence by John Cage,
tape description by Seoungho Cho

Artist Pages Created with Tracy Leipold

I blinked three times

The real phenomenon thematically modest. merely to refer to ph make of the reader a read, shows already a lack of modesty on my Power that could match complete creation

tease to consider "objective" critica at the original poetic phenomenon at gist, being deafened by the keeps describe his feelings. And the resonances, vid method, inevitably intellectualizes the image reverberations in his effort to untangle the skein rpretations. He understands the image more the psychologist. When the point, he it. For the psychoanalyst, the poetic image context. But that's just the image more a language that is different from the poetic fact, was "traduttore, traditore" more jus- o a language that is different from the poetic e a new poetic image, I experie jectivity. I know that I a going to re- communicate asm. When con- ion fro the soul to another poetic image elude causal, such

"I BLINKED THREE TIMES"
 approx. 10 minutes. fall,1993

I tried to make a visual poem about travelin

contrary elements such as the beginning and

and spontaneity, and brightness and darkness

manipulate the situation which has correlat

elements or has no discrimination because a

are already mingled.

obliterating

This work is about my private visual and sp

of landscape itself and imagination derived

emotion of landscape through the travel.

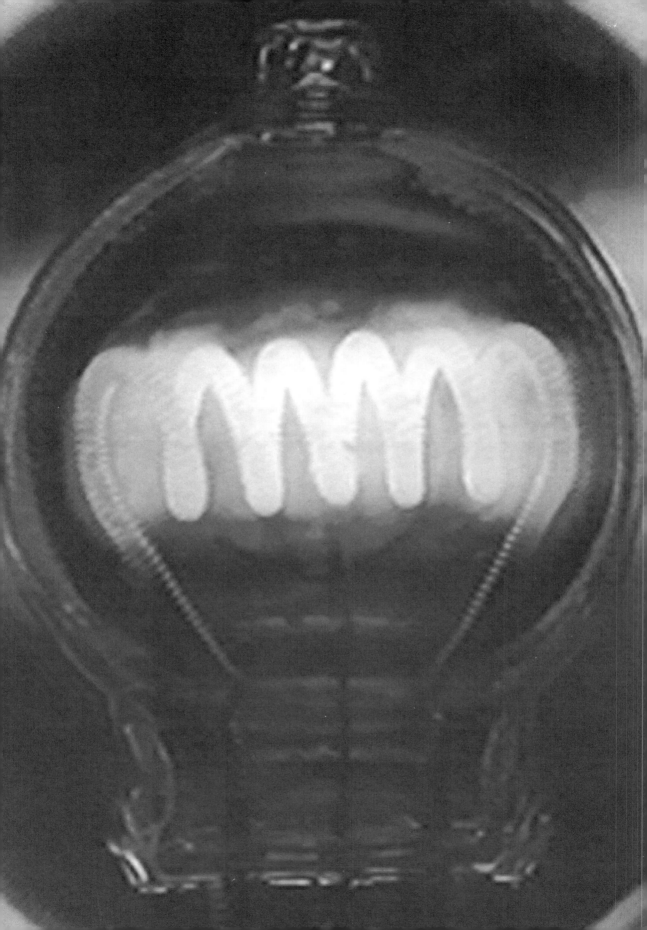

MUSIC: CREDO

I BELIEVE THAT THE USE OF NO

noise. When we ignore it, i
fascinating. The sound of a
stations. Rain. We want to
not as sound effects but
library of "sound effects"
possible to control the ar
and to give to it rhythm
Given four film phonog
wind,

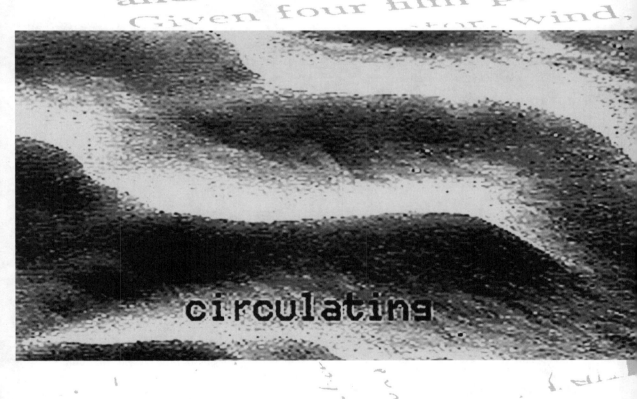

circulating

The following text was delivered as a talk at a meeting of a Seattle arts society organized by Bonnie Bird in 1937. It was printed in the brochure accompanying Anakian's recording of my twenty-five-year retrospective concert in 1958.

DYKE TV

DYKE TV is a year old. It began last June when lesbian activists and media artists Ana Maria Simo, Linda Chapman, and Mary Patierno decided that it was high time that lesbians make TV for themselves. The first show aired June 8, 1993 in Manhattan. Since then the show has expanded to cablecast in 18 cities nationwide, has been screened at numerous festivals, is distributed in bookstores, and is available through individual subscription. Their office remains in New York, but an ever-growing network of stringers contributes from cities around the country. The result is a broad-based collective of dykes making TV for and about dykes, which is TV well worth the wait and well worth a watch.

LESBIAN ACCESS/PUBLIC ACCESS

What does any public access show have to offer anyone in our media saturated world? A thorough examination of public access in the 1990s should take into consideration what we've learned about public access since its inception in the 1970s. Since then we have had to lower our expectation that public access has any inherent potential to democratize television. Media activists in the 1980s (DIVA TV, Deep Dish, Paper Tiger, etc.) responded to the major networks' refusal to address progressive concerns,

working with a cynicism fueled by the AIDS crisis, government inaction and later, the Gulf War. That cynicism also led these groups to develop a distinctly alternative media system that aspired to involve the communities addressed by their programs at every moment from inception to reception. These groups operated with the understanding that the mere existence of "a show about ____" in a cable world of 500+ channels holds little political potential without supplementation.

DYKE TV's strategy looks beyond those earlier prevailing philosophies of public access as the democratizer of television and the short term goal of group visibility. Visibility is a necessary strategy of any disenfranchised group's activist agenda; it is not, however, an end in itself. DYKE TV's power lies in its ability to practice visibility as one component in a more complex design to empower lesbians.

CONSUMERS AS PRODUCERS

Clearly, narrowing the gap between TV production and consumption approaches a more democratic ideal. Still, viewer involvement does not guarantee subversive potential or content.

America's Funniest Home Videos, a mainstream TV show that operates on the illusion of some sort of interactivity, inscribes the viewer as not only a viewer but as a potential "maker," obtusely networking committed camcordartists across the nation into a web of(?). The result is a delayed video-feedback effect: imagine Jane Doe sitting in her living room vigilantly watching week after week for the tape she sent in of a pool-party mishap. One night it appears and lo-and-behold, she has an image of her world appearing on the TV in her very own living room, with friends, perhaps, in attendance. Why is this remarkable? It isn't really, unless you consider that Jane shares an identity with others who regularly watch this program, or produce for it. All who watch participate in its reception system, a system in which the viewer must understand that the show's existence is dependent upon not only viewership, but potential contribution. Direct reference is made to production within the product to be consumed. And, if that's all the show is, Jane and the rest of the regular viewers are caught in an endless cycle, for no other purpose than the show's self-maintenance - TV for TV's sake: product for product's sake.

INCITE

The show seems to be operating on a slickly manufactured illusion, one that is the basis of dominant discourses about community or "americanness" that mainstream media, particularly television, generate in the interest of some notion of nationalism. This illusion is constantly generating copies of itself, relying on these hopeful viewers/producers to create in-kind images of themselves for broadcast.

SO WHY IS DYKE TV DIFFERENT?

It too fundamentally depends on engaged viewers who are potential producers. But while DYKE TV is concerned with its self-maintenance, its scope is not limited to it. Hence, the unifying identity of DYKE TV viewers is not limited to a role in a closed-circuit system, allowing DYKE TV to be "more than a show." At the end of each episode DYKE TV invites its viewers to participate in various ways. An additional byproduct of this pro-production stance is the de-facto activism it necessitates. Scenario: Jane Dyke decides to videotape a local demonstration to send to DYKE TV. Not only does DYKE TV get that spot for its news segment, but Jane Dyke has effectively committed activism in her hometown. This moment propels the program forward towards its goal: to "incite, subvert, provoke, and organize."[1] DYKE TV's Lesbian Avenger roots have much to do with this mode of operation which reflects DYKE TV's goal - "to create a blueprint for community-ori-

ented lesbian programming broadcast throughout the country to enhance lesbian visibility and empowerment."[2]

The show's magazine-like format allows for remote production by women in New York and other parts of the country, and leaves more room for late additions to the show, particularly when the segment intros remain the same week to week. The show strikes a neat balance between serious news features, meandering personal profiles, and humorous, but always informative shorter spots of Dyke relevance.

WHERE IS DYKE TV GOING?

While co-Executive Producer Linda Chapman would like, in a few years and a couple of million dollars, to purchase betacams and produce a DYKE TV slick enough for PBS, it is mostly because PBS offers the capacity of "broadcast" in the true sense of the word. Presently cable access offers only the opportunity for "narrowcast" (i.e., one must have cable to see DYKE TV). So while DYKE TV is the second most widely distributed gay or lesbian television program in the country, it still only reaches a portion of its potential lesbian audience. Even so, everyone at DYKE TV feels that the current expansion of the network they have begun to build remains their primary focus.

1 DYKE TV byline.
2 DYKE TV's mission statement.

IN AN ENVIRONMENT OF INCREASED ACCESS TO VARIOUS MEDIA, WHAT IS GOING TO DIFFERENTIATE SOMETHING THAT IS JUST MORE PRODUCT FROM SOMETHING WITH SOCIAL AND POLITICAL OUT-COMES? We're looking for alternative media that would differentiate itself from **ENTERTAINMENT**. We're looking for shows that contribute to community communication, that allow consumers to complicate their relationship to images of themselves or others in their communities. We're looking for a **N E T W O R K .**

SUBVERT   PROVOKE   ORGANIZE

Snack Bar Open

I'm walking down Poplar Street towards Broad. When I was a kid, we lived on another Poplar Street outside of Philadelphia that I always half-believed was "Popular Street". Every time a commercial came on the radio that

listed the establishment's address as Poplar Street, I would get all excited thinking that it was our Poplar Street. I would get excited when the radio or TV or the newspaper would name something or someone close to me; the little store down the street, or a friend listed with his boy scout troop. Like a happy lightning striking. But unlike our Poplar street, I imagine this street has never felt the shade of its namesake. I take off my ball cap to welcome the sun's heat on my shaved head.

The homeless gather in doorways like pigeons. They wander the sidewalks and foul the stoops. Has that comparison been made before? Maybe I'm thinking of the quote, "Pigeons are like rats with wings." I would think that being anything with wings couldn't be bad, although I don't know which I'd choose; pigeon or homeless.

I step around the flotsam and jetsam common to these city streets. Urban tumbleweeds formed from the guts of discarded cassette and VHS tapes. A fresh pile of dog shit covered by a paper napkin; a warning flag or the owners half-hearted attempt to pick it up. Shards of blue tinted auto glass spilling over the curb into the street, like a pile of shiny cereal. A used tampon as red as a whore's lipstick.

I am walking through the neighborhood east of Ridge Avenue; there are a lot of burned out, bombed out houses. In addition to the decay, there is a funeral home, and a number of community services. There is a Little-People-Head-Start day care center affiliated with some quasi religious institution. There is a church with a sign outside the front door advertising, "HOT DINNERS TODAY", and Trevor's Place. Trevor's Place was started by Trevor when he was only like 14. He saw a report on the local evening news about the homeless living in Philadelphia and he was astounded. He made his father drive into town and he gave his blanket and some sandwiches to the first homeless person he saw. I think they made a made-for-TV-movie about him. Didn't Scott Baio play Trevor? There is another building right down from there that is often engulfing and disgorging long lines of people. It has no visible signs of identification.

I'm walking to the financial exchange where I pick up my public assistance money and food stamps (nobody calls it welfare, not the people in the official capacities anyway). I get $105 in food stamps every month and

$102.50 every two weeks in public assistance money. It may seem like it's free, but you pay with your time. You are "time rich" and the Department of Public Assistance makes you pay out every second. Watching four feature-length films (Batman, Blue Thunder and two I don't remember) over the course of nine hours waiting for an ID card. You are paid to ingest this insidious serum; they don't tell you, but this drug is a distillation of apathy, lethargy and mindless TV watching: the kind you never plan for, the kind that saps away your day.

I don't know what the financial exchange place is called. The only indication of a name is a banner, the kind used to advertise limited-time promotions at fast food restaurants, hung right on the front of the building. It reads, in capital letters, "SNACK BAR OPEN." At night the stores close up like rusted-aluminum, graffitti-besotted, roll-top desks, but the sign stays up. Presumably the snack bar is still operating, a great and churning engine in the world of snack establishments.

Michael O'Reilly

I pass the junkyard that always reminds me of the junkyard in the Saturday morning cartoon, Fat Albert and the Cosby Kids. I'm reminded of Sesame Street when I see the chain link fence lined with multi-colored old doors. There is a dwarf cleaning the junkyard owner's Cadillac. He barely has to bend to scrub the hubcaps with soapy water. The junkyard dog, teats slung low, slinks from behind the car.

It is about ten o'clock in the morning and the girls are out in full force. There are a lot of them; black, white and male. They operate out of the Hotel Carlyle, I imagine. Under the hotel name is the legend, "50 rooms by the week." Some of the  prostitutes get picked up in cars, only to be dropped off soon after. One is dressed like she just came from cleaning the kitchen. Another wearing a Drexel University sweatshirt, simply looks like a fat co-ed. I pass one and she gives me a crooked, tooth-less smile. She is emaciated, strung out on heroin or wasting with AIDS, I guess. She wears a polyester low cut top that only serves to reveal her bony white sternum. When I look at her, I get the feeling that I'm about to have a seizure or that my insides are turning to jelly, not unlike the feeling I had in the hospital: a distinctively unpleasant feeling and time.

She doesn't come on to me, like she would if I was driving by. I can't drive just yet, or drink. Drinking would interfere with the effectiveness of the Phenobarbital; driving would put me behind the wheel in danger of having a seizure. She doesn't come on to me maybe because of the 28 staples in my shaved head. What's the matter, baby? You don't like the Frankenstein of Auschwitz look? I didn't think to count the staples until they were in my hand, the intern plucking them out, one by one, each more scabby and crusty than the next.

A man is standing on the sidewalk peeing on a building. He shakes off, zips up and be-gins moving up Broad. A door to the left of the pee stain opens and counselors herd, direct and wheel people in varying degrees of mental and physical func-tioning towards the waiting lift-equipped white buses. They don't notice the spreading pee stain and walk right through it. Someone lets out a squeal like a goat being slaughtered. Across the street, black men drink quarts of beer and watch.

These men sit in the shade of the marquee over the main entrance to The Met on Poplar street just off Broad. The Reverend Thea Brown (I look hard and find the descriptive male pronouns in the small type) promises to hold services here on Sunday at 2 o'clock in the afternoon. You always have a friend in Jesus, and you can call on him here in this very building come Sunday afternoon. Aside from these signs that the Rev. Brown has put up, the building looks condemned; a singular reminder of what Philadelphia has become and once was.

I round the corner of Poplar and Broad and a mental groan leaps to mind; there is a long line that snakes out the double glass doors of the snack bar place. I cross against the light and make my way through the perpetually double parked cars in front of the snack bar/financial exchange. It sits sandwiched between an auto tag place and

The Hair Weev™ Factory. This factory advertises "human hair creations" at "the least financial." I get in line. The crowd in here is mixed; pretty much evenly divided among whites, blacks and latinos.

I'm generally left alone because of my appearance. I wouldn't want to engage in conversation or ask any questions anyway. Not that my aphasia is that bad that it would not permit me from carrying on a conversation. I am certainly easier to understand now that my jaw is no longer wired shut. It's just that I don't like this feeling that talk-ing engenders. A man taps me on the shoulder. The irrational fear that it might be one of my assailants is replaced by an inward sigh of relief. This man is black. My attackers were white. He asks the time. I don't have a watch.

I am noting the sock and shoe choices made by the people in adjacent lines. I guess this is kind of a hold over from being in the restroom of the mall or school and noting the shoes of the person in the adjacent stall and then later trying to identify that person as they walk around the atriums and through the corridors. A game to pass the time.

I notice white Reeboks and a muscular pair of hairy, male legs. A small clutch purse dangles and swings rhythmically as this man shifts his weight from one foot to another. White sweats topped by a lime green sweater with two small, lumpy breasts. He is trying to keep the breasts very still but prominent. Blue eye shadow, red lipstick and a wig.

At first, I almost laugh when I see him, thinking he is not a very good transvestite. But then I realize that he has a woman's card and is going to try to use it. Probably his mother's card from the conservative choices he has made in his lipstick and handbag. His line begins to move quicker and for once I am glad I picked the slower moving line as I always do in the supermarket. His success or failure is much more entertaining than reading the tabloids.

All that is required to obtain public assistance cash and food stamps is for the bearer to match the picture and for the card to be valid. The computer determines if the account is current and the cashier determines if the person pictured on the card is the same one holding it. I'm sure this guy knew the exact day the public assistance money on that card became available; he'd probably seen people do this makeup thing before. Our respective lines inch closer to the tellers; no one else seems to notice him, at least they aren't laughing or pointing. He gets up to the window and gets his money. There isn't any prob- lem at all. He is back at the snack bar buying something as my turn comes up at the win- dow. He is gone before I get my food stamps and cash.

I step outside and adjust my sunglasses over my prescription glasses. I make my way back up Poplar. I spot what I think is a figure removing a wig to put on headphones. Not watching where I'm walking, I promptly step in a piece of maggoty meat that the junkyard dog has dragged from the curbside trash. Words fail in describing that sound and feeling. The dog growls. The whores laugh.

Come with me. Imagine yourself high over Philadelphia in the summer of 1991. What things will you see ? Can you imagine ? Start out high to the west of the city, flying away from the sunset, fix your eyes on the moon and look for the farm. The antenna farm of seven one-hundred foot towers with blinking red lights. Hug the river through the Conshohocken curve, low to the water but fast. Then under the stone rail bridge and Girard Avenue and bank hard left. Look for the Corinthian columns of Girard College, tucked behind a thick stone wall. The trolley veers right along the wall, we continue straight, past the post office and the Janines lounge. Trevor's place, the Carlyle hotel, the Met and then Broad. It's all there.

See if you can see the black owner berate the white dwarf for not doing the hubcaps properly or the transvestite whore get into the white guy's car. Watch the man piss in the street or the challenged stumble into vans. Listen to the breaking of glass in both homes and cars. Smell the dog shit, the roofer's tar, the rotting meat and diesel exhaust. Taste the roofer's tar. Feel the fetid breath of a Philly summer on your face as you slow in flight to take this in. It's all there. It's always there.

Come with me on this trip, Pennsylvania Department of Public Welfare ID card in your back pocket, pistol kissed in the Broca's area (like the plugs made apparent by a failed hair transplant, this will not fade; permanent). Come with me and I guarantee you, between the Hair Weev™ place and the auto tags store (no one refused !), the Snack Bar will be Open.

Typing is fine, but not speaking. Unwanted syllables jump into words when I least expect it. I can imagine the word or sentence perfectly, it's just that something happens from the time I imagine it to the time my mouth actually says it. I know I owe you a better explanation for what is going on inside my head than that, but I am afraid to articulate it. Afraid of what I might discover through writing about it.   Driving down Girard Avenue is a similar experience to trying to speak. In the winter, the trolley tracks contract and are the same width as your car. It is possible to position the wheels so that the journey will be one exclusively of rubber kissing unblemished

steel, but it is just as likely that you'll be off into a pot-hole, on the rail for a second, and then off again, only to then travel for a full mile on just the rails. My speech is as bumpy as that trip down Girard Avenue.

It is as if speech rides in an unseen car guided by the groove of thought. Speech, at it's best, is an erratic driver kept in check by grooves and rails, like children in kiddie cars at amusement parks. Damage to the brain causes the formation of many aliases and gaps, through which speech slips at every chance, egged on by the random riding shotgun. I am only baggage in the back, thrown from side to side on the vinyl seat like the cassette tapes scuttling crab-like over the dashboard every time we shift grooves. I give into speech and the way this car is driven, knowing I'll finally arrive at what I'm saying, though I'll be a little shaken up.

The way I try to make words and something else plows out of my mouth is like pressing charges: you have no say in the matter, they are just pressed. It's not like in the movies where a kindly police officer asks you if you want to press charges; no one asks you anything and it's all you can do to find the name and number of somebody in the D.A.'s office who is connected with your case and hope it doesn't change tomorrow like it has for the past three days.

There was a whole group of people who crashed the party but only one guy who hit me on the head. The group told the police who among them had committed the actual assault, and he was all I cared about. No reason to drag the other people into criminal proceedings. Calling the many associated authorities, you'd think I was Gomer Pyle trying to return to the phone company the excess change from a faulty pay phone; nobody had heard of not pressing charges before.

Just before I get in the door of the financial exchange, I can see they are still loading the higher and lower functioning people on to the white buses. The building with the fading piss mark has no sign or name. It occurs to me, standing there, that I don't know that much about this Poplar Street. Many of the buildings have no numbers or markings, and I don't want to ask anybody to try to find out what they are. I followed this street straight out from where the sign first indicated Poplar. There is nothing like that at the intersection of Broad and Poplar, where I reminisce about TV shows and how the weekday TV schedule of my childhood telegraphed activity on our Poplar Street. Sesame Street is on and then all the big kids come down the street from school. Once Wee Willie

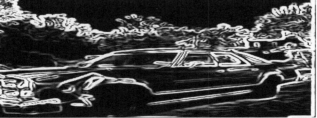

Weber's Colorful Cartoon Hour is over, all the dads come home from the train. It is only now, as I write this, that I realize the breadth and depth of the gulf between this real Poplar Street and the image I had of this Poplar Street from hearing the name in the commercials of my childhood.

Once I get in the door, I choose a line, cross my arms and pray that my line choice is a quick one. The front of the financial exchange calls to mind the betting room of a large racetrack; stubs and tickets littering the floor, the people here itching to get their money, rather then part with it. On the right at the back of the small 20x20´ room, there are video games and on the left there is the Snack Bar. This counter sells no snacks. Instead, there is a vast array of cigarettes, walkmans, cameras and electronic items. These items are like the free radios and cameras you get for subscribing to Time magazine, though it would take a quarter of my public assistance money to purchase the cheapest thing. The walkmen have brand names like Vocor and the printing for the 'paly'[sic] and 'stop' buttons is thin and just cover the unrecognizable Asian characters underneath.

Diderot and The Last Luminare gives a new perspective on the aims, processes and structures of the Age of Enlightenment. It both examines and skews the underlying similarities and differences between the scientific revolution of the past and the contemporary nostalgic constructions of the notion of "progress." Diderot's writings on the function of culture and politics in society and his concept of the distribution of knowledge are made manifest in the plates accompanying the Encyclopedia. These plates structure the video. His subversive model of visual knowledge, designed to democratize information, is used as a springboard to examine current constructions of knowledge, its control, its dissemination and its threatened collapse. The tape is an "updated" 20th century encyclopedia with all of its attendant impossibilities, a ludicrous desire to interrogate larger questions through the structures of the past. In a sense it longs for the speculative order of the Enlightenment while realizing the impossibility of its replication. It is about the gap between these two impulses.

The original plates of the Encyclopedia (1747-1765) were broken down into subject categories that ranged from fishing techniques to mining geology, theatre sets to silk production and all points in between. This video "update" is a project that could exist indefinitely, or could end tomorrow. It is a desperate electronic stand-in, comprised of inherited categories of knowledge which pretend inclusiveness, both comfortable and dangerous. The encyclopedic system, its privileged iconographic representation of labor and craft, and its visual and theoretical 20th century legacy coexist in visually speculative juxtaposition that posits a famial resemblance between our cultural industries, humanist impulses and one of the earliest "modern" compendiums of what was considered necessary human knowledge - Diderot's encyclopedia.

ERIKA SUDERBURG

DIDEROT AND THE LAST LUMINARE: WAITING FOR THE ENLIGHTENMENT (A REVISED ENCYCLOPEDIA)

INTRODUCTION
SPINNING TOP
ORIGIN OF UNIVERSE IMAGE
SPINNING GLASS
RINGS OF SATURN
MOON SURFACE LANDING
PLANET DIAGRAM EXPLODES
RED TOP RETURNS

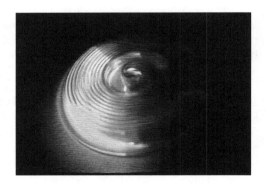

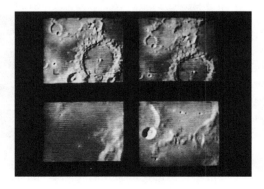

TITLE: LA PECHE

CAT EATING FISH

Diderot writes: I am misunderstood in my own time. The fishmonger avoids me in the street

Sophie reads this letter, burns it and scatters it in much the same way that the her cat's tongue dispenses fish molecules

Diderot writes of matter as motion, energy and spirit.

Sophie wonders when he will learn to eat less red meat and leave his wife

AISLE SHOPPING AT YAOHAN

Waiting for the Enlightenment
We were consumers lost in a vast network, unsure of our buying power, adrift in a shifting matrix of organisms that would live beyond....
digestion, fear and diagnosis.

TITLE: L'ARCHITECTURE

(A glossary of misapplied monuments)

The previous standards collapsed and were replaced by pale fetishistic models carried in small velvet pouches by the distressed

HAND BUILDS SMALL STONE TEMPLE

It was clearly time to decline and fall

TITLE: LES TECHNIQUES ARTISTIQUES
A CAREFULLY LETTERED FIELD

E
Every so often Diderot is locked up in a tower by the censor of Paris for writing various articles:

V
Varieties of scientific theories of the origins of the universe and a satiric and costly reference to God as "the being who does not die"

C
Convincing arguments for the education of women and the narrowness of the empire of public opinion

V
Vehement celebrations of skeptical philosophy and warnings on the dangers of clerics

R
Rousing praises of tableaux painting as the genre in which past, present, and future co-exist at a common point

B
Bantering but praiseful notes on Father Castell's color organ and its multi-colored ribbons designating the sensations of melody and harmony for those who cannot hear.

Or...

The burning of Diderot's philosophical works in 1759 by the public executioner.

A
A few questions on how invisible the stealth bomber could actually be

TITLE: L'ECRITURE
A WOMAN READING

Voice of Ingeborg Bachman and a translator:

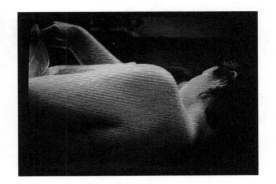

It should not be the task of the writer to deny pain, to erase its traces and blind us to its existence. On the contrary he must become aware of it and acknowledge it once again so we can see it. We all want to be capable of seeing and only that secret pain sensitizes us to experience especially the experience of truth. We say very simply and truly when we reach this condition...
that clear transparent moment....

my eyes have been opened

TITLE: LES TECHNIQUES CHIMIQUES (CHEMISTRY)
CACTI AND SOAP BUBBLES
A SINK OVERFLOWS

The paper chart of his immune system began to resemble cuneiform. This document stayed in the doctor's files. He thought that they should be at home papering the bottom of the medicine cabinet or pinned above the kitchen sink. He called himself the drug trial baby. The frail, public soap bubble waiting to be pricked, decimated or saved.

He had visions of grinding his own pharmaceutical distillates- afloat in a soapy ether- waiting to erupt. He imagined a newly written encyclopaedia section on bursting and being burst open. A section on the failure of universal explanations.

TITLE: L'ART MILITAIRE

Voices of a CNN news team during the Gulf War:

If this is surgical bombing... I don't like being this close to the operating table.

BURNING LOS ANGELES
LOS ANGELES BURNING

We are back now in the CNN bureau/ Do you want to talk to us?/ from the BBC/... can you talk to us?/ we are on line...

BURNING PALM TREE ON THE
HOLLYWOOD FREEWAY OVERPASS
NEAR MY HOUSE

Michael can you tell us what you see in the city of Jerusalem this morning?

HAND LOADING A GUN

Jerusalem is pretty quiet at the moment.. no traffic.... 45 minutes ago we had an air raid siren over in the Hilton Hotel

GUN SHOOTING/ TARGET RANGE

Most people were taken down to the base-ment... great degree of panic and confu-sion......

Larry Register?....... can you hear me
interrupt you?
We are telling our people to get out of here...

SAME BURNING PALM TREE

as soon as they can..
fold it and go!
fold it up and go! and God bless you!
Guys break it down- out of here!!

TITLE: LES METIERS DE LA VIE QUOTIDIENNE
(THE PROFESSIONS OF EVERYDAY LIFE)

Closing remarks on the search for categories and explanations

Diderot: The understanding has its prejudices, the senses their incertitude, the memory its limits, the imagination...

TITLE: END INDEX

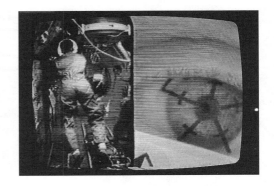

... its glimmerings,
instruments their imperfections,
phenomena are infinite,
causes are hidden

BLACK
SPACE LAB EYE EXPERIMENT

..... Forms are perhaps transitory

Against so many obstacles, both those inside ourselves and those presented by nature....

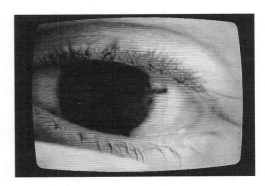

SPINNING RED TOP

We have only slow experimentation and circumscribed reflection...

BLACK
EYE REPEATED

... such are the levers with which philosophy proposes to move the world

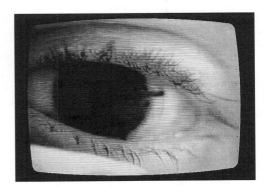

BLACK

END

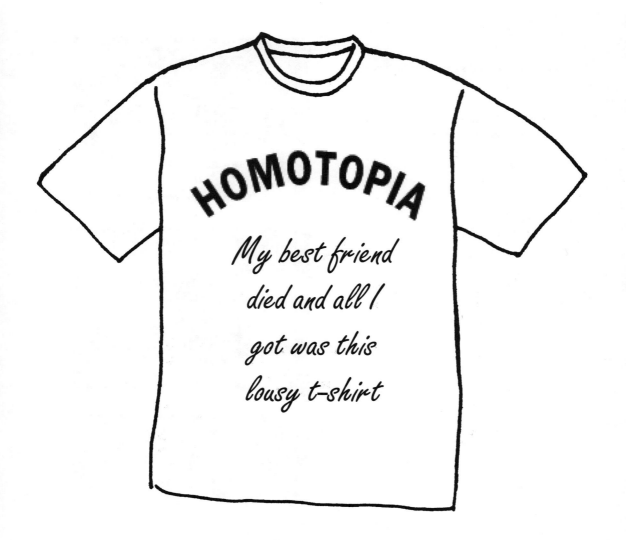

Cynthia Chris / Suzie Silver

Coming Soon from

Unconditional Love Machine ®

The Official Guide to
The New Same-Sex Love, Fun
and Entertainment Capitol of the World

HOMOTOPIA

" . . . A land that I heard of, once in a lullaby . . . "

*Where all your childhood dreams
and adult fantasies come true.*

Here's some Highlights of *HOMOTOPIA* you'll find out all about in our informative, helpful and exciting guidebook

CASTRO VILLAGE (Mixed)

An urban "gayte" way where the revolution never ends. Visit a scale replica of the original **Stonewall Inn** of Christopher Street in New York City. Enjoy a drink with loved ones or meet new ones. Several times each day, "Cops" raid the place and everyone gets to participate in the "rebellion."

Don't miss our startling array of gay and lesbian bars and nightclubs. . . Something and someone for everyone! Wear leather, denim, drag, uniform, or just you Calvins (or is that Tommy Hilfiger now)! Dance in our underground, afterhours, and underage clubs . . . Pay tribute to the spirit of the 70's in our **Disco Inferno** . . . Drop by our piano bar for a sing-along and see our hallowed permanent display of an audio-animatronic **Judy Garland** singing *Homotopia's* official theme song "*Somewhere Over the Rainbow*".

And of course everyday's a celebration at *Homotopia*. At noon, participate in our ever-changing spectacular **Pride Parade**.

DYKESPORTS (Women Only)

A Lesbian field of dreams. Enjoy all the classics - softball, volleyball, touch football, soccer, or rugby. Be sure to visit our **Gym Teacher Hall of Fame** and the giant **First Aid** area. Compare injuries! Make your girlfriend feel sorry for you! Bond with other butches! All this sweaty action will have you heading for the showers!

FETISH/FANTASY LAND (Mixed)

For those of you who may be out of the closet but not afraid of the dark.

Dark Shadows. Ride a bat car through a world filled with gay and lesbian vampires from literature, cinema and lore - scary! - don't get bit. With a special detour devoted to **The Hunger**.

The Dungeons (separate but equal facilities).
For leather and S/M aficionados. Super-advanced audio-animatronics will put you safely through your paces - or you be the master! So life-like, you'll believe our animatronics feel the pain. A large choice of fantasy scenes.

The Fantasmic Orgasmic Theater. Where what you see is what you feel. In an unprecedented display of pyrotechnics, lasers, fog, fiber optics, giant props, and the latest in imaging technologies, 69 performers put on an unforgettable show. (Separate performances for men and women, check schedule) And when you need a break, don't forget to visit the local bars: The **Hairy Bear Biker Club** for men and **Bad Girls** for women.

For those of you who are not hard-core but enjoy a good fantasy anyway visit:

Peter Pan's Lost Boys. Fly thru the air, feel like a boy again. See Peter "cavorting" with his boys, watch the "initiations" of Wendy's brothers . . . and don't miss the classic catfight between those ultimate faghags Wendy and Tinkerbell! This attraction is a favorite of NAMBLA members.

Sappho's Isle. Ride a flying unicorn through a mythical world filled with playful nymph's, goddesses and stately mortals. Watch Aphrodite emerge from the sea! Witness the hunting skills of Artemis! Hear Sappho's lost poems celebrating lesbian love while frolicking nymph's playfully display their charms!

(RADICAL) FAERIE LAND (Men Only)

A nature's wonderland for men to try to find that ever elusive oppression-free masculinity. Join in the wild wig hunt. Get make-up tips. Dance around the Maypole. Participate in self-fertilizing rituals.
This is the place for those into male bonding without bondage. FISH FREE.

A TASTE OF MICHIGAN (Women Only)

Eat or be eaten in a politically correct home away from home for women, womyn, womon, and wimmin. For your enjoyment, **A Taste of Michigan** is surrounded by **No Man's Land**. Separatism strictly enforced. Smoke-free, drug-free, alcohol-free, fragrance-free, caffeine-free, sugar-free, fat-free, animal product-free.

WILD, WILD WEST

Homo Hoedown. Two-Steppin' Country Dance Madness (Mixed - but no opposite sex partnerin', pardner!)

The Mine Shaft. Ride the Mine Train deep underground to watch our hunky, grimy miners deep at work . . . you know what we mean! (On the job safety required for all interactions with the workers.)

Leapin' Lesbians All Cowgirl Ranch. For you rough and ready gals, our ranch hands will satisfy needs even Sissy Hanshaw couldn't "handle." Dont' get the blues . . . hopalong over to the ranch - and bring your chaps and spurs!

I SHOP, THEREFORE I AM GAY

Boutiques for your shopping pleasure. Don't forget to visit the **Pink Triangle T-Shirt Shop**, the **Red Ribbon Tattoo** and **Piercing Center** (real or temporary, to suit all your body adornment whims), and the **Rainbow All Over** housewares store (decorate your home and office in gay pride motif — from toilet paper to wall paper, from letter openers to linens, from canape trays to canopy beds, and from cockrings to wedding rings.

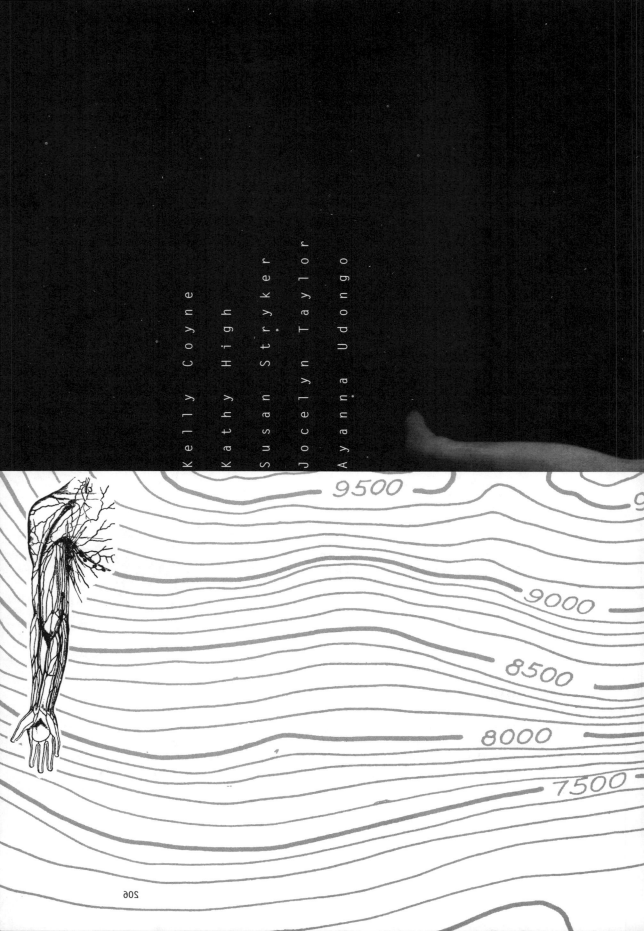

Kelly Coyne

Kathy High

Susan Stryker

Jocelyn Taylor

Ayanna Udongo

9500

9000

8500

8000

7500

KH: Fleshy landscapes abound. The idea of flesh, the sense of mounds of flesh becomes intoxicating and I hunger for it. I dream of stroking flesh, grabbing flesh, devouring flesh. I think of tracing flesh and modeling its contours: flesh that is licked into shape, forged, so to speak, sculpted, cast, stamped, minted, whittled, cut, chiseled, hewn. I think of picturing this flesh, flesh that is out of reach, flesh that is forbidden to see, to touch, to eroticize it, and to eroticize the reshaping of it: I want to navigate a new terrain of the body, laying claim to it for myself, molding it to fit my desires. ¶ Here we want to talk about the corporeal entity, the physical self and our desires to re-shape and re-picture, re-imagine, re-articulate the fig-ure, the human form. The erotic flesh, the severed flesh, the mutilated flesh, the seductive flesh... like something slippery and sinuous... is the site of battles and dominations. This bodily structure is caged in preten-sions and repressions often dictated by laws, by morals, by fashion. To break from this entrapment demands a kind of morphogeny to a new form, the creation of a revolutionary corporealness. LP: Where do metaphors end and flesh, bone, and skin begin? Can we so easily slide back and forth between the material body and its representation? How do we theorize around, through, inside, outside, and all over the body and still recognize its substantive, material, physical presence? How can we hold both bodies at once? KH: I have heard many friends/colleagues of mine say that we've moved into an era that is "post-human," meaning *beyond* human — mean-ing we have moved *beyond* the cyborg (the man/woman/machine coupling) to *become* the machine. There *is* no more split. We now embody the artifice. ¶ I would like to address this mind/body conundrum and speak about our need to literalize our locale even in our new state of being. Even though we may be engaging in a new integration of that which is natural and that which is fabricated, creating an entirely new synthesis, I would like to look at some of the cultural remnants of our current place/moment in history. Perhaps because of this new state of "artificiality," I also see an urgent need for *locating*, and *literalizing* our sense of place in the world and with the body. We seem to have entered a time of essentialist politics, scientific grounding for all cultural definitions, and the need to "name" and "label" everything and everyone. The reconfiguration of our bodies, the articulation of our need and desire to "see" ourselves, and our desire (as they say in the military to command/control and communicate) seems to be a genuine urge to "bridle" nature, but also to create something authentic and new. **LP:** I think it is of particular interest that at the same time theorists are talking as if we are post-human, there is this full-blown resurgence of biological determinism in popular culture and scientific discourse that you bring up above. Perhaps it is the instability of bodily signifiers that strikes fear in the heart (hey, did you get that from a baboon or what) of certain purveyors of popular discourse. While the fear this slippage provokes, on the one hand, speaks to the power and possibility in that contested space, this backlash of biologism has real effects on real bodies. I'm not sliding off into the notion of a beaurocratic body, I'm thinking more mundanely about things like gay-bashing in the Village and the ramifications of current syllogisms that make the leap to link IQ to race.

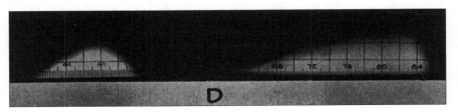

Renegades

by Jocelyn Taylor

THOUSANDS OF YEARS AGO, before recorded history, there was a black or asian woman who spawned the rest of humankind. Scientific research confirms that our origins rest in the southeastern hemisphere. Stretching the information just a tad, we could also conclude that initial sexual expression existed there as well, and that reproduction wasn't the sole reason for intimate contact. It is a little known fact that among the household items found by archaeologists at ancient sites are dildos and other similarly fashioned objects. It was our sisters of color that provided the momentum for sexual expression and pleasure.

In the memory of those ancestors, I look at the current territories of desire and sexual expression by women of color. Now, in the Age of Television, we are constantly faced with a barrage of sexualized images intended to conform our urges into a homogeneous model that tells us what is or isn't desirable. Our transgressions and taboos have been predescribed by these models. Visions of people of color, differently-abled and differently-shaped individuals, and lesbians and gays, in mainstream representations have historically been problematic and something extraneous on the image landscape.

The particular impact of racism on how we imagine erotica has magnified the need for self-perpetuating, self-promoting imagery. There's always the danger of being objectified or eroticized by a media machinery that thrives on the narrowest interpretations of the sexual. In addition, Black women, are plagued by remembrances of sexual servitude. From the beginning of our arrival to the New Land there has been the co-optation of our bodies, our pleasure, and our interpretation of the erotic. It's been difficult to retrieve all that. Dawn Suggs' short piece, *She Left the Script Behind*, opens with a shoot-in-progress for a film in which a black female slave accepts and enjoys the attempted rape by her master. As the slave struggles beneath her attacker the lines between reality and fiction become blurred and uncomfortable. The actress rejects the role saying that she "just can't do it," but not before she causes physical injury to the white actor in the role of the master. *She Left the Script Behind* is a film, not a video, which expresses a fear and an anger that just hasn't gone away.

Black women have remained in the dangerous category "exotic" which has often meant being the thing to be taken, used, and discarded. So, assuming the position of "object of desire" can get a little unruly. If the video/film conveys transgressive themes (S&M, power, gender confusions) the work can be scarier and therefore more problematic. Often we are distrustful of the occasions when we do get to see ourselves in sexualized postures. We realize at the same time that the frontier of erotic imagery is incomplete without us. Being "desired" has its consequences, yet we must desire and be desired in order to experience our fullest erotic potential as human beings. It is no wonder that there is an element of radicalism within erotic work by women of color who want other women of color. Every effort re-shapes the model "object." The work of black women videomakers re-creates the ideal "object." Now, these objects can be ourselves. They are also outside ourselves in places that haven't been explored by dominant media. We're speaking a new language, carving a new niche in the visual terrain.

Frequently, we focus on ourselves as subject, object, and audience. In a recent screening of videos by black lesbians at the Lesbian and Gay New York Film & Video Festival, a large percentage of the works presented contained the makers themselves. The cross-over of on-camera participants demonstrated an interesting in-breeding of intention. More than an agreement of, "I'll be in your video if you'll be mine," the repetition of faces from video to video seemed to express a contracted purpose of creating and stabilizing a territory for the images of black lesbians. In a sense, the mirror within a mirror reflection of the producers and the participants in the work exemplified a definite transformation of the image landscape. It was both an effort to make up for the years of invisibility and a protection against an unwelcomed "gaze." A cliche of "makers" and "lookers" is more capable of developing an agenda for a com-

Still from **Frankie and Jocie**, 1994, by **Joceylyn Taylor**.

munity of under-represented, sexually marginalized women; black lesbians specifically. As for the audience, the majority of viewers were lesbians or women of color themselves. The whole scene was an example of a complicit arrangement of approval and acceptance.

On the other hand, producers are still stuck with attempting to transgress warped expectations by viewers from the "outside." Since the combination of video, sex and lesbianism are elements within heterosexual pornographic representations, audience expansion of lesbian erotica is tricky. Much depends on the forum, the actual place where the videos are being shown. Recently, P.S. 1 Museum of Contemporary Art sponsored a screening of erotic work by lesbians of color as part of an installation entitled *Boudoir-In-Exile*. As the coordinator of this particular event, I arranged the format of the presentation, including an introduction of each tape by the artists (all of whom were present), and opening comments by a cultural theorist. My intention was to present the work, talk about specific themes, and open up dialogue about sexual representation by lesbians.

On the night of the event, I took a visual survey of the audience. Most of the viewers were straight, white men. While *Boudoir-In-Exile* implied an investigation into sexual exploration, the lesbians were interested in talking about exploring sexual visibility. The straight audience was more interested in participating as voyeurs. The makers and myself attempted to block the process by stopping in between each tape in order to allow the producer to talk about her work. We hoped that strategy would help us to control the mood of the screening. It didn't quite pan out as we'd hoped. A member of the audience went ballistic. He didn't want to be told what he was watching. He just wanted to watch. The confrontation was so disturbing that we switched to Plan B: show all the tapes and then talk about them. While the tapes were running, we formed a lesbian huddle to re-think the situation. We decided to ask the audience what they thought they were watching. We met with more resistance. Someone wanted to know why we needed dildos if we were lesbians. We were dealing with folks from the museum mailing list and passersby from TriBeCa, many of whom had no context for lesbians' sexuality and didn't know the difference between a man and a sex toy.

Well, we weren't necessarily interested in teaching our audience the in's and out's of lesbian sex. Our male audience was poorly equipped to discuss desire and media from a lesbian perspective. How easy it would have been for our "exiled" viewers to shield themselves from that challenge. There we were, sitting on a huge red bed with the television on one end and the audience and producers at the other. It was an intimate setting indeed, hyped with 42nd Street visuals and innuendo. We lesbians couldn't quite escape the role as "teacher" nor could the audience help from performing as uneducated "kids." They had never seen lesbians of color in deference to themselves, had never witnessed the burdened discusssion of Sexual Visibility by Lesbians of Color in Media. No, we didn't want to instruct our viewers. It was enough to assert that we have revived the energy of the "first sisters," and with cameras in hand, continue to change the territories of desire and s e x u a l i t y .

Opposite: still from **24 Hours a Day**, 1993, by **Jocelyn Taylor.**

Aftershocks:

Re-Shifting the Sexual Landscape Through Language, Image and Action

by Ayanna Udongo

Nubiànt, (nu-bee-ahnt) 1: a person who seeks a greater understanding of sexual pleasuring for personal and societal enrichment 2: a sexual healer 3: one who believes in the life force powers of sexual communion and shares their knowledge with others 4: a seeker of sexual excellence.

PROFILE: *In general, most practicing nubiànts can be any sex, any race, any age, any size, any social-economic class, or sexual preferences. They are sensuous, connected to nature and the universe, creative, spiritual, self-confident, expressive, sensitive, playful. Dedicated to a life of teaching with compassion. Ever-seeking inner healing for themselves and humankind.*

Sometimes, I describe myself as a "try-sexual," a person who is willing to *try* a broad range of sexual and sensual encounters. I am also an eroticist, one who practices the art of erotica in the forms of video art, performance, storytelling and dance. I use the term *sexualist* when I'm asked about my sexual preference. This term allows me to define my own sexual territories. I am without question a *nubiànt*: a being in search of sexual excellence.

I grew up as a lonely and imaginative teen who found great solace by getting lost in the illusionary world of television and film. This was during the mid-60s where there was a hot bed of unrest constantly bursting upon the tv screen. There was the civil rights movement shaking at its very foundation, and no one knew what the aftermath would hold. In the meantime, I was creating a revolution of my own, shaking up (literally) my own little world. Learning to make love to my body while encountering imaginary lovers was a nightly adventure. They eagerly came to me, lovers like Kato (Bruce Lee), Tony Curtis, Rock Hudson, Pam Grier or Mr. Spock. Each of these individuals possessed a certain look or power that I found very exciting. Each encounter took me to exquisitely unknown places where my fantasies were fulfilled with numerous lovers and my virtue still remained in tact.

Ever since I was a high spirited adolescent, I learned about the button-pushing power of the word s-e-x and its ability to provoke a broad spectrum of responses. It was a major source of amusement as a kid, but as I grew older it became a serious concern. Thirty years later, this word still has the power to provoke the same reactions. Why? Why is a man a stud and a woman a nymphomaniac?

Highly charged words like "bitch," "bulldagger," "ho," "cunt," "nympho," "ball buster" are loaded terms meant to demean and intimidate the recipient. In Western history sexual language has been a powerful tool for men's privileged use alone. And women have had little or no recourse. In the game of sexual politics, men primarily have been free to exploit women at their discretion. It's about physical, mental, and economic power and control. I believe women have the potential to begin a healing process and become empowered once they have the freedom to explore their bodies through the eyes of another woman, separate from a male domain.

I use video to explore all of the sensual and sexual possibilities. I challenge myself to create new terms and language within my work and try to apply it in my daily life. Words like *nubiànt* — I was trying to find a word that defines a person who is sexually confident, someone who genuinely honors the gift of sexual communion and generously shares that knowledge with others. No such word existed. This discovery inspired me to create *Moon Song of the Nubiànts*, a video about the existence of a sexual culture in the future: where the life force powers of sex are highly worshipped and honored; where the erotic is recognized as the center of balance and harmony. These sexual artisans are the descendants of the first Nubiànts who originated from the Black countries of Africa. My primary motivation was to explore, going back through time, how European intrusion distorted Black African women's sexuality and perceptions of themselves as women.

THE IMAGE

I was raised on the moving images of television and film. My mama was constantly telling me to get my head out of the tv. Everything about film and video had a mesmerizing effect on me. And as a socially rejected teen I submerged myself into the world of illusion so deeply I eventually evolved into a media-morph, someone whose life is so transformed by moving media that they believe it as truth. My sexual urges forced me to veraciously consume films about love and desire. (I was transformed one fateful day when I saw *Barbarella*, with Jane Fonda.)

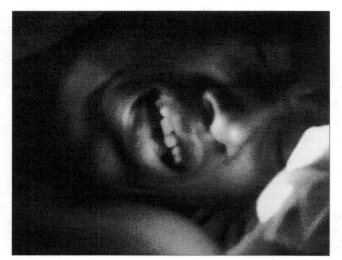

Even though I saw a myriad of stories about love, I was becoming restless and frustrated: where were the images of myself, my sister, girlfriends and grandmother on the screen? The ones that did appear were so tragic and had limited desirability. I began searching for positive images of African-American women.

It was a lonely journey trying to find representations of African-American women who were admired for their sensual and sexual power, beauty and passion. Where were they? Certainly not in the fine art museums, or immortalized in bronze in public parks. Certainly not in enough great works of literature. My last hopes were dashed in the dust as Hollywood films and television refused to give Black women proper respect. I became more agitated as Elizabeth Taylor played Cleopatra, Bo Derrick wore cornrows, Cat Woman (Eartha Kitt) didn't get to make love to Batman, and Pam Grier never got the roles that were worthy of a woman of such intelligence and beauty.

Above and opposite: stills from **Edges,** 1993, by **Ayanna Udongo.**

I decided to become a sexual revolutionary, a resistance fighter for all women to rightfully pursue and reclaim their independence. I realized that I would have to go back into our past in order to investigate the negative representations of Black women in the present. The effects of the North American slave trade had so brutalized African women that it has left a deep wound that still influences many of today's attitudes and perceptions about her.

That perception could not have been more evident than throughout the Anita Hill and Clarence Thomas hearings. I was bewildered and disturbed by the lack of solidarity between women, especially African-American women, behind this event. This unfortunate event forced me to reflect upon some of the reasons why women are so immobilized when they need to defend themselves and each other.

Edges was created in direct response to those hearings. I realized that many women (myself included) have been raised to accept the good girl/bad girl syndrome as truth. I painfully watched Anita struggle to do the "good" thing and still get labeled as a bitch. With *Edges* I was able to release my pain for her and briefly explore how the disempowering process begins in our lives.

The entertainment fields of music and film are aggressively objectifying Black women. However, there is a sexual movement taking place as more and more positive sexual images are being produced by African-American women video producers like Jocelyn Taylor, Michelle Parkerson and Cheryl Dunye, just to name a few. These women possess the courage, passion and spirit of conviction intense enough to provoke the viewer into re-thinking misconceptions and stereotypical perceptions of African-American women. They acknowledge freely the power of the erotic, coming full circle to the point where Black women can openly reclaim their sexual dignity without shame or guilt.

It is my mission to present images of African-American women in as many diverse roles as possible, exploring the potential for new and alternative ideas for positive change. The challenge is in creating work that will effectively engage and persuade those who are the exploited and disempowered on a daily basis. Personalizing the sexual and the political allows me to interact with the viewer on a more intimate level. Hopefully, we are able to connect because of similar experiences.

I'll end with this inspiring quote from Audre Lorde in the hopes that it will encourage future women of color to embrace and practice the powers of the E R O T I C .

Only now, I find more and more women-identified women brave enough to risk sharing the erotic's electrical charge without having to look away, and without distorting the enormously powerful and creative nature of the exchange. Recognizing the power of the erotic within our lives can give us the energy to pursue genuine change within our world, rather than merely settling for a shift of characters in the same weary drama.

      — AUDRE LORDE, "USES OF THE
        EROTIC: THE EROTIC AS POWER"
        IN <u>SISTER OUTSIDER</u>.

On Orlan

by Kelly Coyne

Orlan is a French multi-media artist who began a project called
The Reincarnation of St. Orlan in 1990. She began by using a
computer to create a composite image derived from her own face,
the "Mona Lisa," and old master paintings of Diana, Psyche,
Europa, and Venus. These figures were chosen because they embody
certain character traits Orlan finds admirable. In an ongoing
series of cosmetic surgeries (seven to date), Orlan is trans-
forming her face to conform to this composite image. The surgery
rooms in which this transformation is performed literally become
operating theaters, multi-media spectacles orchestrated by Orlan
as she is operated on using only local anesthesia. Between surgeries Orlan raises funds by selling images derived from the
surgery process, as well as *Reliquaries* — small pieces of her
flesh imbedded in panels with text.

Interview with Penine Hart *

KELLY COYNE: What are the most popular misconceptions about Orlan?

PENINE HART: Well, I think the worst thing that happened is that
people seem to think that she is just a publicity hound and that she really is
in this for her own narcissistic fix. And people have failed to realized how
courageous it is to take this on as a project. People fail to realize the
touching reliance and the touching belief she has in art — that she could
give over her body.

KC: To say "I give my body to art" with this sort of seriousness, to not be tongue in
cheek...

PH: Yes, with absolute seriousness. ¶ The one thing that *has* irritated me

* Ed.'s note: Penine Hart is the NYC gallery representative for Orlan.

most, since you put it that way, is the failure to realize that she has absolutely given herself over for her personal idea of what it means to be an artist, and how to be an artist means to dare.

KC: One of basic things that seems to be blown up in the media, and which I'm still confused about, is this notion of the composite image which is her template for surgery. Is it physical or psychological?

PH: What she means is that the characteristics that she has chosen from each of these goddesses reaffirm something inside of herself that she wants to bring to the fore. For instance, having a prominent forehead indicates stubbornness and intelligence, the same with a strong chin, the same with far seeing eyes — someone who is willing to look into the future and take chances. That's what she means by the psychological portrait.

KC: So, she wanted Mona Lisa's forehead because of the physiognomy of an intelligent forehead?

PH: Exactly, here's a quote:

> They all have some of me: Psyche is always sticking her nose in things, Diana travels a lot, she is a goddess who doesn't surrender to men; Venus has the drive of birth; and the Mona Lisa is a beacon, she is the most enigmatic in the history of art, she is unavoidable.

KC: Now I understand it as a mental or psychological ideal, but I can't help but be fascinated by how these features are coming together. She is not striving for beauty and she's clear about that.

PH: Yes she's clear about that. Well, it's quite noticeable for me since we first met. She's a very charming looking woman. Now she has a completely different look. ¶ I don't know.Her cheeks are really pudgy, her nose is way too small — of course that's going to be fixed, but that's what it looks like now — and these silicone implants above her eyebrows are monstrous looking, like the Bride of Frankenstein.

KC: Yes, that's what everybody was talking about at the conference. (*Illustrated Woman*, San Francisco, February, 1994.)

PH: And she laughs about that — she laughs about that as if it's like a new monster from Star Trek.

KC: So it is the grotesque she's interested in in this transformation — or are the grotesque effects incidental to her plan?

P H : It is incidental. She wasn't striving to become grotesque, but she does realize that there is certain irony because there is an element in what she's doing which is monstrous, and so that it should look monstrous is not exactly out of the question.

K C : Is it true that with the forehead implants that they were placed there to reference the Mona Lisa?

P H : Yes, but not to look exactly like, but just to reference.

K C : Just to reference... but wouldn't it have been possible to create a more protruding forehead and not just place cheekbone implants there?

P H : It would have been possible, yes.

K C : But she chose to use cheekbone implants instead...?

P H : She and the doctor discussed it and decided that this was the solution they preferred, and I think there was a bit of her perversity in that.

K C : Why doesn't she just have an artist or herself design custom implants that do very interesting things to her face and push that side of things?

P H : She doesn't want to have two noses, she doesn't want to be a freak in a zoo. She wants to make her point and do it in the best way possible, but she doesn't want to be ridiculous.

K C : But those forehead nodules sit there on the border...

P H : They do, and I think that's something she welcomes about them. It's something that amuses her and that is a little perversity and she likes that, and she likes to push that, but at the same time she didn't want two eyebrows on one side of her face.

K C : So that is one little tweak of perversity, but she won't be playing with those ideas anymore?

P H : No, but someone like this has to be perverse, right?

K C : Oh , it is incredibly perverse, so how do you draw the line? Why not do this or that?

P H : It's not practical for one thing. She has to work with the reality of what the surgeon will provide, they won't make two noses

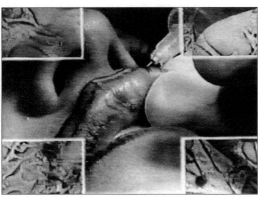

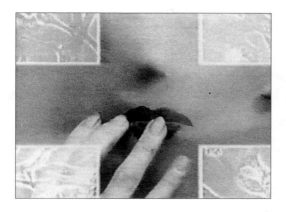

because they can't make two noses work, but they can make implants in the forehead work. She is working with bio-medical technology as it exists.

KC: I guess then one of the issues would be the ethical limits of the surgeons, what they ultimately consider unnecessary, or harmful.

PH: That's one of the questions Orlan wants us to consider when we look at her.

KC: Does she have a definite idea what the final physical image that she'll end up with is, or is she discovering this as she goes?

PH: She does, she has this computer composite portrait, but she absolutely understands that it's going to change as she goes along with those changes. It's as if in the process you take some chances, and she welcomes those chances as part of it.

KC: So it's the process which is central?

PH: Oh, the process is the whole thing, the result doesn't matter at all. The result is absolutely immaterial. What she looks like at the end of this is immaterial. The whole thing is about the process, the transformation, the metamorphosis over many months and years.

KC: To address the actual videos — once the initial shock fades from watching the surgery — which probably never happens for some people...

PH: Trust me, it never does!!

KC: ...Or at least once people get used to it enough, they then notice the circus atmosphere she generates within the surgical space, when the surgery might be enough visual stimulus alone. Could you talk a bit about that relation to the operating theater, and why that is such an essential part of the transformation?

PH: I think that she has always spoken of her work as interventions, and it has always had an element of the theatrical, she has always been the actress and she has always thought it to be a very important element: The One Who Sees—you know, the spectator—"the one who sees," and so she sets it up as though it is a theater. So, even the surgeons are dressed, and they are part of the theater, and they are part of the chorus that she is directing. That's an important element of it all, that she directs every aspect. So, that's why she stays awake, has only local anesthesia and continues to bark out directions.

KC: What are her sources or inspirations for this sort of performance?

PH: Well I think the iconography of religion. I believe she finds those rituals theatrical and she wants to use that in her own way.

KC: There is that trope of martyrdom, the mysticism of the relic. Is this just referencing the self-sacrifice to plastic surgery and the martyrdom to beauty, or since she is Saint Orlan, does she consider this a spiritual transformation?

PH: Yes she does. I think it's several different levels. Personally, I don't think that it can be pinned down to one or the other. I think that she is referencing, yes, self-sacrifice, "I give myself to my art" is one of her phrases. It's important also that the title of the videotape you saw was *In a moment you will see me, and in another moment you will no longer see me.* Those are the words of Christ. Those are the words of the Christ in his passion, and that's important.

KC: At the *Illustrated Woman* some of the audience seemed concerned about her spiritual well being, and concerned about the lingering effects and psychological impact of this surgery. They had a belief in the wholeness of body and spirit which Orlan was contradicting by saying things along the lines of "my body has never been particularly important to me" and "my body is a costume that I change at will."

PH: On the other hand, she has often talked to me, and for interviews,

about what she wants — to reduce the distance between the internal and the external.

KC: Really?

PH: She is expecting a wholeness by trying to make her external features match her internal characteristics. She actually wants to reduce the distance and bring the whole closer together. ¶ It's interesting to me that you say she didn't respond that way on that occasion.

KC: It didn't seem that way, but then it was very confusing with the signer and the translator, and the blood and gore playing on the video behind her...

PH: I've seen her misunderstand questions before and answer something else. Some of that confusion has to do with language.

KC: So, I think that's really interesting, I've never heard that anywhere before, that she desires a reconciliation between her body and her mind — which speaks to a pre-existing split between her body and her mind.

PH: Yes that's one of her more important quotes. Here's a bit of it :

> *the skin is deceptive, one is never what one is,*
> *you can have the skin of a crocodile and*
> *actually be a small dog, you can have the*
> *skin of an angel and actually be a jackal...*

It sounds clumsy because of the translation, but that is some of a passage that she always reads before starting on an operation, and she always uses that text and she uses it because she wants to make exactly that point, that she thinks there's too much distance between the external and the internal and she's trying to bring the two things together.

KC: So she sees this as a universal, human split?

PH: A human split, yes.

KC: And not her own, personal split? Because she is often being accused of being self-loathing or dissatisfied with her body.

PH: Yes which is amazing because she a very attractive woman, with a nice body as well.

KC: And what's happening through the surgery is changing that.

PH: Yes.

KC: What about all those charges I see of what Barbara Rose termed "pathological behavior" or what some reviewers refer to as her mental instability — people assume she has to be crazy to be doing this.

PH: Well, sometimes people do crazy things because they feel for one reason or another forced to. They act in crazy ways but they are not actually crazy. I don't believe she is crazy, I really don't. She is very lucid. ¶ I'm not saying, though, that she doesn't kid herself about certain things. For instance, I think she is in a certain amount of denial about the pain and the potential danger, but that is probably because she has to in order to get through it, in order to stay strong. ¶ There's actually a whole medical journal written about her, it's French. There's a picture of her on the front with her name across the front, and half her face superimposed with the Mona Lisa, and inside there's article after article discussing whether or not she's crazy, and the conclusion is that she isn't.

KC: That must be reassuring.

PH: It's funny to see an entire magazine given over to this.

KC: Well, I think that's one of the most interesting things is the discourse, the incredible amount of discourse that surrounds her work.

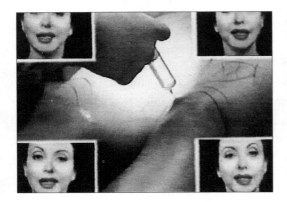

PH: Well, that's what I enjoyed about having her show here, it was one of the most intense periods of my life.

KC: Continuing on the insanity line, I wondered when I was reading when insanity suddenly became a disqualifier for "great art." I was amused to see them either trying to prove her crazy and thus disqualify her as an artist, or trying to prove she is not crazy and defend what she is doing as ar .

PH: I'm glad you brought that up, I mean it's OK for Van Gogh to be crazy, but it's not OK for her to be crazy.

KC: But her program is a feminist program? She considers herself a feminist artist?

PH: Yes, she considers herself a feminist artist.

KC: So it's important to her that the surgery scene implies the voyeuristic way women are viewed — making the dissection of the body literal and all of that...

PH: Absolutely, that's very much part of it, and the other part of it, which can seem contradictory at times is making the point "Look, I have chosen this, this is not *happening* to me. I am not an object."

KC: Is there anything about her transformation that has surprised her, or anything that she has learned as an artist, that she did not expect, and I mean more on a mental than a physical level?

PH: Sure, here's how she describes it: when she was learning to become an artist she felt she had to put on a mask, a self defense mask of a very aggressive person, and one of the reasons she is involved in this project is to take off that mask of aggression and find a more vulnerable, tender self. Although she was going for that, I would answer your question by saying she has actually been surprised to have found that.

KC: Even though she wanted to take it off, you mean she was surprised by how vulnerable she became?

PH: She found herself to be more vulnerable. Yes, that was part of the process, that she expected to be a more vulnerable person in the end result, to be able to take off her mask of aggression.

KC: That's interesting cause it seems to go back to that trope of martyrdom — the passivity of the martyr or the vulnerability of the martyr.

PH: Yes.

KC: Where is she in her progress of surgeries? I had heard it was a series of seven surgeries, but she just had her seventh. Was it prolonged?

PH: It was never a set number — she always imagined that there could be as many as a dozen surgeries. She's had her 7th and now she envisions a maximum of two or three more because she was able to reach many of her goals in the 7th one, and she actually is, believe it or not, not a masochist, and she doesn't want to go on forever. Definitely not more than two or three more.

KC: So, one is to lengthen her nose. What else is left?

PH: Further work on her chin.

KC: Why has she undergone liposuction?

PH: They are removing fat from her thigh and butt area to use in her face, and some of it gets used in the relics she makes.

KC: I see, but the sculpting of her body is not part of the program?

PH: No, it's not.

KC: So, its just fat farming?

PH: Yes.

KC: How is she going to know when it's time to end?

PH: It will sort of depend on the next surgery, she doesn't want to say definitively now that there's only going to be one more, and it's going to be everything because you really don't know that in advance. So, she's going to see how it goes. If she reaches enough of her goal to satisfy her after one more, then she'll stop. That's what she interested in...

KC: An interesting question for me is *what* will she be when this is all over.

PH: She will become a new person, and she doesn't know what that is yet because she hasn't reached it. She is still in the process of transformation.

Four stills from ...**In a short while you will no longer see me... then a short time later... you will see me again...**, 1992, by **Orlan.**

225

The Unmasking of Orlan

Rumor has it that Orlan presented a necklace containing a preserved piece of her own flesh to Madonna on a French talk show. Apparently, this shocked The Shameless One for a moment, but she quickly regained her composure and told Orlan "This is very pretty, it looks like caviar."[1]

I wish I could have witnessed this media moment, a savvy attempt by Orlan to shake Madonna's cool, and perhaps genuinely to pay tribute to her in an acknowledgment of kind-ness. Madonna generates her publicity as inseparable from her body image, and so does Orlan. The difference is in the message. Madonna's message is her self — her image is the meaning. Orlan is also rendering her body as a message, but what that message is, exactly, is the question at the center of all discourse about her work.

I saw Orlan speak at the *Illustrated Woman* conference in San Francisco this February (1994). A charismatic woman in cat-eye sunglasses and a black, corseted dress, she came on stage preceded by a signer and a translator. A video projection ran behind her, showing one of her surgeries. Both the Orlan on stage and the Orlan in the operating theater gave me the impression of a woman of enormous will. Close-ups of her flesh being pulled from her face made difficult viewing for many in the audience. Yet I found the difference between the Orlan pictured in this documentation and the Orlan on the stage before me more disturbing. Of course her features were altered, but she seemed physically fragile, and older than the woman on screen. But most sensational were the two large, lima bean shaped lumps above her eyebrows, which caused whispered speculation throughout the audience. It was obvious that her transformation had nothing to do with beauty, but instead investigated the borders of the grotesque. However, after her presentation and a long Q&A session, I was still unable to explain her program to my curious friends. Orlan always speaks through a translator, and this may account for some confusion or misinterpretation. Beyond this, Orlan's intent as artist is highly idiosyncratic, and I believe she bears much of the responsibility for the confusion around her work. Only after seeing her speak, reading every article and review on her that I could find, and speaking with her gallery representative in New York, Penine Hart, have I begun to see the more subtle points in her work. The question is, how hard do you have to work?

Reading the press on Orlan has left me less interested in Orlan's Real Meaning and more interested in mapping out the terrain formed by the discourse around her work. I expected the popular press and venues like *Eye to*

Flavr Savr, digital image, 1994, by **Kelly Coyne.**

Eye with Connie Chung to capitalize on the sensationalist aspects of her work, but the reactionary interpretations of her work by art critics working for major papers and journals surprised me. I guess what Madonna has shown all along is true: it doesn't take much to shake up the establishment.

> *The biggest danger I face as an artist*
> *is that people will become so seduced*
> *by my body, by the body in the process*
> *of performance, that they will*
> *cease to perceive me as an artist.* 2

The most active point of controversy, comment and criticism around Orlan's work is her use of the composite image as *(continued on page 330)*

Across the Border

A Discussion between Susan Stryker and Kathy High on the Anarchorporeality Project.

SEPTEMBER 23, 1994

Dear Kathy:

It was great to talk to you the other day. I'm really looking forward to working with you.

I've enclosed several items to give you a sense of what I've been up to for the last year or so of my life...

PROJECT OVERVIEW

The way I envision what I've tentatively labelled the *Anarchorporeality Project* is as a series of transsexual surgical operations performed upon me, and documented/interpreted in various media by other artists as well as by myself. I intend to accomplish several goals in undertaking this project.

The first is simply to chart the contours of contemporary transsexual experience from a transsexual perspective. Not only do I want to record the surgical procedures that most nontranssexual fixate on, I want to document the bureaucratic process of actually getting access to surgery to show how the current medical system imposes some tough choices on transsexuals about how we exercise power over our own bodies.

Second, I want this to be overtly political work—not in the sense of being didactic or moralizing, but at a more sophisticated level. Transsexuality is officially pathologized the way homosexuality was officially pathologized until 1973, and I see the project I'm undertaking as part of a broader effort to alter public perceptions of transsexuality as well as to dismantle the oppressive legal, medical, and psychiatric regime that currently regulates transsexuality. I feel this is important work not just for my own special interests but because it involves a critique of a biomedical establishment that operates coercively on most people. The deep rationale for undertaking this project is to shift the grounds on which a transsexual project justifies itself. I've chosen to do gender politics in the arts field because I see in body performance art work a set of precedents that can be harnessed to my broader purposes.

I want to see exactly how far I can push a claim—that I'm changing the shape of my genitals and secondary sex characteristics for aesthetic and artistic reasons, not because I am eligible to receive a DSM-IIIR diagnosis of 302.5(c)—gender identity disorder. I consider making a viable claim for transsexual body art to be a major step toward depathologization.

In a forthcoming essay on the photography of FTM transsexual Loren Cameron, I suggest that:

> transsexuality itself increasingly needs to be considered an art form. The more we pry body-alteration technologies away from their pathologizing rationales, and the more we divorce them from futile attempts to shore up the bankrupt notion of a "true sex," the more the decision to reconfigure one's flesh relies on purely aesthetic critera. "What's your pleasure?" rather than "What's your gender?" could well become the operant question for transsexuals in the rapidly approaching 21st century. This suggests that "transsexuality" as we know it could easily become a relic of the twentieth century, a label designed to incarcerate and stigmatize the transformational potential of all human identity, as well as the capacity for its technologization. This is not to say that genital reconstruction and other surgical techniques will disappear in some imagined future of proliferated possibilities for meaningful expressions of identity; desire cannot be so easily detached from the form of one's flesh. That is why the political struggle currently being waged by the population consolidated under the transsexual sign—the so-called transgender liberation movement—is so crucial. It is but one of the initial cultural arenas in which the ability to practice consent over the technological means of our own embodiment is being fought for.

Of course, pursuing this project means actually doing work of artistic and critical merit, but I am capable of that, at least as a writer and conceptualist. My lack of skill in other media is the primary motivation for wanting to collaborate with other artists. At the very least, photography, film and video would play an important part in documenting the project's unrepeatable work in the medium of living human flesh; I imagine, however, that visual arts could play a much larger interpretive role. Transsexuality (to my way of thinking about it) is intricately bound up with the manifestation of gender in the visual realm. Visualization and gender identification are in fact explicitly linked in several psychoanalytic theories—the gendered subject is consolidated through recognition of its projected mirror image. Through its disarticulation and redistribution of the constitutive elements of gender, transsexuality offers an opportunity to witness the temporality of this gender construction, while the visual arts—especially film and video—supply a means to investigate gender's temporal performativity through the representation and manipulation of gender's spatial display.

The project that I've envisioned would neccessarily entail a critique of some contemporary body art work that uses plastic surgery, especially that of Orlan (and especially since she is the person whose project most resembles what I propose, and the person to whom I have been most pointedly compared). I want to show how the kinds of fleshly alterations Orlan undertakes uphold rather than undermine dominant standards of embodiment—she is not contesting the regulation of the most heavily policed regions of the body. My project would allow me to do precisely that.

Finally, I find the conceptual and intellectual terrain my project ventures into fascinating in its own right—the intersection of gender, sexuality, feminist politics, biomedical technology, and media. This is a terrain we all live in and contend with, and I would look forward to contributing something novel and provocative to the cultural discourses on these issues.

STAGE ONE

The initial part of the project is, to put it as bluntly as possible, for me to cut my balls off, and to make a short film about the process that explores the issues surrounding the procedure.

Castration alone is not a routine part of male-to-female transsexual surgery for most middle-class white transsexuals; most surgeons prefer to do the orchidectomy (or orcheotomy, as it is sometimes called) at the same time they do the genital reconstruction. It is more common among transsexuals from lower socio-economic positions because it is a relatively simple and cheap body-alteration technique that can be fairly readily obtained. Castration is also medically advised upon occasion, primarily because removal of the testes permits the administration of lower doses of estrogens (which can cause liver damage and other adverse effects after prolonged high-dosage use). I'm interested in exploring the class issues around the procedure—poorer people must often content themselves with a bodily "disfigurement" that the middle-class can afford to renaturalize and erase.

I'm also interested in looking at geography and the physical location of the body, which are always pertinent issues in the cultural construction of identities. Location profoundly affects the points at which one exercises choice about one's body, and where one loses it. In the United States castration requires a psychiatric approval letter, a three month waiting period, and costs upwards of $3500—but the medical care is generally quite good. There is an unliscenced clinic in Tiajuana that will do castration on demand for a thousand dollars—but the quality of care is considerably less. There is also an underground circulation of pornographic home movies of castrations and thus an underground knowlege of how to do castrations outside of (or covertly within) medical settings. I want to examine the trade-offs involved in these three different routes to castration, and the kinds of "border-crossings" they entail.

I would be interested as well in investigating the differences between acts and identities. Historically and cross-culturally, the act of castration has been associated with several different identities—the Hijra, the Galli, eunuchs, and the castrati, to name a few. What is the relationship between these historically and culturally specific identities and the late-twentieth-century western European male-to-female transsexual? What is the difference between a man castrating *him*self, and a preoperative MTF transsexual castrating *her*self? What are the implications of any answers I come up with for current theorizing about the Foucauldian distinction between acts and identities in the history of sexuality?

Finally, I would be interested in the theoretical—especially post-structuralist feminist psychoanalytic—aspects of castration and it's role in the formation of the gendered subject. On the one hand, "castration" functions metaphorically as the definitive gesture of consolidating a feminine subject position in the signifying economy. On the other hand, physical castration is the only surgical manipulation I can think of practiced by MTF transsexuals that deforms (rather than reconsolidates) a dominant morphology of the body—that is, transsexual surgeries are about making part of one kind of body look like a part of another kind of body, rather than simply breaking a form. Theorizing from the situation of the castrated MTF transsexual body would provide an uncommon vantage point from which to examine some of the most hotly contested problems in critical theory, feminism, and cultural studies about the relationships between sex and gender, body and identity.

PRACTICAL CONSIDERATIONS

The bare bones of the matter is that I want to have somebody film me being castrated. How all the isuses I've outlined above get addressed are open for discussion. Perhaps they, too, will be part of the film; perhaps they will be addressed in other media—lecture, photography, panel discussion, whatever. I've talked to the surgeon in Tiajuana, who is fine about us doing photography/video during the procedure. I've also begun investigating the possibility of getting the surgery locally (as well as cheaply and clandestinely), through some contacts I have in the S/M community. I also have contact information for surgeons in the Bay Area and Los Angeles who require psychiatric recommendations. I do have my official diagnosis letter proclaiming me a bona fide transsexual, and know psychotherapists who would write the surgery letter. If all goes well, I'd like to do the surgery in early 1995.

On the noncorporeal front, I have a public lecture scheduled for November 16, 1994 at the Art Institute of Chicago to discuss this project, and am currently working on a proposal for a performance/presentation at The LAB in San Francisco for the 1995-96 season. I am also beginning to write grants and explore other means of funding the project. Finally, I am contacting other artists with whom I can collaborate.

I hope you're interested in what I've outlined above. Please let me know what you think. Feel free to use any of the material I've sent, including this letter, in any way you think might further the project.

Looking forward to seeing you in the not too distant future, and talking again before that,

Sincerely,

Susan Stryker

Dear Susan,

It was good to hear from you and to hear about this project. It brings up a lot of issues for me. I will try to explain what I am thinking about it and also how I am envisioning this project.

As I was pondering the identity of a MTF transsexual and what that actually means to me, I ran across this citation in an article by Judith Butler where she talks about the relationship of gayness to straightness:

> ...*imitation* does not copy that which is prior, but produces and *inverts* the very terms of priority and derivativeness. Hence, if gay identities are implicated in heterosexuality, that is not the same as claiming that they are determined or derived from heterosexuality, that is not the same as claiming that that heterosexuality is the only cultural network in which they are implicated. These are, quite literally, *inverted* imitations, ones which invert the order of imitated and imitation, and which, in the process, expose the fundamental dependency of "the origin" on that which it claims to produce as its secondary effect. 1

Although this quote deals with the areas of hetero/homosexualities, and does not touch upon transsexual issues, I found it useful. I acknowledge the invisibility of transsexuality within many homosexual/bisexual contexts, and am wary of the dissing and othering of transsexuals and their preferences. But, for me, the subversive/inversive relationship between straight and gay in looking at cultural definitions of identity was useful in clarifying gender and transsexuality. So, please allow me to refer to Butler here.

Rather than an imitation of "womanness," perhaps another interpretation of woman is being produced with MTF transsexuality. Perhaps transsexuality is an inversion of the natural parts, a redoing of nature per se. What does it mean to "perform" as a woman in this culture, anyway? In your transsexual womanness I see your development of a *new* woman, an *inverted* woman. The "monster" which some may consider being created here, is much more a hybrid, a synthesis of the essence of dualisms: nature and culture perhaps. But if we step outside of those binary situatings, and consider the overlaps, the combinations as essential, I can begin to see your interpretation and mine so charged and rich for exchange. As you quote in your letter: "'What's your pleasure?' rather than 'What's your gender?'" But also, "What's your pleasure?" rather than "What's your pathology?"

I am excited about doing this project with you, because it challenges me

as a maker and a viewer as well. I have wanted to propose working together since we met at *The Illustrated Woman* conference last February. The
investigation around gender and medical technologies *needs* to include a discussion of transsexuality. There are so few videos that look at the topic of
transsexuality in a way to include recordings of MTF operations. This video
could be an important inclusion in an ongoing dialogue about both transgender issues and the discourse of medical technologies or the critique of
technological determinism and hierarchies. I believe your participation in this
project is to define the political groundwork of the theory of gendering and
transsexuality, and mine is to determine the use of the video, the politics of
the "handling" of the pictures, and the choices inherent to the medium.

I have to admit I am experiencing a fair amount of resistance to the idea of
taping your castration operation. I don't believe what I am experiencing is
resistance to your change, or to the fact that you are a male-to-female transsexual. This is something I am wary of, and have thought about a lot. As
you have said: "The attribution of unnatural monstrosity remains a palpable
characteristic in most lesbian and gay representations of transsexuality, dis-
playing in unnerving detail the anxious, fearful underside of the current cultural fascination with transgenderism. Because transsexuality in particular
represents the prospect of destabilizing the foundational presupposition of
fixed genders upon which a politics of personal identity depends, people
who have invested their aspirations for social justice in identitarian movements say things about us out of sheer panic that, if said of other minorities,
would see print only in the most-riddled, white supremacist, Christian fas-
cist rags." [2] But I believe my resistance is towards the act of cutting to alter
your body. I have resistance to cutting in general (I have never had surgery
and have gone to great lengths to *avoid* having it). And maybe it is the fact
that you are choosing to cut off your <u>balls</u> that presents a problem for me.
(And the notion of cutting off the "penis" is so closely married with the
notion of *castration* especially in psychoanalytic associations that I tend to
trip up on it all the time.) So, if that is the source of my resistance, am I ultimately resisting your choice and your change in gender identity? I can't separate it right now. Is it the *cut* or *what* is being cut? Why am I focused on
this aspect? (I suspect my reactions are typical of those of a non-transsexu-
al.) This I must examine some more with your help.

I don't see this resistance as an overwhelming problem. I think that my
resistance can be used to our advantage in the tape. I suspect that other
people who come to this tape will be experiencing similar resistance, and if
we can successfully explore this area we can present a shift from a judg-

mental viewing to one which remains open. "Just as the words 'dyke,' 'fag,' 'queer,' 'slut,' and 'whore' have been reclaimed, respectively, by lesbians and gay men, by anti-assimilationist sexual minorities, by women who pursue erotic pleasure, and by sex industry workers, words like 'creature,' 'monster,' and 'unnatural' need to be reclaimed by the transgendered." [3] I would like to work with you in your "transgender rage" to make a tape that will positively call attention to transsexuality, to make that which is presently invisible much more visible.

This notion of "heroic doctors still endeavor[ing] to triumph over nature..." is intriguing to me. This notion of medical science conquering the body, mapping and charting its terrain is a history I am familiar with critiquing. But this instance gives different possibilities. Where did this surgical practice come from? When and where was it practiced first? References to the history of transsexual surgery would be useful to include in this tape to give a context to the medical establishment's control over the genderization of the body, as well as its reproductive capacities, and so-called "well being."

If we do go the Tijuana route, I would like to consider the possibility of talking to the doctor before (or after) you have the surgery performed. I would like to discuss with him why he is involved in this kind of work: for the money, because of the fall-off of U.S. clients who are, like you, skirting the regulations of the system; or is there a particular research he is interested in around genital surgery? Or perhaps there is a politic behind his practice that engages with the transsexual experience. Perhaps he only deals with a certain class of people and is committed to that socialist practice?

The surgery itself is the most challenging to consider shooting because surgery in general is difficult to watch. I think it is a political act to show this surgery in this context. But how to present it to depathologize it, without spectacle, without sheer sensationalism sending the audience into fits of convulsions? This is my question. It seems a definitive act, but ultimately it is really only one part of the entire process for you. So, that bigger process must also be shown as well as this "act." I propose that I come to visit San Francisco and that we spend some time together. Perhaps we can map out some other ways to trace this history from your psychological involvement in your girlfriend's birthing, through the decision for your surgeries, and beyond.

To be successful, I would like to see this tape move people to understand how you have become involved in the pleasure side of the issue rather than simply the gendering. Rather than depict you "at war with nature," I would like to have you claim your gender, "constituting yourself on your own terms." [4]

I am not so concerned about shooting the surgery for myself. I know what happens to me as I shoot — I distance myself through the lens and worry about banal details like keeping things in focus and composition of the frame. Also, my viewfinder is black and white, so I will be further distanced from the color of the blood, etc. But many questions remain: How to shoot this surgery? do we want a spectacle? should I shoot it as a dance where I circle the surgeon and you on the table; or as a detailed microscopic shot with the lens in macrofocus; or as a unmovable still tripod shot with medium framing? What does each framing and movement within the frame suggest? How will it further distance the audience or include them in this process? Do we want them to "feel" pain, to experience nausea and discomfort? Or to be a witness and a collaborator, aligned with you, or the surgeon, or surgical assistant?

Lately, I have been really worried about the preponderance of cop shows on TV. What concerns me mostly is the identification of the camera with the cops themselves. The audience begins to adopt the position of the authority themselves, the viewer policing with the police. This psychology I would like to try and subvert and use to our advantage. I would like to identify the surgery not as an invasion, a mutation, but as an extension of your power and a transformation, much like the birth of a baby transformed from its inside world to the exterior with such force that it must be agile to survive. I want to demonstrate your agility, and your survival.

To be continued and continued. When shall we get together to work some of this all out? Look forward to hearing from you soon.

Best,

Kathy High

1. Judith Butler, "Decking Out: Performing Identities" in *Inside/Out: Lesbian Theories, Gay Theories*, ed. by Diana Fuss, London, NYC, Routledge, 1991, p. 22.
2. Susan Stryker, "My Words to Victor Frankenstein Above the Village of Chamounix: Performing Transgender Rage," *GLQ: A Journal of Lesbian and Gay Studies*, Vol. 1, No. 3, Fall, 1994.
3. Ibid
4. Ibid

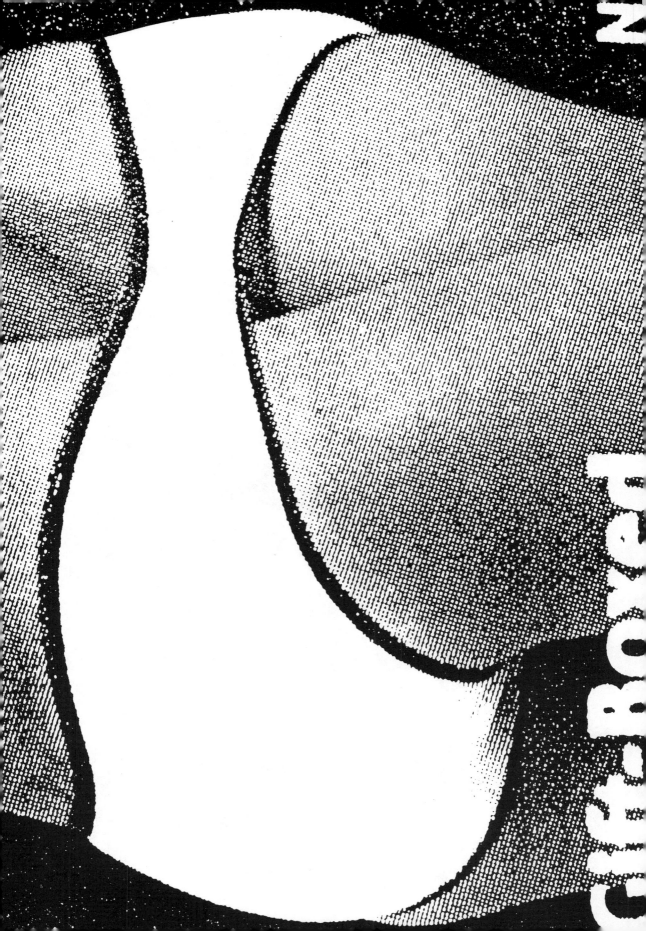

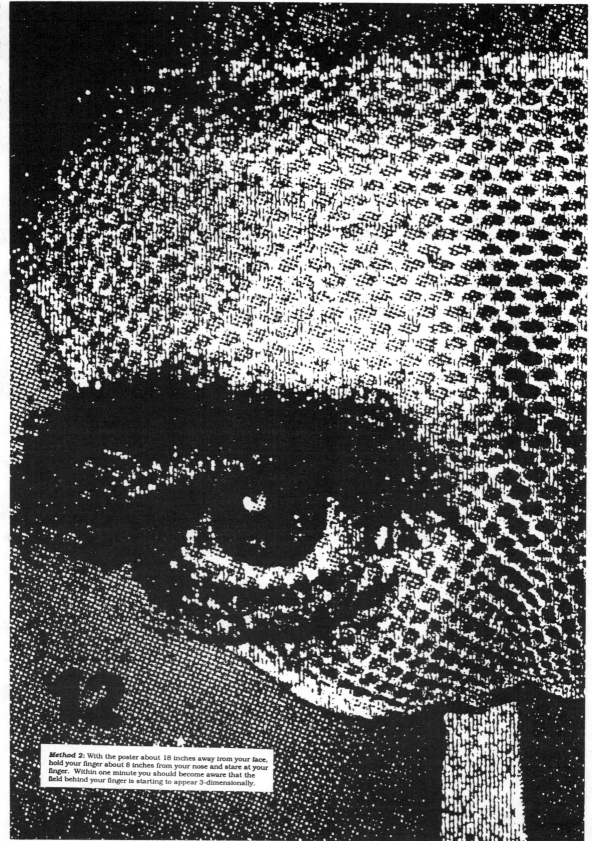

Method 2: With the poster about 18 inches away from your face, hold your finger about 8 inches from your nose and stare at your finger. Within one minute you should become aware that the field behind your finger is starting to appear 3-dimensionally.

Braille and Sex

Dale Hoyt So Jordan, your pieces haven't been shown a lot on the east coast. Mostly on the west coast, right, and partially in Europe. I'd say probably your main elements are text, body and landscape and that sort of sounds like, you know, the standard props every one is using these days, like charcoal, oil and acrylic; and yet the way you assemble those elements are unlike anything I have ever seen. It's an amazing antidote to what I think is really disturbing in the art world, especially the trend toward declarative art making. Nothing approaching irony, telegraphing to the audience—which is what TV does essentially. The mechanics of broadcast television are actually in comparison more mysterious than standard video art now. So could you talk about what mode of communication you feel is at work in your pieces, or whether you are trying to communicate anything at all, or is that an infantile simplification?

Jordan Biren Oh no, not at all. But before I answer those questions—I covet that image in <u>Braille</u>, the way <u>Braille</u> opens, more than anything I've seen in any other work.

DH Thanks—which image? The image of the dots on the screen?

JB No, no, I'm sorry, the second image.

DH Well, of course I did the titles in braille which were worthless because you couldn't feel the text on the screen. I wanted to start off with a worthless image.

JB The close up of the wave.

DH It starts on a wave.

JB And slow—the camera slowly pulls away . . .

DH Pulls away to reveal that it's actually a sort of K-mart painting.

JB In a room of terrifying normalcy.

DH Yes, my parents living room.

JB Right. That's where I see such enormous similarities in both of our work, but we can talk about that later. Well, first of all I know exactly what you are talking about in the state of the way video now communicates. I've divorced myself from it. The thing that it lacks that my work doesn't is at least an opportunity to imagine, a chance to flexibly use your mind in regards to content. I try to avoid any sort of pedanticism. But—ah—I like to keep the way my work constructs itself as mysterious as you've just described it. So, I don't really have a very concrete answer. I can say that the one thing I attempted to do in the last tape, which we're not going to talk about, is to just reduce everything to an irreducible state. That doesn't say that it meant anything, that doesn't say that it conveys anything; it just simply is and it was very successful in that way.

DH But you know, it is very tempting to compare your work to a sub-genre of structural film called monomorphic films which meant that there was a one simple or several simple elements tied together, but your work is by no means minimalistic, there's content all over the place and your last tape <u>My Mother's Family</u> has an enormous amount of content, pictures, words.

JB There's plenty. But if you want to look at this or my other works as autobiographical, having any meaning like that, then the issue of personality—memory, reflection, history, or whatever, takes over. The pieces close down, just shut off. Like turning the monitor off. They're over. I've dissociated myself from anything that brings that sort of closure to work.

DH They're also basically, again, declarative. But I do think it is interesting that you have co-opted some current props like transgressive language, your gore narrations, and yet to completely different ends. I find that fascinating because a lot of what you see in your tapes are elements that you would see in other work from this time period and yet you've completely stripped them of their connotations by differing their contexts.

JB That was the purpose of using those texts and the reason each specific one was chosen was, if for no other reason, out of pure laziness. I went for the most aggressively—ah . . .

DH Transgressive.

JB Transgressive, OK, the most aggressively transgressive text because I didn't want to deal with the issue of text. Now I don't work that way. Now the text—in fact things have inverted in my work. There was always a place for text in my tapes, but in the beginning, text was added later and generally I'd come up with it very fast, as fast as I could. Then I actually started lifting it, and I lifted as fast as I could.

DH Were any of those sections from American Psycho?

JB No.

DH Well when I first heard it it sounded a little bit like it.

JB He probably used the same sources I did. It's just from those lurid "real crime" paperbacks.

DH And the only way people can classify the work is by zeroing in on these texts and sort of perceiving it as the entertainment value of the work.

JB It's a funny thing, the paradox—it's impossible to show these works without people getting stuck on portions of those texts. But there seems to be a complete failure to understand that no graphic images accompany those texts. They're creating every single image and if they're horrific, then there's a complicity involved that I find very interesting.

DH And then we have Madonna who tried to pretty much patent sex, trademark the word sex. But Madonna calling her book <u>Sex</u> and you entitling your tape <u>Sex</u> are like two authors so disparate that you not only seem to be not speaking the same language but coming from different planets. So the fascinating thing about your <u>Sex</u> to me is that you really don't know what's going to happen next because everything up to that point in your work I'd perceived as a single texture or a single surface. As elliptical as <u>Sex</u> is there really does seem to be a diagramming of some kind going on. There's also classic references, the piece of music you use is also the music they used in <u>Un Chien Andulou</u>. Did you know that?

JB The Liebestod—no. I was very surprised when I first showed this tape, someone said that they were moved by it. I was flabbergasted; I had expected something else.

DH Talk to me about my work—landscape—<u>Braille</u>.

JB Well, there are much more important things about landscape than what is generally accepted as being landscape. So with <u>Braille</u>, first of all it's pretty hard to ignore the way it starts. I'm not so sure what that sound is. It's slow, pitches are lowered, tracks move backwards, it's a mix of dark, grating sounds. The overall effect is perfect with the camera set focused solely on this wave. I have a photo of a wave in my bedroom. Just a wave. It breaks in an unexplained ocean. In <u>Once Upon a Time in the West</u>, the man who is lame and never leaves his private rail car that moves him around the west, periodically gazes at an oil painting of a wave that hangs on a wall. No context—just a wave in an unexplained ocean. In <u>Braille</u>, the camera begins to slowly pull back and you see that you were within the frame of a typical Sunday painter's seascape. The audio is itself so much of a figure. It changes, transfigures, as the camera recedes. Now we're in a room. We've exceeded the frame of the painting. By this time I think the music has completely normalized—it's become like store music, mall music.

DH Muzak.

JB Yeah. Now that we're way outside its frame, we can see we're in a room that's just like the painting. Anyway, the point is you've gone though a very slow progression from inside a landscape with no context, which is terrifying and exciting, to a room that should be comforting and familiar but is in fact way more terrifying because it's far too normal.

DH Yeah—sort of a thesis statement. There's two other allusions—of course it was partially based on the zoom mounts that occur in <u>The Shining</u> which I just thought as far as tempo and structure were beautiful, that take place in Florida in Scatman Crother's motel while he's watching the snow storm on TV. So, structurally that was kind of used as a template. It's also, of course, a reference to <u>Wavelength</u> by Michael Snow which is a zoom *in* on a wave. Let me tell you how <u>Braille</u> came about. I had made <u>The Complete Anne Frank</u> and had necessarily had to depict her story in a claustrophobic way. Where as when you're looking at a landscape you're everywhere but where you are, you're somewhere far away; or what Hollis Frampton called photography:

something that is absolutely elsewhere. So after <u>The Complete Anne Frank</u>, as an antidote I wanted to do something more expansive.

JB I find Braille so unexpansive in a way I like, and that's why your incorporation of landscape in <u>Braille</u> works so well for me.

DH But there's another reason why I use landscape so much in Braille. I had seen a snuff film shortly before I moved back to Rochester to be with my parents. One of the reasons why I moved back was because I suffered a nervous breakdown that was precipitated by accidentally walking in on this snuff film playing at a party in SF. So suddenly this horrible wash came over me that maybe taking people's images is really bad and maybe this is really sort of a sinister process this photographing people. OK, I am in Rochester and I vow not to take a picture of another human being for an entire year. The other restriction was locale—I would not photograph anything that I could not see from—everything had to be shot from within a view of no more than a 20 foot radius from my bed. In other words, I could go into the living room 20 feet but I had to stop. So the landscape I do use is artificial photographs, paintings, or the onion fields in the backyard of the house. While Muzak does have this over normalized sinister interpretation, to me Muzak actually was something that was sort of like my mother's heartbeat because it was playing in our apartment constantly. But it was also a portrait of my father who was dying. To get my father to cooperate with any kind of portraiture, I had to pretend that I was doing something else with it other than talking about him. So it's also about him and about being at the end of his life and at having perceived life as music that is not to be listened to, which is the way he describes it.

JB The best line from the tape.

DH It's the selling point Muzak has built it's industry on—music that is not to be listened to.

JB The first time I saw <u>Braille</u>, on a gut level, an intuitive level, all the complex and disparate elements fit. It was like the pieces of the puzzle all falling into place with no doing on my part. It was one of those large experiences watching the tape. It seemed acutely personal.

DH It's not. It was using emotions—I was basically using the tragedy of the situation as raw material rather than using it as a source of titillation.

JB It's not in the tape, you aren't given any information.

DH But you are given information. You're given the textures of the office, you're given information. I mean, to me the most manipulative image in <u>Braille</u>, but also successful, is the zoom in to shag rug where the complete video screen is a close up on the shag rug.

JB Incredible. Carpet is the family business in LA—I grew up with carpet. To invert the tape, rather than give information, to all of the sudden break everything apart into pixels of indiscernible carpet fibers.

DH That really is the texture in so many peoples lives.

JB And also I think the way you used landscape, because as you said earlier the landscape was comprised of shooting photographs, shooting a painting, shooting out the window, shooting the interiors—those choices show what I've always liked about your work, an innate intelligence in the way it is constructed—the way you chose to acquire the landscape and then integrate it, the edit.

DH Landscape certainly has some default romanticism and attractions to it and one of them of course is being outside yourself, expansiveness. You can't look at landscape and not reconsider your relationship with nature.

JB But what about a skewed landscape? The reason I get so involved in your tape is that I cannot get outside of it. I wouldn't allow myself to even when the shot does go outside to the onion field—there's something peculiar about those fields, especially the first one which has, as I recall, long gangly blades of grass looming in the foreground.

DH Shot from a low angle. And of course it was colorized a little bit. And of course the dead garden variety plants that have died in the completely padded office.

JB I think that landscape is a fiction. What really can be differentiated out from anything else by calling it landscape. The places depicted by the imagery of my tapes are the places I went to with a camera to shoot—they're just being seen from a different point of view, videotape. The thing I appreciated most about <u>Braille</u> is it all took place in my head—it all took place in your room, it all took place in the twenty feet from your bed, it all took place through a window.

DH The last naturalistic landscape you see is the onion field and lightening coming down, which was not that easy to get, but was largely inspired—on a purely anecdotal level—by a rivalry between two art school teachers of mine. Both had used lightening in their pieces, and both had thought of the other as using their concept of lightening. It's really interesting for people to say, well, I authored this natural phenomenon, it's my possession. And that I actually got to have lightening in my piece and that it was edited to the beat of a Muzak version of <u>Funky Town</u> was my final comment, who cares. So in other words even landscape becomes synthesized into something artificial which in fact is reality, because shag carpet is as real as real as . . .

JB God yes, it's every bit as real a landscape as—I grew up in LA. For me its landscape is always a torturous experience. It can be quite exquisite as well as, outside few other places in the world, the most horrific place in existence. The extremes make it one of the most present cities, an urgent place. I mean it's a very real place that must exist as it does under a lingering and persistent sense of acute unreality.

DH You can't really see the landscape because of smog.

JB That's what LA is all about, that is it's landscape.

DH And of course smog is a natural phenomenon, it's always been there.

JB The smoky basin, in more halcyon days. It doesn't bother me, it's integral to the scenery. LA is extremely important to me because, I don't understand it, I had to leave it, and my family is still there. I wanted to go back to LA for a tape I was working on and get involved within the most gruesome landscape it had to offer. But it was impossible. I had criteria for the search. In seeking the grotesque, the grotesque became sought after. And when I found the worst of views they became the best because they were exactly what I wanted to find. The grotesque LA was the same as any other sort of LA—none can be separated out from the other.

DH It's very easy to dismiss LA as being sort of plastic and flat. It's something much more dramatic and sad.

JB Last December I flew into LAX, rented a car and got on the new Century freeway. Driving a new freeway is an indescribable experience. This freeway goes through a very complex part of Los Angeles. You can't know this though because you can't look up or down into anything—you're driving at the same horizon line as the endless sprawl of flattened city on all sides of you. The grotesque vastness of the city completely disappears as you drive towards connections to other freeways. It inspired me to re-do an older tape about LA that failed as a tape but had points I'd set out to get at that are still valid, even more so now.

DH I grew up in the country. That changes my opinion of landscape because nature to me means being in a state of constant fear because I was beleaguered all my life by hillbillies in upstate New York. It's was scary. The first time I felt safe in my life was when I was 17 years old and I went New York City. I went straight from being a farm boy to being a city boy. The appeal of landscape has nothing to do with nature as far as I am concerned.

JB Nature is bullshit. I can't understand it being separated out as if somethings, and what are they, are un-nature. How can determinations be made that some natures are not natural. I think these divisions come from agendas, they don't come from morality. I don't understand morality, really. It's a far reaching thing, complex, indecipherable and innumerably leveled, where agendas are only black and white surface simplicities. The morality in nature and landscape has been subsumed by agendas used to determine political divisions. And who are these people that determine where these divisions lay. That's where much of my work comes from. I like to hang out at the place I imagine people need to determine these divisions and just sort of go nowhere, conclude nothing. I think that's why probably my work has been a little difficult to look at. It sits in the cracks between what people consider to be things. A few years back I heard Vito Acconci say of the sixties that everyone was looking for themselves as if they were going to find a jewel. It was so jarring—the suggestion, in the way he phrased this, that possibly in the end we'd find something far from a jewel. Suggestions like that keep me working in those places described by the divisions between things.

DH One the most truly transcendent, spiritual, global experiences that I've ever had was being at a Muzak Christmas party. One time during the year do you hear a vocal on Muzak and that's when they play the Hallelujah Chorus at midnight on Christmas. And tears come to these people's eyes because they know that one of the cardinal rules is NO VOCALS but when they hear that voice coming over the Muzak it's like the magi. I'm done. Are you done?

JB I'm done.

DH What did we just do?

Transcribed from recorded conversation–
July, 1994, San Francisco, by Phoebe Brookbank

Opposite: top, from BRAILLE, Dale Hoyt, 1987; bottom, from SEX, Jordan Biren, 1990

SEEING OURSELVES WATCH: LESBIANS & EXPLICIT SEXUAL REPRESENTATION

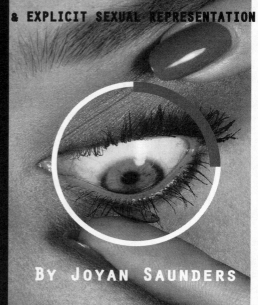

BY JOYAN SAUNDERS

At this point in time, there's certainly no shortage of sexually explicit lesbian imagery, but that wasn't always the case. Queer video of any kind has only been around for a few years, becoming an acknowledged trend in 1986 when Bill Olander curated "Homo Video: Where We Are Now"; which was purportedly the first New York exhibition devoted exclusively to videotapes by gay men and lesbians. That show, at the New Museum, was written up in Art in America by a lesbian critic who noted that the gay men's tapes tended to focus on explicit sexual activity while the women's tapes were dominated by talk. (1)

Shortly after that, another lesbian critic made a similar observation about a sexuality program at the AFI festival in LA. I had a vested interest in the commentary since my work was included in both shows and referenced by both critics vis a vis this observation that lesbian videotapes were all-talk and no-action. (2)

IT'S NO BIG SURPRISE THAT

Assuming that this was an accurate conclusion, why were lesbian producers seemingly so THE PRO-SEX INITIATIVE much more circumspect, than gay men in the way they dealt with sexuality? PREVAILED IN OUR CIRCLES. This question was given very little serious consideration at the time - and there was a certain AND IT WAS IN THIS RATHER insinuation of prudery - the idea that women are just more conflicted, more uptight about the HEATED ATMOSPHERE THAT whole down-and-dirty side of sexuality. It was also suggested that some more dogmatic dykes LESBIAN CRITICS PUT OUT THE might still be loyal to Laura Mulvey's critique of voyeuristic pleasure (3), or else they were CALL FOR A MORE IN YOUR holding on to the old co-optation idea that 'I don't want to show women doing it, because men FACE STYLE OF LESBIAN VIDEO WORK. might get a kick out of it too'.

Of course, by that time, in the late 80's, Mulvey's anti-pleasure agenda had come under considerable fire on the feminist academic circuit (4), where the porn debates or sex wars had been going on for a number of years - between the 70's styled antipornography movement and the pro-sex camp. It's no big surprise that the pro-sex initiative prevailed in our circles and it was in this rather heated atmosphere that lesbian critics put out the call for a more in-your-face style of lesbian video work.

Subsequent to this development, if there was no sex in your work it could too easily give the impression that one was anti-sex, anti-pleasure, and anti-porn etc., etc. Supply and demand kicked in and now lesbians have been delivering the goods in a big way for the past several years. However, not everyone has felt an equally compelling urge to dive in head first and perhaps we are now in a position where we might be able to develop a more generous analysis of that choice.

To start with, I think it might be interesting to look at the a priori privileging of the visual and it's bearing on women's work. So what if lesbian producers, past or present, would rather talk about sex in their work than show it? Does that need to be a problem? We're still 'talking about' sex - same subject different sign system. And a preference for the verbal is only a 'problem' if you subscribe to the assumption that the verbal is somehow inferior to the visual. And not surprisingly that's the prevailing assumption in a culture which privileges the visual to such an acute degree, but why not upset the whole apple cart and interrogate that system of values, why not be vocal about opting for the verbal?

The state of the art in earlier women's work would seem to support the notion that many women have tended to prefer the verbal over the visual. And historically, although women haven't been the primary consumers of pornographic imagery, they've always been ardent consumers of sexual representation in literary form. This preference for pornographic texts over pornographic pictures has been discussed by Ann Snitow with respect to romance novels (5) and, more recently, Andrew Ross has commented on the phenomenon (6).

From my perspective the most important thing is that the girls are getting their jollies - but I still feel like I need to explain why I might not be getting my jollies in the highly visual way that boys do. So, I thought it might be useful to begin with spectatorship and consider whether voyeurism operates in an analogous manner for the male and female spectator.

THE STATE OF THE ART IN EARLIER WOMEN'S WORK WOULD SEEM TO SUPPORT THE NOTION THAT MANY WOMEN HAVE TENDED TO PREFER THE VERBAL OVER THE VISUAL.

A great deal has been written about the subject since Mulvey's article but what rings most true for me, still, is John Berger's early observation that women are avid spectators of themselves:

"SHE HAS TO SURVEY EVERYTHING SHE IS AND EVERYTHING SHE DOES BECAUSE HOW SHE APPEARS TO OTHERS, AND ULTIMATELY HOW SHE APPEARS TO MEN, IS OF CRUCIAL IMPORTANCE FOR WHAT IS NORMALLY THOUGHT OF AS THE SUCCESS OF HER LIFE... WHILST SHE IS WALKING ACROSS A ROOM OR WHILST SHE IS WEEPING AT THE DEATH OF HER FATHER SHE CAN SCARCELY AVOID ENVISAGING HERSELF WALKING OR WEEPING".(7)

Berger is proposing that in the most banal of circumstances, and in the gravest of situations, women are obliged to continually watch themselves, as if through the eyes of another. This practice may play itself out somewhat differently for lesbians and heterosexuals. But, even though I'm not sexually involved with men, they are nonetheless heavily involved with what Berger calls the success of my life: So, I literally need to watch myself. And I tend to believe that, generally speaking, this is something women internalize, to some degree, irrespective of sexual orientation.

From there, one may reasonably assume that this habitual self-surveillance has some broader implications for female spectatorship. To extend Berger's example further in this direction one could ask: While she is sitting in a darkened theatre looking at a sexually explicit film, for example, does a woman not envisage herself sitting and looking?

AND SUPPOSING
SHE DOES
WATCH HERSELF
LOOKING?

And supposing she does watch herself looking in this manner, might it not affect her experience of the images she's looking at? I imagine that it does. Because, the film is asking her to experience voyeuristic pleasure - and voyeuristic pleasure operates on the precondition that one's gaze is unimpeded and unidirectional, so that we can look at people, or images of people in compromising positions, while we ourselves are unobserved.

But, what I'm trying to get at here is the idea that a woman may not entirely have this prerogative, since she doesn't altogether look without being observed; She observes herself in the act of looking. And if that is true, then we may have a mediated relationship to voyeurism and a more detached perspective on the imagery we're looking at.

Assuming that this is the case, it could serve to explain why sexual images may be somewhat less appealing to certain female spectators. A sexual text may be our porn of choice because it bypasses the whole voyeuristic problematic. The reading of a text doesn't invoke voyeurism, which by standard definition means looking at actual bodies or pictures of them.

Of course, we may still watch ourselves (a la Berger) in the act of reading a sexually explicit book. The difference is that when we watch ourselves read, our pleasure still flows freely, because pleasure in the pornographic text is not predicated on an unimpeded voyeuristic gaze like it is with the pornographic image. In other words, even though we may still be watching ourselves, in this case, it doesn't have any effect on the activity we're engage in.

In talking about the significance of the sexual text, I don't mean to suggest that there aren't plenty of us who take pleasure in sexually explicit images or that there aren't more and more of us working on lesbian porn. But I find it hard to ignore that, in the big picture, it's men who have produced and consumed the lion's share of sexually explicit images. I find it easy to go on the defensive about that, but I find it more interesting to entertain the possibility that women have simply chosen to serve their desire by another equally gratifying means.

That is the theory, but one needn't feel particularly bound by these ideas in terms of one's practice. I believe that a certain amount of contradiction, or slippage, between theory and practice is always more provocative than a strict correspondence between the two. What I've found most troubling in my own practice is the fact that explicit sex presents something of a stylistic dilemma. It's always seemed to me that convincing representations of explicit sex generally involve either bare-assed, documentary style naturalism or the kind of crafty simulation one sees in narrative fiction. Which poses something of a problem because, in my kind of experimental narrative work, characters rarely ever do anything remotely naturalistic nor do they act - in the sense of simulating intense physical or emotional states.

I've always felt that a good earthy, docu-styled fuck, or an 'authentic' enactment, would really go against the grain of work like this, because the work is so obviously constructed and it intends to undermine the authority of straight documentary and narrative genres. But increasingly, I find that this contradiction is beginning to have a certain perverse appeal. I start imagining an apparently uncooked, authentic moment in the midst of obvious artifice - and I see that it might serve to point up the constructiveness of the 'natural' after all.

1). Martha Gever, "Video: Where We Are Now", Art in America, July 1987, pp. 43-49

2). B. Ruby Rich, "Only Human: Sex, Gender and Other Misrepresentations", 1987 American Film Institute Video Festival, (Los Angeles, AFI, 1987), pp. 42-44.

3). Laura Mulvey "Visual Pleasure and Narrative Cinema", Screen 16, no. 3, 1975, pp. 6-18.

4). Most notably; Powers of Desire, ed. Ann Snitow, (New York, Monthly Review Press, 1983); Pleasure and Danger, ed. Carol S. Vance, (Boston, Routledge and Kegan Paul, 1984).

5). Ann Snitow, "Mass Market Romance: Pornography for Women is Different", Powers of Desire, pp. 245-263.

6). Andrew Ross, "The Popularity of Pornography", No Respect: Intellectuals and Popular Culture, (New York, Routledge, 1989), pp. 171-208.

7). John Berger, Ways of Seeing, (London, BBC 1972), p. 46.

DESIGN: NANCY SERENSKY

She was deeply afraid of offending other people or coming across poorly in conversation. Every social interaction would trigger an avalanche of doubt and self criticism. After a conversation, she would replay the scene in her mind, analyzing and evaluating each word and gesture. Although nothing was said outright, she felt she was picking up on signals that the other was giving off, signals that told her she had either offended, come across as snobbish, appeared nervous, said something stupid, not maintained appropriate eye contact or had been insensitive. A strange look on the other person's face would throw her into a frenzy of self questioning that could last for hours. Were her perceptions accurate? She was never absolutely sure.

MARIA VENUTO

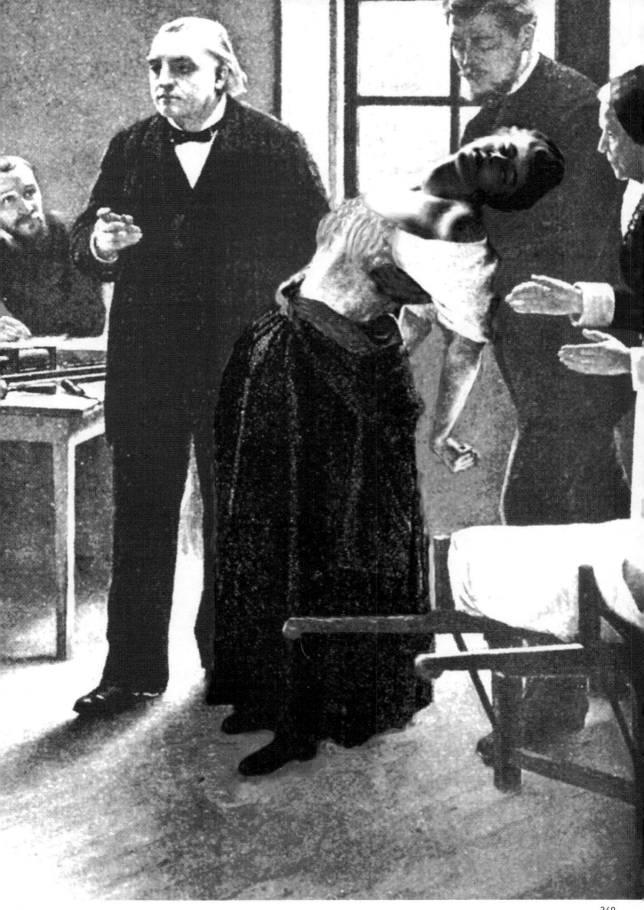

"I don't want to be shoved into a box and put into a category. That person said I was gay and he never asked me; he never approached the subject... I think it was just wishful thinking on his part. Ultimately, people will see what they want to see in the whole aspect of what I do and my motivations. I'm not embarrassed about the word 'gay', but it's not in the least bit relevant. I'm beyond that frankly."

"I'm quite convinced that homosexuality doesn't really exist."

MORRISSEY Lead singer and lyricist, The Smiths*

Girlfriend In A Coma, The Smiths, Sire/Warner Bros. Records

OFFICE VISIT: June 12, 1984
<u>Medical History</u>: No Hospitalization. Atopy, springtime. No medication allergies. Right clavicular fracture, age 6 or 7. Had all the usual childhood illnesses. No Mono.
<u>Family History</u>: Father 64, Mother 57 with thyroid disease, brother 22, sister 20.
<u>Social History</u>: Grew up in Baltimore. Studied film at New York University, finished 1982. Working in video. Saw a psychologist in 1980, and again recently. Single, heterosexual.

*As quoted by Johnny Rogan, Morrissey & Marr: The Severed Alliance, Omnibus Press, 1993. Pages 198-99, 210.

Robert Beck

PHONE CALL: January 30, 1986
Reassured about AIDS.
OFFICE VISIT: October 14, 1986
No pleuritic pain, dyspnea. In Europe two weeks
of September: Upper respitory infection when
leaving Amsterdam. Blood streaked sputum. Left
ear stuffed. Throat pain. Weight loss. Fever.

Bigmouth Strikes Again, Robert Beck, June 1986

BIGMOUTH STRIKES AGAIN

Sweetness, sweetness I was only joking
when I said I'd like to smash every tooth in your head
Sweetness, sweetness I was only joking
when I said by rights you should be bludgeoned in your bed
and I now I know how Joan of Arc felt
as the flames rose to her roman nose
and her Walkman started to melt
Bigmouth, Bigmouth
Bigmouth strikes again
and I've got no right to take my place with the human race
and now I know how Joan of Arc felt
now I know how Joan of Arc felt
as the flames rose to her roman nose
and her hearing aid started to melt
Bigmouth, Bigmouth
Bigmouth strikes again
and I've got no right to take my place with the human race

OFFICE VISIT: December 20, 1988
Found new office, moved corporation. Past
week, sore throat that evolved into chest cold
with sputum. No fever. No pleuritic pain. Not
well again. Minimal drip, worse than usual.
Insomnia. No medical problems in family.

Panic, Robert Beck, August 1988

PANIC

Panic on the streets of London
Panic on the streets of Birmingham
I wonder to myself
Could life ever be sane again
On the Leeds side-streets that you slip down
I wonder to myself
Hopes may rise on the Grasmeres
But Honey Pie, you're not safe here
So you run down
To the safety of the town
But there's Panic on the streets of Carlisle
Dublin, Dundee, Humberside
I wonder to myself
Burn down the Disco
Hang the blessed D. J.
Because the music that they constantly play
IT SAYS NOTHING TO ME ABOUT MY LIFE
Hang the blessed D. J.
Becasue the music they constantly play
HANG THE D. J., HANG THE D. J., HANG THE D. J.

GIRLFRIEND IN A COMA

Girlfriend in a coma, I know
I know - it's serious
Girlfriend in a coma, I know
I know - it's really serious
there were times when I could
have 'murdered' her
(but, you know, I would hate
anything to happen to her)
NO, I DON'T WANT TO SEE HER
Do you really think she'll pull through?
Girlfriend in a coma, I know
I know - it's serious
there were times when I could
have 'strangled' her
(but, you know, I would hate
anything to happen to her)
WOULD YOU PLEASE LET ME SEE HER
Do you really think she'll pull through?
Let me whisper my last goodbyes
I know - IT'S SERIOUS

"Girlfriend" In A Coma, Robert Beck, October 1989

Hospitalized: October 2, 1989

Medical Attending Admitting Note: 30-year-old white male. 4 days of 103 tempature, vomiting, sore throat, nausea, neck pain, headaches. No cough. No history of recurrent strep. Homosexual contact, single partner past 5 months, never before.

Paul Brenner

Toni Dove

Keller Easterling

Pam Jennings

Judith Russi Kirshner

Muntadas

Florence Ormezzano

Elisabeth Subrin

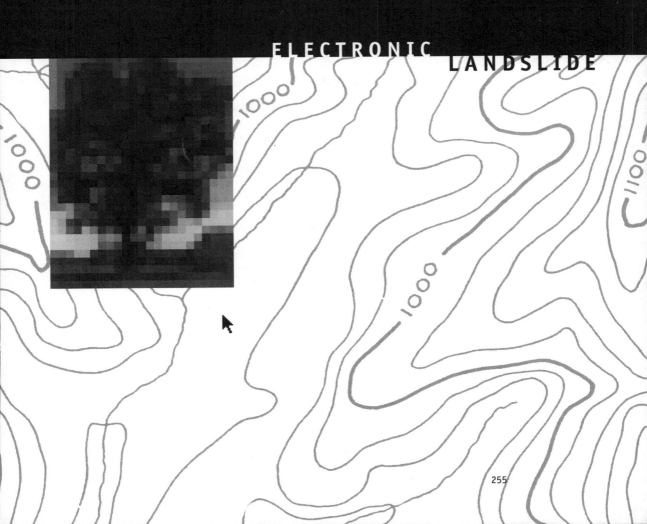

ELECTRONIC LANDSLIDE

255

KH: Question: If we are created in a test tube or pitri dish, and all communications are changing to digital bits and factoids, what will our art work look like? How will it be distributed, via genes or fiberoptics? Which one should I buy stocks in? ¶ I asked a friend of mine the other day if she knew where the systems computer for America On-Line was housed? In what state or city? She acted incredulous. "It doesn't matter." She responded. "I know it doesn't, but I want to know where my messages are traveling." She looked at me as though I were crazy. Maybe I am. Maybe I am being too literal. Is it our attachment to locale that remains dominant? Where is "@" at? ¶ You know, I am interested in the topic of the electronic landscape, because we are slipping so quickly and easily into this arena of new media, in an *electronic landslide*. What is our electronic reflection? Is there an architectural model for the virtual landscape, a geographic history of metaphors to pull from for these communication models? ¶ While the media reportage continues as an almost unconscious chronicle of our growing interest in "technofutures," electronic communications, human egg manipulation and genetics are probing deeply into questions of human identity, creating conditions with which we have no prior familiarity. The Internet access gives me a sense of free-floating, "traceless" maneuvering, without the product of tactile ephemera or hard copy to document my existence. Cyberspace allows one to define oneself, outside of oneself, and perhaps, at the same time, also being the closest realization of "our reconfigured embodiment." ¶ *Spoken in a dreamy voice:* I do want to navigate new cybersites, the virtual, the possible, the unmanifested, the potential. The place where time and place coincide, posing the connections between virtual geography and virtual time (interactivity). In this intersection between time/place there is no absolute. **LP:** Call me old-fashioned, but it's hard for me to jump right on the hyperwagon at the promise of the continual and endless possibilities of who I might be—personae play. I've tried to be other people, looking at every new place as a possibilty for re-invention, and while I've always had to bring my physical body along with me, I'm not sure it has been the determining factor in me being the same old, same old. It seems no matter what road I'm on, my driving is always the same—reckless. And while I want to believe in the most utopian applications, I can't help but think that the chance to "be all that you can be" will be available to those who have been quite a bit already. **KH:** In efforts to redefine the "superhighway," each definition still articulates a space, a locale, and acts as a metaphor mapping this "place." The terms used to describe the "superhighway" are varied and intriguing in their literalization of the people's ideas of Internet cyberspace: a playground for ideas, a small town with a Main Street, an interstate highway (does that require a "drivers license"?), an electronic marketplace, a universal mind, a network, the Net, a corporate global datanet, a wired world, a pool, a pond, a stream, a raging river, an ocean, the town dump. **LP:** Sometimes I sit and try to make images for the metaphors, but they always end up looking like some poorly rendered outtake from the *Jetson's*. It really is difficult to deal with the immateriality of the Internet. It doesn't fit with comfortable and familiar perceptions of the world. So this ceaseless process of giving form—through analogies— is about trying to render the invisible visible. Culturally, we're still hung up on empiricism, with vision as the definitive sense. We want to see it to know it, and I think it will take a long time for this to change. Hey, I still get stuck thinking about where all that data is in my computer.

Network Ecology

by Keller Easterling

AT-TVA: NETWORK ECOLOGIES

There are rich and poor examples of one infrastructure informing or imitating another: television and radio, fax and teletype, highway, parkway, and railroad, and more recently, information highway and interstate highway. This latest parallel is a curious one. "Information highway" is a blunt and inaccurate term to describe the network's efflorescence and immateriality. If anything, the idea that our new networks might resemble the generic landscape of the highway is less a promise and more a threat from those that stand to benefit from its standardization. But this blurred distinction and other useful confusions surrounding information networks help to initiate the contemplation. AT-TVA (Appalachian Trail-Tennessee Valley Association) benefits from a consideration of these the newest infrastructures in a more complex reciprocity with the existing, comparing their development as technologies, their place in cultural consciousness and their organizational operatives.

America typically replaces its infrastructure networks in ways which generate redundancy rather than interplay. From this site of multiple infrastructures, AT-TVA develops theoretical ground by blurring distinctions between them, borrowing intelligence from each, and examining these networks as cultural persuasions, part of a mental infrastructure, as well as physical and spatial manifestations.

THE AT AND BENTON MACKAYE

Though typically viewed as a recreation trail within the federal park system, the Appalachian Trail, as it was originally conceived in 1921, was actually intended to be the central spine of a complete reorganization of the eastern seaboard not around metropolitan formations but rather around the geological formation of the Appalachian Ridge. Though the intervention was modest, it proposed an essential reversal. The Appalachians, as a reservoir of natural resources, might sponsor industry and community independent of the big city. The central spine of community development from Maine to Georgia would be, not vehicular filtering out to pedestrian, but rather a footpath filtering out to streets and rails — a footpath around which crystallized an infrastructure of land.

This quite radical scheme was conceived by eccentric theorist and self-proclaimed "regional planner," Benton MacKaye. MacKaye was a member of the Regional Planning Association of America, and pursued a hybrid practice in the areas of forestry, labor, hydraulics and highway planning. He was a planner when planning was a relatively new endeavor, not evoking ineffectual bureaucracy but rather its opposite — holistic thinking and a spirit of political and physical reorganization. Ideas of technocracy, popular during this period, also called on the "planner" or "manager" to deliver technical expertise and political leadership. Following a more dilute federal program of technocracy, planners entered government service during the 20s and 30s, as did MacKaye both in the Department of Labor and the Tennessee Valley Authority.

Aligned with members of the RPAA and other left-wing thinkers of the time, MacKaye's romance with primeval wilderness and moralizing about what he called "metropolitan invasion" is less pertinent to contemporary conditions than his recognition of the landscape of development as another nature, an "industrial wilderness." Even more significant was the *way* in which he theorized about this "wilderness of civilization" as kind of geological formation read not for its shape but for its recording of change and movement. Like undiscovered territory, this

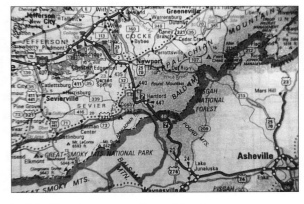

Road map of northern edge of Great Smoky Mountain National Park.

landscape awaited *The New Exploration*, as MacKaye's most well-read book is titled. For MacKaye, the manifestations of either geology or development were understood as activities and movement rather than morphology. MacKaye thought planning was discovery and exploration, not invention. "Its essence is visualization — a charting of the potential now existing in the actual. And so with planning generally: the final thing planned is not mere area or land, but movement or activity." [1]

America has generally privileged those forms of engineering which generate commerce or support defense. (For instance, on the west coast, traffic engineering has been privileged over the engineering of land use which considers the seismic sciences.) But MacKaye's was the science of Geotechnics, a hybrid science and a perceptual art which involved theorizing through a mixture of art, ecology and engineering, linking technology and the humanities — the "composite mind" of many engineers artists and cultural practitioners. Land-based engineering was on a par with other sciences.

MacKaye theorized about infrastructure by blurring distinctions between different kinds of paths and thoroughfares, thinking about highways as "cement railroads" and the AT footpath as a "wilderness levee" to contain east coast metropolitan development and what MacKaye called population "flows." MacKaye imagined a technology of "world integration" like our communication networks provide, but he envisioned these networks tuned not only for commerce and communication but also for land-based exchange and ecological balance — what he called a "terrestrial lacework." When appropriate and coincident, new infrastructure recognized its proximity to old grooves and reread culture through the lines worn into the land. The continuous footpath from Maine to Georgia like the Mohawk trail, the Natchez Trace or any of the other paths and ruts marking the country with the flow of people or animals.

This method of theorizing involved finding space in alterations of perception. The AT was a kind of prototype for MacKaye's theories about landscape as a cultural and personal mnemonic. As a boy growing up with a family of free thinking dramatists, inventors and scientists, he devised "expeditions" through the woods where features of the land, flora and fauna acted as mnemonic devises to prompt the recitation of literature, poems, songs or geological sagas. Landscape was found in the mind as well as in the world without and MacKaye placed equal emphasis on that virtual landscape and its reciprocal analog in the real. He likened "visualization" to a "psychological conversion" of the land's resources. The practice involved using time spent in perceptual contact with the land as the parameter of a virtual environment wherein repeated perceptions were stored and cross-referenced with prior knowledge from history, geology and other endeavors of culture. He consciously shaped mental systems into virtual *space* within which understanding and interplay were multiplied without conscious control.

TECHNOCRACY AND TVA

Early technocracy theory grew, on the one hand, from a socialist critique of capitalism fueled by post World War I and depression era economies, and, on the other hand, by the very forces which were partly responsible for these economies: Taylorism and Fordism. Spearheading one branch of the movement was Thorstein Veblen, whose many ruminations about the fallacies and affectations of capitalism hinged on a critic of those business structures which generated inflated profits and wasteful distribution. A better leader, Veblen argued, was the Engineer who already embodied the ethic of the worker and could scientifically rearrange the doomed business system. An appropriate system based on units of energy rather than an artificial system of prices would provide more equitably for everyone.

Another key player, Howard Scott, attended Veblen's New School discussion group. Scott was a self-styled technocrat and village bohemian who dressed in a kind of engineer's costume. While influenced by Veblen, he led his own charge as the head of several organizations and journals. The Technical Alliance, of which he was at one time "chief engineer," even engaged Benton MacKaye, Stuart Chase and Frederick Ackerman.

Another group formed at Columbia University around the Department of Industrial Engineering, headed by Water Rautenstrauch. Rautenstrauch and Scott met and pooled their efforts. By 1933, a kind of Technocracy manifesto was published in *Harpers* and another was published in *The Nation*. Differences of opinion dissolved the union and the "Technocraze" diffused into a number of other groups and leaders, but ideas about the position of engineering and planning resurfaced during the New Deal. The Federal government expanded its practice of employing professionals in management roles or using technical expertise as a means of galvanizing legislation — a practice which continued into the development of the military industrial establishment and on into the present.

Tennessee Valley Authority projects are significant emblems of the positivism and heroics associated with technocracy as a political movement. Formally, the dams not only refer to the power of electrification and hydraulics but also the political power of more centralized resource management. Forms and scale expressed the fitness of engineering and celebrated the benign strength of the worker. MacKaye wrote to friends from his TVA post that there were two camps of thinkers he wished to avoid: the landscapers and the engineers. The landscapers looked to land as a visual display providing a romanticized representation of Tennessee mountain countryside. The engineers valorized the image of technology in a way which reminded MacKaye of little boys with model trains. Both groups treated with visual aesthetics what MacKaye regarded as more indeterminate activity.[2]

With TVA, the Tennessee River joined the Mississippi in a long-standing confrontation with the arrogance of the Army Corp of Engineers. This public effort reassigned the use of huge amounts of land and displaced a population of people and wildlife, which, like many economies, was blunt and even cruel in its interplay of parts. Thousands of acres of refitted land served by controlled waterways and huge corridors of power easements are the remaining artifacts passing through the AT-TVA site.

INTERSTATE, PARKWAY AND SCENIC HIGHWAY

Recalling another episode of technocracy, the Interstate highway passes through the mountains, crossing the Appalachian Trail and linking up with TVA waterways. In the postwar era, traffic engineering was the template of legislation which pervasively altered the American landscape from the dimension of the highway to the turning radius of the driveway. Parkways like the Blue Ridge were part of an early highway history which included MacKaye's formulations. Parkways were either first urban parks with roads going through them or later a means of accessing the wilderness and country side. Parkways were, by their very nature, limited access roads with long stretches of uninterrupted driving through undeveloped or undisturbed land.

The interstate highways resembled this organization, but for another purpose speed. The templates of traffic engineering were curvatures associated with vision and attention span in motion. As the Interstate highway system merged with the agendas of commerce and defense, the "greater elbow room" persuasion with which traffic engineering and highways were typically paired became even more perverse. For all the claims of patriotism, for all the pictures of Conestoga wagons used in its promotion, the Interstate was one of the most centrally controlled and bureaucratically directed chapters in American history, one which continued an American tradition of standardizing something as specific as land into a generic product. And for all of the New Deal ideas of a national network of parkways or land, the interstate highway system was the connective tissue which America sponsored.

In the 60s, pairing highway development with the aesthetics of beautification was equally curious. Highway beautification policy applied a dilute version of English landscape garden aesthetics to a form whose real and more recent landscape history seemed neglected or forgotten. In 60s gov-

Highway diagrams from government publications.

Below: (Left) Visually disjointed arcs and tangents versus (right) a continuous coordinated ribbon.
Opposite: Screens of trees or shrubs are used deliberately to narrow the corridor at some points by permanently blocking from view objectionable landscape features.

ernment literature, encapsulated histories of the parkway were referenced as supporting precedent for the "scenic" highway. Highways were seen to create anticipation and visually enhance the natural beauty of the "scenery." Traffic engineering was a kind of natural topography. When the curvatures of traffic movement were coincident with the natural topography, (making dynamite unnecessary) traffic engineers congratulated themselves for their environmental appropriateness.

The absurdity of these beautification efforts only matches the piety that is often a part of some contemporary environmental or neo-traditional movements attempting to grapple with this landscape. Efforts to be "natural," blend with nature, worship it, frame it, preserve it or declare some cultural moment as more authentic and appropriate are like our episodes of romance with technology, an aesthetic rather than a process.

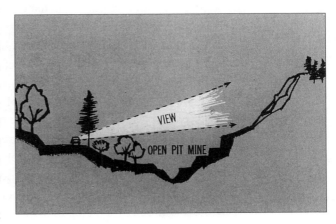

This technical/aesthetic object and its often dominant engagement with the landscape is the ensuing generation's fascination. However uniform its template, however generic the development product that it generates, the position of the Interstate highway, paralleling so many different kinds of infrastructure efforts and passing through so many different kinds of land, is undeniably powerful.

NEW NETWORKS NEW OPERATIVES

The newest networks of information systems will be largely invisible or coincident with existing lines, but their presence may make some existing architecture obsolete and leave reconstituted sites open to new programs.

These technologies, like others, are associated with persuasions that launch them into culture or facilitate their legislation. The newest kinds of telematic and cybernetic information networks, as technologies finally immaterial enough to be pliable to individual thought, are the captive mascot to many multiples of theories and persuasions. Cyberspace is haunted with everything from gender theory to sci-fi, "terminal" dystopias to technology as a second nature as expressed by mid-century corporate jargon, federal regulations, or the subversive spirit of the hacker. Internet is a massive anarchical network promising to complicate and diversify a generic broadcast of television transmissions, thus interfering with the ambient standardization which has characterized our culture since mid-century. Computer code is even treated as a kind of genetic code where technology is posited as a second nature or an enhanced nature of cyborgs, cyberplasm, warm-blooded computers, wearable, contact lens-sized computers and on and on. Accompanying persuasions invoke the word "frontier," "democracy," "connectivity," and "anarchy" to describe this new world, even though the Net is, in practice, as pedestrian, violent and exclusive as other social groupings or communities of exchange.

That we use the word "cybernetics" to refer to both mental and electronic systems is some indication of another strong persuasion. Perhaps misguided by some claims of artificial intelligence, or our habit of analogizing brain and machine, we sometimes think of electronic systems as if they were comparable to neurophysiological networks. The computer can simulate our conception of the growth of neural networks, but often rather than being seen as a tool for modeling greater understanding of the mind, it is placed in competition to make a machine that will equal or surpass the mind's complexity, displacing the real riddle of consciousness in the pursuit of technology. We have begun to think of virtual mental space as that which is somehow inherently linked to cyberspace and, privileging the wrong site, we train ourselves to manipulate predictable software systems that will stimulate these virtual, often fairly banal spatial analogs. The most interesting work in this area veers away from the jaunty acronym "VR" to explore a reciprocity between virtual systems and the real, but the primary reciprocal site, the mind and more precisely, mental *space*, that electronic systems facilitate, receives less conscious focus. Making mental environments, virtual spaces in the

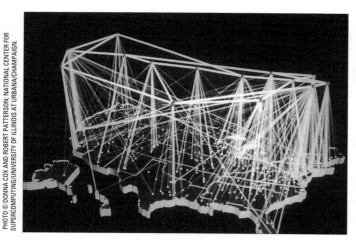

Map of Internet Traffic.

mind, spaces of powerful and unpredictable cross-reference, like those explored by MacKaye is also an act of consciously training distinct mental faculties. Furthermore, adjustments within this neural architecture can replace the need for physical rearrangements by adjusting the persuasions which position them in relation to culture.

Cyberpunk affectations and AI ambitions aside, electronic technology does maintain a proximity to the neurophysiology of consciousness as a responsive tool, a tool which begins to go fast enough to represent some of the mind's spatial operatives. Also, the *behavior* and *economy* of electronic information systems — employing operatives of consolidation, collapse, disappearance, layering, erasure etc. have all become cultural operatives which potentially challenge our romance with primeval nature, ecological piety and technofilia, just as atmospheric environments challenge electronic realities.

AT-TVA

AT-TVA reasserts a mental architecture by adjusting persuasions and perceptual templates to develop sites in the mind and reciprocal sites in the real. Interstitial network space is an expanded architectural field where actions are considered over morphology. Building can then be the making of economies between pieces — to recondition, recircuit and consolidate at points of interface and crossing — to complicate the generic templates we have applied to the landscape. The patterns of a changing interplay or economy of parts *is* an architecture — an architecture where, adjustment and subtraction can be growth.

Examining the crossings of the AT footpath, the TVA dams, the huge power easements and automobile infrastructure, and attempting to view process and action rather than aesthetic, it becomes clearer that there is no sweet primeval nature to preserve — only changes with different periodicity — from geologic time frames to that of the speediest technology. AT-TVA discovers territory of interface between the strands of infrastructure using intelligence from MacKaye, the newest networks, and an awareness of those forces which neutralize interplay and sponsor aesthetic or generic products.

1. Benton MacKaye, "Regional Planning and Ecology." *Ecological Monographs*, July, 1940, pp. 349-353.
2. Benton MacKaye to Stuart Chase, July 20, 1935.

Interpretations on the Electronic Landscape

Conversation with Toni Dove
by Pamela Jennings

PAMELA JENNINGS: I have found that there is very little talk about artists' work using advanced technologies other than interfacing with the Internet, computer bulletin board services or hypertext.

TONI DOVE: Yes, there seems to be the Internet and the whole explosion in multimedia and CD ROM, which is probably a preparation for the interactive television arena, which will probably eventually collapse the Internet, television and computers together. It's an interesting territory right now because it's not standardized yet, and so it offers a window of opportunity for artists to perhaps have some small impact on the developing vocabulary. The danger is it becoming standardized, since much of the impetus behind it is direct delivery of advertising. People tend to move towards the paths of least resistance. This can shut down other more eclectic paths through technology, because of a difficulty at securing funding and support.

PJ: The learning curve is so steep for anyone, independent or corporate, wishing to create an interactive project. It takes much patience and determination to see a project completed.

TD: Yes, it's really new and people are just beginning to experiment with it. And the whole notion of interactivity and its potentials is very complex. Yet currently, it's being produced as a very simple concept where you navigate through a book. Some of the major CD ROMs have quite simple interactivity at this point. The whole notion of navigation and non-linearity is a problem in terms of programming, in terms of authoring tools and in terms of creative people's access to developing tools. It's an interesting problem and it's in a state of evolution. As an artist, you're sort of involved in a territory where you're building a piano in order to compose the sonata. I often find myself in this situation.

PJ: That's a great analogy. It's trailblazing.

TD: Yes, you have to build the instrument in order to make the piece. Although I'm interested in the new technologies, I'm not a programmer. I'm a techie to some degree, but I'm not somebody who can sit down and play with chips and rewire circuits and stuff. Although I am learning, I don't want to be exclusively involved with the programming end of things. I've found that what happens is that all your energy and focus goes into the technology. Then the work becomes about the technology and not the content. One of the ways that I've discovered to deal with that is to work with a programmer. It's been both very interesting and frustrating. Sometimes it can be like eating with a fourteen foot fork because you want to do things and you have to do it through this conduit in order to make the behaviors happen. It's a collaboration with another person's ideas and with a whole set of possibilities inherent in a programming language. I'm interested in developing some kind of an authoring system for interactivity that can be a base that I then can work from. If I find that it's an interesting place to work from then I'll be able to build on it over a period of time, so that I don't end up with each project starting almost completely from scratch, which happens to a certain degree anyway.

PJ: So you're developing specialized software that you can always use as a foundation?

TD: Yes, I'm using some existing systems and then I'm developing some new links between systems that work for what I want to do. And I try to

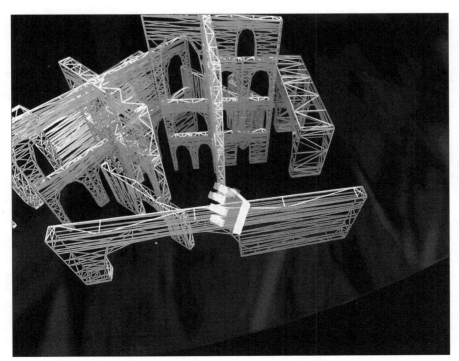

Frame from **Archeology of a Mother Tongue**, 1993, a Virtual Reality project at the Banff Centre of the Arts by **Toni Dove**, in collaboration with **Michael Mackenzie**.

keep it simple. But it never is. I found when I was working on the Virtual Reality Project at Banff, *Archeology of a Mother Tongue*, that I had been used to working with technology that I had never worked with before, but was not used to working with technology that nobody had ever used before. So we were kind of making up the vocabulary as we went along. It was quite fascinating, but in that particular case we were working with very high end equipment. It's problematic to some degree because you have a piece that becomes vaporware because nobody has the equipment to run it on, nobody has access to the equipment. It's fascinating and I would be interested in doing it again, but it's not something I would want to make the base of my practice because I want my work to be more accessible.

PJ: The Banff Centre for the Arts Virtual Reality project, *Archeology of a Mother Tongue,* has basically been presented through video tape.

TD: Right, it's been shown a few times as a Virtual Reality installation, and it will probably be shown again. As the equipment becomes more accessible it will become an historic artifact. That's not uninteresting to me, but it's not exactly the territory that I want to exist in.

PJ: How has the issue of access to high end versus low end effected your work?

TD: It's definitely a real issue because this is a very technologized society. The whole culture is very focused on new technology. But access is very selective. I think there's a trickle down factor with obsolete equipment that has tremendous acceleration because technological developments are moving so fast. That sense of access is constantly increasing, for example, DJ's doing hip hop scratching with LPs. That's a really interesting manipulation and reuse of information and data that's based on essentially an obsolete technology. I think that's always been an extremely interesting territory for artists. The artist's book movement escalated with lithography displacing letterpress and letterpress becoming a cheap and accessible technology. As artists we are also interested in getting our hands on the best and newest stuff, to see what it can produce.

PJ: So then we try to get to Banff.

TD: Yes, you go and work in these places. But it's not necessarily always the most interesting place to work from. I've used a lot of slide technology in *Mesmer-Secrets of the Human Frame* and *The Blessed Abyss — A Tale of Unmanageable Ecstasies.* I'm using less of that right now because I'm getting involved in desktop video, but I've always been interested in mixing high tech and low tech and being able to create some kind of collage where you can develop an aesthetic out of a bunch of technologies. Most of these

Opposite: Installation view of **The Blessed Abyss—A Tale of Unmanageable Ecstasies**, 1992, by **Toni Dove**.

are developed for corporate use in some way and have imbedded in them an aesthetic and a way of working. I think that this is true across the board with technology. There are never, obviously, neutral tools. Uses of color and concepts of resolution start to become built in as part of an aesthetic that isn't necessarily the best or most interesting way to use equipment. Maybe the sharpest clearest image, or the most colors may in fact make your work look more like a Mitsubishi ad than what you were interested in. I think it's really interesting for artists to work with a variety of tools and to keep questioning commercial aesthetic standards.

PJ: There doesn't seem to be a concern or desire to bring independents into or creating a space for independent's work within the proposed five hundred channels and interactive television.

PHOTO © T.CHARLES ERICKSON

TD: No, I don't think they're even slightly interested. I don't think that that's planned ever. I don't think there was a plan to encourage independent production in film. But I think what they discovered was that they could make money from independent film projects, that there were smaller audiences perhaps, but also smaller budgets for films that could actually make money. That's the bottom line. If that works, then those things survive.

PJ: It's a passion.

TD: Yes, it's a cuckoo passion. And that's another reason why I want to start to be able to standardize what I'm doing to some degree. So that every time I do a project, I don't need a whole knew set of equipment. Also as you're working closer to the bleeding edge, the access to the equipment becomes trickier because some of it isn't rentable, some of it's very expensive and there are less people who know how to use it and work with it. It also brings with it a certain kind of attention which I think is interesting and alarming at the same time. I found for instance, when I did the VR piece, that I got more press and more publicity around that piece even though fewer people saw it and fewer people knew the content of it. There would be a still image here or there. Or a tape that would float around. And yet that piece got tremendous publicity. That's very seductive. This happens if you're working in an area of technology where there's a lot of publicity and interest. I kind of tripped into it by accident. I wasn't particularly interested in virtual reality or interactivity. As a result of working on that project, I got fascinated with a couple of aspects of interactivity that I didn't get a chance to work through in the context of that project, which I'm working through now. One of them had to do with the idea of immersion in a narrative space. The sensation of walking around in a movie, of actually being inside of a narrative space. And the other aspect, was a certain kind of virtual illusion that results when a physical action produces a response in video and audio. And that can be a powerful and actually sensual experience. That interested me because it seemed to subvert or undercut some of the rhetoric of dis-incarnation that surrounds a lot of new technology. So those were a couple of things I wanted to explore a little bit more.

PJ: Can you further explain what you mean by dis-incarnation?

TD: Well I think that people tend to think of the relationship to technology as being dis-embodied and non-physical, virtual. There's an anxiety that surrounds that. People not being able to touch their work, of it being imma-terial in some way, and excluding the body. I think in some ways that the explosion of interest around issues of the body is related to that anxiety about the disappearance of the body within the technical sphere, for instance, the Internet. There's all sorts of discussion about developing com-munities and gender confusions and realignments, and all kinds of things that can happen in a virtual community because of their non-physical nature. I think that is part of what's made the whole contemporary theoreti-cal examination of the body an interesting frontier of discussion.

PJ: What do you think about the concept that there are opposing philo-sophical camps happening in the discourse on new technology? One in which the physical body is no longer deemed as having importance in terms of communication and identification. Rather it is symbolized by abstrac-tions. And another discourse where technology is viewed as a bridge to unite bodies and minds across gaps where the physicality of individuals may prove to be a hinderance toward communication.

TD: I don't think that I would set it up as a polarity. I think that it's more complex and fluid than that. The technologies themselves are changing so rapidly, they're so new, our access to them is changing so rapidly. You know, who has access, who doesn't have access. And our familiarity with whole territories of technology is shifting constantly. For instance, in the process of designing an interactive piece or designing a CD ROM, you're dealing with a situation where the recipes for production and reception are not yet standardized. So there isn't anything given in terms of your user and their familiarity with the system. There are certain kinds of things you have to be self-conscious about, in that context, because you know you have somebody coming in who won't know how to use it. There won't be things that are familiar that will funnel them into some way of doing things, so you really start from ground zero. You have to think in terms of people's sense of agency. I think it's a very interesting thing because it can cause you to think in critical terms, in terms of the social ramifications, the behavioral ramifications, the political ramifications, the economical ramifications, all the ramifications of each move that you make in developing some kind of syntax for use. The piece that you design now five years from now, when there's a different level of familiarity with use, will be used differently and seen differently. That's a very odd and interesting situation to be in, to have that sense of instability and transience in relationship to the work. It's so new. It's developing so quickly that ideas around it, for instance, the idea of relationships to technology that are technophilic, technophobic, that have to do with dis-incarnation, incarnation, all these kind of things are complicated and integrated into this whole very rapidly evolving set of issues which at this point is kind of primitive. So I don't think you can codify it in a way where you'd say there's an approach that would look at it one way or the other. I think that they're all folding into each other and breaking up and reforming. It's very quick right now. With my own ideas, I'll work with something for a while and I'll start to have a critical take on it and that will collapse and shift.

      PJ: Creating new foundations for navigation through what can be called interactive work is really pretty broad.

TD: Yes, it is pretty broad. Even the word interactive I think is kind of weird and problematic, because I think in some ways it's a false icon. It's produced by notions of advertising that deliver a fraudulent sense of empowerment and agency. In other words, you replace intellectual challenge with multiple choice. You give people a sense of activity and empowerment that implies choices that aren't really there. It's interesting the way a rhetoric develops around things. If you look at the telephone, which is one of the first interactive technologies, and the kind of rhetoric that has developed around "being there." You know, "Reach out and touch someone." And that's similar to a language that's developing around virtual reality. This whole notion of being there, touching someone, of being connected as some kind of community. That is, in fact, the opposite of what's happening. You're not there at

all. But then there's a whole new technological sphere in which communications are made and increased, so a completely different kind of community is evolving. And it does exist as community. I don't know, it's interesting.

PJ: I think that doing work that's "interactive" is more manipulative. Even though there's the rhetoric of choice, the choice is what the maker or artists decides to give the user. In a way you're leading a person down a pathway that says, "You , the user, can think you're deciding the way you're going. But I, the maker, have already decided your fate."

TD: Also, as an artist I have to say that I'm not particularly interested in creating tools for other people to be creative with. I'm not interested in something that has a tool base, or something that is a place for other people to make things. Because I have a vision or a concept of something or an experience of something that I want to deliver. And in some sense I guess you can say that that's always been manipulative. I'm more interested in responsive environments. In creating an environment that has a personality that reacts to a user. I'd like to explore the cinematic environment into something more immersing. It's interesting to me because it suits certain concepts of narrative that I have. I think of narrative as a wandering accretion in a three dimensional cube. And I've never been involved in story or plot in a traditional sense. I tend to work with narrative as an accretion and look for different kinds of engines that move it through time. I think it's tricky. The problematic side is that if you don't have a traditional engine, you have to be careful that you do have some kind of engine or you end up with cinematic wall paper, or a trance state that doesn't produce a trance. Already within the interactive realm there's a number of cliches developing to replace some of the traditional vocabulary of plot, like suspense that is built up based on conflict. This has been replaced in the game arena by dropping somebody in a pit and giving them 30 seconds to get out. I think that there are more complex possibilities for creating a dimensional narrative, and it may not be something that is completely non-linear. It may not be non-linear in a looping random access logic tree structure. It may be something that you move through in some linear fashion but has a different sense of dimension.

PJ: Like depth, on the z plane.

TD: Or parallel realities, or just a more complex three dimensional time space. It's like asking a set of questions, or opening up a potential set of streams of thought, or giving people a place to explore an idea, or setting up something that gives a person a place to think from.

PJ: I find sometimes that I have a tug a war between my desire to make a set of images designed for the user to sit back and watch, and trying to figure out when and where to put some form of interactivity or "choice."

TD: I think that we're so imbedded in the notion of linearity, that when you first start thinking in terms of non-linear structure it's a very self conscious procedure. I can plot out a video that's linear or an installation. It may not be a traditional plot, but it has a time base — a beginning, middle and end. I can plot that. But at this particular point for me to plot something that's interactive is much more difficult to preconceive. I can preconceive chunks of it and then I have to set it up and get in it and see how it works and then do that again. Perhaps others, especially music people who have been working with interactivity for longer and have a more complex and deep concept of the possibilities of interactivity, can think about that space in a very different way than I can at this point. So I understand what you're saying. I find that as the length of the projects I work on expands, because I'm interested in work that I can develop in a more complex way, I'm getting more involved in the notion of story. Not necessarily in a traditional way. I have to figure out how to design that story so that something happens, so it isn't like wallpaper, and I've been thinking a lot about what kinds of narrative engines I use. I think that there are two things that I tend to work with: one is a kind of escalation of emotional environment that often happens through the use of

Opposite: From **Casual Workers, Hallucinations and Appropriate Ghosts**, a video installation at the 42nd Street Project, 1994, by **Toni Dove**.

sound, and the other one is the developing of a philosophical concept that is subliminal to the text. So that the text is being produced as a fictional space or as a poetic space, but there's an idea driving it underneath that has to do with the thing that you're trying to say. That becomes a kind of hidden engine for how you go somewhere. But then figuring out how to design that inter-actively so that there is satisfaction that you get from things happening — does it need chronology or not? What moves people through a space so that it doesn't feel like being caught in a revolving door? There's a method used often now that involves a logic tree where people are making these incredi-bly complex pieces that have very detailed programming and branching. And it's like, I don't know, it's like serving peeled, stuffed grapes to 40,000 or something or washing your kitchen floor with a Q-Tip. There's a labor inten-siveness to it that I find extremely unappealing as a creative process. It has a level of tedium. I think it's also a process that will be replaced as authoring tools become more sophisticated. That's another aspect, how these tools are going to develop. And how creative artists are going to have access to these tools. And how the tools will be less about high level programming languages and more about intuitive graphic interfaces.

PJ: It seems like that would be crucial in order to bring more artists and independent producers into this field?

TD: Now it's very complicated and not standardized. Right now, every CD ROM company is either licensing an authoring system or developing their own authoring system that they can then expand and work on. It's very complicated, it's very labor intensive, it's very time consuming. And it's a kind of nightmare. Most of the multimedia places that I've worked at are chaotic and crazy. There are endless amounts of files in different places and people keep re-naming them and they end up someplace else.

PJ: Well that's exciting. But it's also a bit harrying at times.

TD: It's a pain in the neck sometimes. I find that there are limits to how much I want to be invested in dealing with that level of technology in the pieces. Because there's a point where I'm spending so much time doing that and writing grants, that I don't get any time to work. So, I find that I'm starting to focus in on learning certain sets of tools that I can work with directly. And then I can hire out certain kinds of other things to people who have certain kinds of expertise in certain other kinds of tools. For instance, I'm working with MAX, an interactive programming language. I have to know more about MAX than I know right now in order to be able to understand the potential of the language, and to understand how to think in that language, even if I'm not going to be able to do very sophisticated things with it myself. If I don't understand how it works, what's easy, what's difficult, what it does most effectively, then I'm working in a dark room with the lights off. It can be very difficult to do what you want to do. Because I would be making choices that are not in step with the flow of possibilities in the technology.

PJ: MAX is actually on my reading list this summer. I have about a ten inch pile of manuals that I hope to peruse.

TD: MAX is like the Manhattan telephone book. It's very daunting. Especially I think if you're a non-musician.

PJ: It almost seems logical that music would be the perfect transitional art form between spectator forms of art and interactive forms of art. Music has always been poly-modal in the realm of composition, counterpoint, harmony and dissonance, and a collaborative process in terms of communication between the makers, performers and audience.

TD: There's an abstract quality to music. And a way in which music is not text based that allows for certain kinds of non-linear development that also makes it interesting as an interactive language. Also because the technology for interactivity and the digital production for sound has been in place a lot longer than it has for images. There are a lot of people who have been working with that for a while, and some of the interactive strategies that people have developed are more sophisticated because they are often producing interactive situations in which a performer is working with something that is more like an instrument. Instead of being aimed at a "dumb" user or someone you assume has no experience with a situation, they're often designing something for someone to learn as if it were an instrument. There is a level of craftsmanship and technical acuity and sophistication in the kinds of interactivity that happens because it's performance based.

I think I've learned the most about interactivity from music people. George Lewis, who I met up at Banff, is one of the people who first began to make me think in different terms about some of the possibilities. He said that instead of setting up this predictable tree of already mapped out solutions, what you do is build a kind of machine. And then you would enter that machine and see how it behaves. If it does things that you don't like you might be able to trace that back into the program and change it, or you might not. So that you're basically developing these interconnecting sets of responsive machines. That was the beginning of an interesting way for me to think about it.

I found that when I was working with sound, I was used to being able to work in a linear way where I usually develop a performed text that has a sound environment of some kind or another. I'd get sound sources, I'd create sound sources, I sampled and processed things. I work with sound very similarly to the way I work with images — a processed collage aesthetic. I had a lot of control over nuance and layers and connections and all different kinds of things that I used to make these musical spaces. And when I started working on the Virtual Reality project, everything had to be programmed. And it had to be programmed in a way where someone walking through the space would find that if they stopped and just started looking around for five minutes the sound environment would continue to be present, and it wouldn't sound like a needle stuck in a grove. So we started making these drone machines that took several samples and then re-sampled pieces of those samples and created different kinds of processing and different sets of repeating random parameters so that there was a sound atmosphere that had a continuing evolving changing shape with enough different parameters so that it didn't sound like it was repeating itself. Then within that you could bring in local sounds and sound events that were more linear. At first that seemed clumsy and difficult and problematic to me in comparison to what I had been working with, because I didn't feel as though I had as much control. And I didn't feel that I could get the kind of nuance and delicacy that I could get with the other system. But I also found that I had to just drop that way of thinking, and get involved in these rooms, these little machines. I had to let go of a whole way of thinking before I could begin to discover what the potential nuances were of this other way of working. Because I hadn't experienced it. And that to me was a breakthrough in terms in being able to think about the possibilities of how to structure concepts of interactivity.

PJ: There is a strong psychological undercurrent to your work.

TD: I'm interested in models of subjectivity. And creating characters that are personal representatives of social constellations and issues. And psychoanalysis has provided us with one of the few extant models of subjectivity. It's often problematic, fluid, shifting, changing and never ultimately satisfying or complete. But I've found that it's been a very useful source of information for developing characters. I do a lot of reading before I do a piece. I do a lot of theoretical reading and it helps me create social and psychological and economic armatures that I can use to build characters.

PJ: When you're initiating a new project, does the concept for the work come first or the desire to work with a certain technology? Or does this happen simultaneously?

TD: It's usually simultaneous. As a result of whatever previous project I was working on, there's usually some sort of spill-over of something that interested me that I didn't get a chance to follow through. Or some new technology that I've come in contact with that has certain things embedded in it which interests me — certain special effects, behaviors or possibilities. So I'll start with those and at the same time I'm thinking about other kinds of metaphors. So the two things develop simultaneously. So it's sort of a combination of concepts and special effects.

And, of course, I've always been fond of magic. And technology produces certain kinds of special effects, and certain kinds of things that can be extremely powerful. I'm usually drawn to some aspect of technology that has a certain magical component for me and that will give me ideas that will generate other kinds of things. I usually work that way — special effects based. I get ideas from Hollywood movies. I don't watch television that much, because I've become such a movie freak. But I have been taking a look lately at advertising. And a lot of the computer technology is starting to surface in advertising. It's interesting, because a lot of that, if you have time, you can reproduce that "relatively" inexpensively on the desktop. And that's very interesting to me, that I have tools to make images plastic. The whole notion of photography and film as a documentary medium is toast, it's finished. It's become a completely plastic and manipulatable arena. Which is what I always wanted to do with it anyway. So it suits me quite nicely.

This last piece I did on 42nd street, *Casual Workers, Hallucinations and Appropriate Ghosts*, is a seven minute video that loops. And most of it was done on the computer, about three minutes of it was done entirely on the computer and the rest was done as a rough cut on the computer. It was really exciting to me as a way of working. I'm interested in being able to do more work like this. I'm gradually learning a certain set of tools and ways of working that I find really interesting. It's definitely taking up my attention.

JULY 16, 1994

Electronic Home in MOOland

by Florence Ormezanno

*I have a new home in a village on the west coast.
It's called BayMoo. It's not a house of paper but a
house of words. One can go there by getting a modem and
paying a local provider to drive on the internet.*

What is the Internet? A slow phone line connecting your computer to several computers in the country (access to free softwares, libraries, news etc...).

What is a MOO? (=Mud-Object-Oriented). Just a piece of software that allows several people to interact synchronously, reading texts/objects. It started as MUD (Multi-User-Dungeon). MUDs are games for "young" people who enjoy playing. So people thought MOO should be the same kind of play with a more social slant, like a big Club Med... Well, some are, like LambdaMoo (type "telnet" then "open lambda.parc.xerox.com 8888"), and some are more interesting! Recently teachers and artists started numerous MOO places that have specific educational purposes (language teaching, programming, biology, etc). Other places are built by artists who are experimenting with electronic life, performance art, poetry, ascii art (!) etc...

All Moos are open to everybody! One starts by getting "a character name" and a password that goes with it. You become an active participant and are allowed to build. Your character stays in the city, asleep when you are off-line, active when you log on.

I, myself, started in PMC-Moo, a post-modern criticisms style Moo. Then I was invited to go to BayMoo:

*After the light, take the route of your local internet
provider, then telnet to mud.crl.com 8888. There you can
build rooms like an architect, write your words all
around the space.*

Little by little I met some people, I had Moo Mail and read Moo News. I made a studio for myself where I started building my art work. I got myself a video camera, video tapes (I'm usually a video artist), a car-trampoline to jump from place to place and a few robots to keep me company. I learned some simple programming, and made objects that give you texts to read or teleport you elsewhere when one manipulates them. This is what fascinated

```
┌──────────────────────────────────────────────────────────────┐
│ ≣□≣≣≣≣≣≣≣≣≣≣≣≣≣≣≣≣≣  Felix  ≣≣≣≣≣≣≣≣≣≣≣≣≣≣≣≣ ⊡│
├──────────────────────────────────────────────────────────────┤
```

Date: Tue, 21 Jun 1994 13:31:50 -0400 (EDT)

From: Florence Ormezzano <ormezzo@panix.com>

To: hamhigh@echonyc.com

Subject: session in Baymoo

> A VISIT TO BAYMOO, the Reverse Studio:
>
> note: [indicates what I typed]
>
> [telnet]
> [open mud.crl.com 8888]
>
> ...
>
> Reverse Studio
>
>   >
>   >   <─────────────--
>   >   <─────────────--
>   >>>   ──────────>
>   >>>>>   Flipping move
>   >>>>>>>   in process!
>   <<<<<<<   <───-
>   <<<<<   ──->
>   <<<   <───
>   <   ──->
>   <   <─
>   < <   ->
>
>   Do you feel blood coming to your brain?
>   You are looking at things BACKWARDS!
>   Your feet are stuck on the CEILING.
>   Hang in there you might get used to it.

279

me most about those sites: the ability for everyone to expand the *city*. Each Moo becomes an elastic, flexible environment that changes its shape quickly, under the fingers of all active participants. It was difficult and interesting to be there working and creating in an open space with all the people passing by, (that was my choice, one can have the option of being private).

Now my space is in PMC-Moo like a touristic site almost, called "The Reverse Studio." You can find it in the village or go there by typing @go #1485. There are five rooms, the first one keeps you hanging on the ceiling and has several objects to investigate, the second one is a Temple to the Goddess Inanna which contains my robot Epinemides. You can talk to him (he will teach you the paradox of the liar). Or you can go to the Cathedral of Chartres and pray to Our Lady of the Pilar and our Lady of the Underground (in the Crypt). There is also an ancient well that you can jump into and arrive far out along the Seine: in Paris (the Paris site is by another artist: Honoria).

After a while I forgot the letters. The words became
a tool. I'd rather carry them around, give them orders
and they'd play jokes on me.

Of course you should keep in mind that so far Moo universes are only made of texts! And one of the contradictions of this simple first dimension experience is that it feels very much like an (interesting) virtual reality. You are acting with words. This results in an ambiguity of what is what. For example, the video camera they have there... You turn it on and it records: what is in the room, the description, the people talking, their actions. The recording in question is a little text file we call "video tape!" So one can say that in the Moo there are several layers to the words, different uses of the language in the same space. Acquiring multiple levels of signification, words can BE (an object part of a general quota), ACT (with some programming), express my talk, my thought or my action (communication), or finally be a description, prose or a poem.

Another experience I have is with a collaborative project called Hight Pitched Voices. Caroline Guyer, who started it, is an artist/hypertext writer. She created a "list" of women who were interested in creating together. We have regular mail conversations (using the list) and started writing in Hotel-Moo. Tom Meyer, the wizzard of Hotel Moo, transformed the original Moo software and made it compatible with the hypertext program called Story-space. Although the Hotel Moo is not the only means of our common work, it is, for sure, a fascinating one. We can connect to the Moo at the same time from different parts of the world, writing together, making instant connection and travelling together throught texts, making comments...! In essence,

```
>

> [look backwards]

>

>From one way to the other.  When the extremes reach a common point. If

you really hate this up side down position, try to find some middle

POINT.

>

> [look point]

>

> A reversing tool for uncomfortable visitors.  Type middle point to see.

> [middle point]

>

> Florence decided to reverse her position :

>          oooooooooooooooooooo >>>>>>>>> <<<<<<<<< oooooooooooooooooo

> Florence is in between the floor and the ceiling, lost in the inter-

val...

>          >>>>>>>>>>>>>>> ooooooooooo   ooooooooooo <<<<<<<<<<<

> Oh Noooo!  Florence almost made it on the floor, but was pulled again

towards the ceiling!

>

> [kneeling]

>

> The Temple

>                        |~\

>                        |  `-\

>                        |      ^`\

>                        |        "=-._,-.-

>                        |                |

>                        |                |

>                        |                |

>                    _____

>                      _____

>                 Open your ears! she said,

>              The eyes wide open!, they answered.

>
```

most Moo spaces are the ideal Hypertexts spaces: typing a word takes you to another room (= a window), to another text. You can travel with links, and its Internet aspect gives it some curious spatial elements.

I wish I had another 5 pages to talk about the project called WaxWeb by David Blair. Some of you might remember his video/film feature called *Wax, Or the Discovery of Television among the Bees*. This video/film has now been developed into a collaborative project in hypertext format and can be found at its logical place in Hotel Moo. With the collaboration of Tom Meyer and David Blair, WaxWeb bloomed into a Mosaic document combined with its own Moo site. Mosaic is a visual interface that until now has never been made interactively changeable... In WaxWeb Mosaic one can add comments and new text and make hypercard links to add to the original video/film *Wax*. (You can also run the WaxWeb Moo at the same time if you wish to interact with other visitors!) So once again, *Wax*, after having been the first film broadcast on the Internet, is now the first fiction film entirely available on the Internet! It has all the video elements in Mpeg, the sound track in four languages, and all extra materials related to the script, back stories, including critiques and other texts by collaborators. I am sure you will be able to read about it in the future, and I believe they have some surprising developments on the way.

I hope this gives you a good image about what a Moo could be. But, of course, if this all sounds strange and obscure, the best way to find out about it is to try it and see for yourself!

At the main prompt type:
`telnet` (return)
`open TheAddressOfYourChoice ####` (return)

Here are some addresses you can try:
`mud.crl.com 8888` (BayMoo in SanFrancisco)
`duke.cs.brown.edu 8888` (HotelMoo at the Brown University)
`bug.village.virginia.edu 7777` (the new Moo site for WaxWeb)
`http://bug.village.virginia.edu 7777` (the Mosaic site for WaxWeb)
`purple-crayon.media.mit.edu 8888` (the MIT one)
`hero.village.virginia.edu 7777` (PMC-Moo)
`lambda.parc.xerox.com 8888` (the original one, use caution)

For the other addresses I suggest you use a gopher program and search for "MOO", you should get a long list! Or once you get in a Moo, ask people. *Word of mouth* is good, too.

Good luck!

```
┌─────────────────────────────────────────────────────────────────────┐
│≡□≡≡≡≡≡≡≡≡≡≡≡≡≡≡≡≡≡≡≡≡ Felix ≡≡≡≡≡≡≡≡≡≡≡≡≡≡≡≡≡≡≡≡≡≡ ▣│
├─────────────────────────────────────────────────────────────────┬───┤
│                                                                  │ ⇧ │
│    > This is the TEMPLE of Heaven and Earth.                     │▒▒▒│
│    >                                                             │▒▒▒│
│    > [look Temple]                                               │▒▒▒│
│    >                                                             │▒▒▒│
│    > A temple dedicated to INANNA and her sister ERESHKIGAL.     │▒▒▒│
│    >                                                             │▒▒▒│
│    > [look Inanna]                                               │▒▒▒│
│    >                                                             │▒▒▒│
│    > Inanna is the Goddess of Love, Morning and Evening Star.    │▒▒▒│
│    >                                                             │▒▒▒│
│    > [look Ereshkigal]                                           │▒▒▒│
│    >                                                             │▒▒▒│
│    > Ereshkigal is the goddess of the UNDERWORLD, from where no one returns.│▒▒▒│
│    >                                                             │▒▒▒│
│    > [look Underworld]                                           │▒▒▒│
│    >                                                             │▒▒▒│
│    > Ereshkigal is jealous of Inanna's power and beauty.  She KILLS Inanna.│▒▒▒│
│    >                                                             │▒▒▒│
│    > [look kills]                                                │▒▒▒│
│    >                                                             │▒▒▒│
│    > Ereshkigal is mourning her sister's death.  She cries for her inside│   │
│    and for her outside.                                          │   │
│    She gives birth to her sister!  Inanna Is again!             │   │
│                                                                  │   │
└─────────────────────────────────────────────────────────────────┴───┘
```

The File Room

Introduction by Paul Brenner
and Elisabeth Subrin; Essays by
Judith Russi Kirshner, and Muntadas
with Randolph Street Gallery

Introduction

by Paul Brenner and Elisabeth Subrin,
Randolph Street Gallery

The File Room is an illustrated, computer-based archive of incidents of cultural censorship around the world and throughout history. The project was initiated by the artist Muntadas and produced by Randolph Street Gallery (Chicago, IL) with the support of the School of Art and Design and Electronic Visualization Laboratory of the University of Illinois at Chicago, the Chicago Department of Cultural Affairs, and a large network of other organizations and individuals too numerous to mention here.

    The File Room was produced by artists and curators and as such does not presume the role of a library or an encyclopedia in the traditional sense. Instead, the project proposes alternative methods for information collection, processing and distribution, to stimulate dialogue and debate around issues of censorship and archiving. Links to other electronic archives and databases internationally, as well as multiple accounts of the same "incident" and a wide range of contributors, challenge *The File Room* visitor to make her or his own decisions about what constitutes an "accurate" account of a censored work of art or historical incident.

    The project was mounted as a public installation at the Chicago Cultural

Center in summer 1994. At the time of the opening of this installation on May 20, 1994, the archive also became accessible via the Internet, where it remains active on the World Wide Web, a large and quickly growing network of databases providing integrated text, image, sound and video capabilities.

The File Room database was developed in Mosaic, a new hypertext-based software program which allows easy point-and-click access to the vast resources on the Internet. In addition to one-way information access, a *File Room* "visitor" can add cases to the archive through the on-line submission form, as well as comment on the content of the archive. In this way, the archive is not a static entity, governed and defined by its creators; rather, *The File Room* invites the interpretation and participation of its global audience.

The File Room is continuously accessible via the Internet, through Mosaic or any WWW browsing software, at the following URL:

http://fileroom.aaup.uic.edu/FILEROOM.html

Muntadas and The File Room
by Judith Russi Kirshner

For more than twenty years, Spanish artist Muntadas has orchestrated remarkably complex installations whose content — the analysis of the institutions of cultural and political power — changes with each situation in which the work is presented. This nomadic character is a hallmark of the work and the career; but in a structural pattern characteristic of the artist, the work instantly contradicts its own mutable quality and is housed or recontextualized in the very form of the institution being examined. Projects earmarked for museum visitors, such as *Between the Frames* (1983-1993) and work for public spaces, are planned according to the anticipated audiences. The permanent appearance of the installations, whose architectural refinement is evident and often elegant, belies the evolving mass of information they contain. Other levels of meaning are revealed in the design of these architectural pieces, for they are conceptualized to function semiotically, not merely to frame the situations they critique.

Muntadas' latest project is *The File Room*, which examines the massive history of censorship. He began his research on censorship five years ago and imagined a space suggesting bureaucratic enclosures, dimly lit chambers claiming forbidden materials. I am persuaded that Muntadas's work derives from a postmodern impulse to salvage and recuperate rather than a utopian urge to rescue and affirm. The overbearing walls of black file drawers and low-hanging light fixtures in *The File Room* give material presence to the sinister arena of censorship. Viewers participate, as did the artist, in a conscious political performance as they search at computer terminals for examples of censorship or, if they choose, enter their own cases into the archive.

For its introduction in Chicago on the first floor of the Cultural Center, an enclosure constructed from 138 black metal file cabinets holds 552 cabinet drawers. The project's interactive component consists of seven color computer monitors (linked to a central server) installed in file cabinets around the room. With a click of a mouse at any one of these terminals, viewers can access case histories of censorship by geographical location, date, grounds for censorship or medium. At the center of the room is a desk with another computer at which visitors can enter their own examples. In May 1994, the project opened with more than 400 entries on censorship from antiquity to the present. Under theater, for example, *The File Room* lists multiple occasions from the fifth century B.C. to 1967 in Athens, when Aristophanes' classic plays were banned for reasons of obscenity and anti-war themes. Another literary example is Salman Rushdie's *Satanic Verses*, while recent entries from popular culture include: television host Ed Sullivan's request to Jim Morrison of The Doors to alter a line in his song, "Light My Fire;" the banning of Steven Spielberg's film, *Schindler's List* in Jordan; and, from personal experience, the Chicago Public School's attempt to confiscate materials handed out to high school students by the Coalition for Positive Sexuality. Entries can also be logged in through the Internet and new archives of texts and images running on other Internet sites worldwide are added to *The File Room* through hypertext links. Hundreds of individuals from around the world log on as daily users. What originally had been private becomes public, as audiences become archivists and consumers of an expanding collection of source material.

Archives are begun when groups of individuals — families, cities — accumulate material that documents a particular activity or series of events. More systematic than the diaristic activities of those who keep journals, archival methods of saving are nevertheless inspired by the profound desire to mark events or to record something for posterity. Whether personal or political, archives have roots in antiquity and are prompted by a belief that what occurs is noteworthy, deserving of future consideration. Record keeping provides evidence: source material for future historians collected in the present serves as factual evidence of the past. The opposite of the archival institution, censorship has an equally long history, but represents erasure, withdrawal from memory. On both personal and public levels, with subjective and objective justification, the need to control what is spoken, written

Opposite: Rows of black metal file cabinets and mounted computer monitors in the File Room installation.

or acted has often occurred as an adjunct activity of authoritarian regimes and religious movements.

The File Room's material condition, however, is rooted and objective; before it was designated and transformed into a municipal exhibition facility, the Chicago Cultural Center housed the main branch of the city's public library. Indeed, the landmark building was constructed in 1897 as a library by the architectural firm Shipley, Rutan and Coolidge. Muntadas chose the Chicago situation because the Cultural Center functions somewhere between the public space of a street and the specialized space of a museum. Since the

organizing principle of *The File Room* is that of an archive, its place in Chicago's Cultural Center becomes doubly resonant. Architecturally, its rationale and history coincide with the subject matter of Muntadas's project to reintroduce censored material into the library. Furthermore, its civic constituency, the fact that it is physically open and accessible to the public, underscores the openness and fluid character of the archival process, always growing, never complete. A similar lack of boundaries and psychological uncertainty marks censorship and self-censorship, since what can be stated and what cannot is always debatable, open to redefinition and potentially infinite.

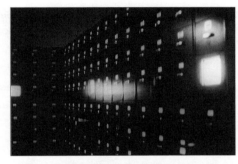

Taken to an absurdist point, *The File Room* in this scenario can never be complete. It holds out the promise of rendering invisible images visible, censored texts legible. Indeed there are archives of online books which can be accessed from within *The File Room* case record. A direct hypertext link will bring up complete texts of Machiavelli's *The Prince*, Hawthorne's *The Scarlet Letter* and Whitman's *Leaves of Grass*, as well as other literary works which have been marked by censorship at one time or another. For the most part, Muntadas's oppositional critique is lodged against and in relation to an institution or ideology. While *The File Room*, like many of his social sculptures, was initiated on a metaphorical level as an archetypal space, with a set-up that evokes the claustrophobic spaces of Kafka, the artist has pushed beyond its perceptual boundaries into a fourth dimension: the space and time of the Internet, the so-called information superhighway. Dialectically poised between reference to past function and present high-tech usage, *The File Room* exists in an uncertain temporal situation and in an equally unresolved conceptual terrain, the puzzle of censorship — who wields the power, what are its targets, whom does it aim to protect?

Rejecting the comfort of extreme positions left or right, Muntadas locates his work in the gray zones between the poles of populism and authoritarianism, censorship and self-censorship. Intentionality becomes a problem as his artistic negotiations are more complex, less conclusive and self-critical of his own position as the single authority who collects the cases. These material and intellectual shifts, which in retrospect seem almost preordained, also displace Muntadas's artistic authority — his role is more like that of an editor of an anthology — as he leads a collaborative team of programmers and researchers who worked together to design the Mosaic program and to undertake research for the archive. Indeed, there is the uncomfortable sense that the project is too open-ended, too haphazard and subjective with few, if any, criteria for selection besides every case for itself. In an essay by Hans Magnus Enzenberger, Muntadas locates some insights into the problem of censorship sprawl:

Structural censorship does not operate with absolute per-
fection, in a 100/100 way. Usually it works following the
rules of the calculus of probability. Messages are miti-
gated, altered or brutally eliminated depending upon their
degree of incompatibility... While censorship oriented
toward production cleans up the core of the cultural
industry (publishing, television, cinema), policing censorship — since it is complementary to the first kind of
censorship — leans the periphery (fanzines, small press-
es). The first kind of censorship is unobserved, so much
that the second is noisy. And this second one likes
to give spectacle, having people talking about it; its
actions are meant to be demonstrative. [1]

The paradox of *The File Room* is the fact that like its content, it cannot be controlled or concluded; potentially it could include all cultural and political production from anytime, any place. *The File Room* changes according to its user's willingness to contribute, to engage in a dialogue and debate the contradictions of censorship without reaching a resolution. It is striking that Muntadas has veered away from his own agenda of deconstructing spectacle and mass media to expose its internal mechanisms in order to provide a global frame of reference for this massive collection. It is perhaps inevitable that certain subscribers to America Online have already submitted an entry about the infringement of their public speech by forum hosts on Internet. According to one subscriber, members of an bulletin board are having their "posts pulled" by this commercial service provider for violating the vague admonition against vulgar or insulting language and explicit talk about sex. In fact, even euphemisms are being pulled for content, although America Online denies its adherence to any specific code of electronic proprieties. Ultimately, *The File Room* is subject to the same constraints of its own cultural logic; it can only be concluded if someone pulls the plug or censors the file.

I would like to thank Sue Taylor, Paul Brenner and Muntadas for their assistance and insights.

1. Hans Magnus Enzenberger, "Lo dico, non lo dico, no, lo dico...," translated by Caterina Borelli from an article reprinted this year in the Italian newspaper, *L'Espresso*, copyright 1977 by Pardon and L'Espresso.

Introductory Notes to The File Room
by Muntadas with Randolph Street Gallery

Was there a time or place in history in which censorship did not exist? Was there ever a group of human beings that was able to survive without censure? These questions precede and introduce *The File Room*, and locate censorship as a complex concept ingrained in our conscious/subconscious reality. Despite the impossible nature of attempting to define censorship, *The File Room* is a project that proposes to address it, providing a tool for discussing and coming to terms with cultural censorship.

The File Room began as an idea: an abstract construction that became a prototype, a model of an interactive and open system. It prompts our thinking and discussion, and serves as an evolving archive of how the suppression of information has been orchestrated throughout history in different contexts, countries and civilizations.

The process of suppressing information, of people in power attempting to hide images, sounds and words, must itself be viewed in perspective. The organizing principles of *The File Room* archive recognize acts of censorship in relation to their social settings, political movements, religious beliefs, economic conditions, cultural expressions and/or personal identities. The means of censorship are understood in equally broad terms and techniques, from behind-the-scenes structural censorship that regulates and controls access to the means of production; to obvious physical restrictions of single instances; to subtle, pervasive, and often invisible psychological methods.

Countering the closed circle of power systems, this project gains its

Above: The File Room's computer terminals. With the click of a mouse, viewers can access case histories of censorship by geographic location, date, grounds for censorship or medium.

meaning through a group effort of individuals, organizations, and institutions. Naturally, this project must be self-critical and self-reflective about the contradictions and possibilities of its own organizing system, the nature of subjective editing, and the limited amount of research that can be accomplished in a given period of time. *The File Room*, rather than being presented as a finished work, is being made publicly available at the point of its initiation. It is an open system that becomes activated, "filed" and developed through the public process of its own existence.

The interactive process of Internet (which remains at this moment a free system for dialogue and information) allows *The File Room* to become a social sculpture, as it moves back and forth from its 3-dimensional installation to an unknown dimension in the Net. When people activate and contribute to this artifact, they will challenge these dimensions and the questions, contradictions, and limitations of attempting to define censorship. The interactive technology is being utilized to add new points of view, complete missing information, challenge notions of authorship, and to reflect direct voices and opinions wherever possible.

As the debate over free and open telecommunications grows, so too will *The File Room* reflect decisions of why, how, when, where an individual point of view may be removed, can't be seen, heard, or read — each decision resonating with the implications throughout past and future of new technologies, marketing strategies, political decisions, and "moral" control.

As Hans Magnus Enzensberger has written, whoever "believes censorship to be an abuse has not understood. Without its tireless twin, self-censorship, censorship could not work. Self-censorship outruns in elegance and shrewdness everything that the most vicious (censor) could imagine. Its target (often met) is the prohibition to think. Whoever believes that they are immune, is the first victim." Let's consider *The File Room* as a cultural project: an open prototype where participation, possibilities, and challenges will be tested.

MAY 1994

FRONTIER WANDERINGS

writings and computer generated images by
Pamela Jennings

Sunday March 28, 1993
MacDowell Artist's Colony
Peterborough, New Hampshire

This evening from Colony House to the Lodge, I walked. Halfway with my eyes closed — only using my ears and nose to guide me. The fresh spring rain has created a white mist above the persistent snow. With the sky cloudy, this night was dark — no billions of stars to guide my way. The road is bordered with tall pines. Their branches hanging overhead creating a tunnel of blackness and mist. If I looked to the right I could see dark grey fields of white snow also bordered by blackness. Way in the distant, a studio porch light glimmered, defused by the spray. I walked with my eyes closed — fantasizing running into her — lost, wandering, looking for me. Electricity shot through my body. I stood still on the road for a few minutes — eyes closed, imaging her touch. A great quiet noise swelled up inside and let loose in a silent pantomime.

Spring 1994, New York City

It got to be embarrassing, the number of times I entered Radio Shack and hid myself for what seemed like hours among the electronics displays in the back of the store. There hung thousands of small plastic bags sealed with a stapled piece of cardboard sporting names like triac, resistor, capacitors, diodes, LED and relays. Should it be 470 Ohms or 4.7 Ohms? What the hell is an Ohm and will it blow up my computer? I was on my way to building my first breadboard and micro computer. I quickly became obsessed. One more visit to Radio Shack and the clerks would have addressed me by my first name. But I think they probably just said, "Here she comes again, it must be her first time building something, because she doesn't seem to know what she wants." I actually found that reading the Mouser Electronics catalog to be an exciting challenging adventure.

April 2, 1993, Peterborough, New Hampshire

There is an owl in the woods behind this house. She calls her missing mate somewhere deep in the woods. "Where are you?, Come here— immediately. Keep me company. It's cold."

Spring 1994, New York City

Sitting at the work bench, with my little black file box filled to the brim with electronic paraphernalia, I began my trip. Reed switches, mercury switches and thermistors — everything in <u>this</u> world is either on or off. Creating the illusion of in-between requires the wizardry of programming and if/then statements. I never knew that at the age of thirty, I would become so attached to a world I use to shrink back from in fear during the college days.

April 9, 1993, 11PM, Peterborough, New Hampshire

I just walked from my studio to the Lodge. It's literally pitch black outside — like charcoal. I couldn't see my hand before me if my life depended on it. I don't quite know what it is — the thrill I seek tempting a meeting with the unknown. My only active senses were touch, as my boot soaked a foot deep into the mud, the smell of the pine and the sound of the stream so crisp and alive in the darkness. I was slightly afraid this night. With the snow — a false sense of security arises that everything else is dormant. But as it melts — the reality of the forest becomes more prevalent. With my eyes at daytime I can see how violent those "quiet" woods are — limbs ripped from their origins, ground ready to open up and swallow what ever steps above.

Spring 1994, New York City

The brain of my great experiment was seated inside the complex matrix of a hobby computer chip called the Basic Stamp. An appropriate name given its size. My first soldering job — the wires and connections so tiny on that stamp. Only a steady hand and much concentration could complete the job. I made it past that hurdle. The stamp now looking like Medusa's beautiful locks, I began my journey through the breadboard labyrinth of voltage, resistors, triads, photo cells and relays. Like my journeys through the untamed woods of New Hampshire, instead of red trailblazer markings, I had electronics diagrams.

April 9, 1993, Peterborough, New Hampshire

Yesterday I went for a walk to find the Log Cabin. Past the well preserved structure was a trail blazed in red. I followed it. Some of the snow hardened and with gentle pressure, could support my weight. But every once in a while the structure proved to be weak. My foot crashing thigh long to the solid ground below. If I caught the fall quickly enough, I could lightly jump with pressure from the other leg and halt the fall to the ground beneath. Soon I gave up trying to conquer this trail. The snow too deep.

Spring 1994, New York City

The experimenters breadboard is a series of perfectly aligned holes. Beneath the surface lays a complex matrix of connections attaching some holes and leaving others out of the loop. The pattern not too difficult to understand, but a monster to manipulate. I had eight input/outputs, two relays and a photocell to squeeze onto this 2 x 3 inch plastic base. I felt more like a landscape designer than a beginner electrical engineer — "no I can't put those inputs there, because there won't be enough room for the relays and triacs", and "I can't remember which side of the transistor is positive?" This quest was worse than the Rubic's Cube. Leaning, with intense concentration,

over this breadboard, needle pliers and flashlight in hand, I bent and twisted and pulled and pushed tiny wires into place. I created a miniature community with rectangular blue structures, strange two and three pronged trees, and weeping willow wires bridging furiously between positive and negative voltages. Will it work?

March 6, 1993, Peterborough, New Hampshire

Text etched into the plexiglass pages of the electronic sculptural book, <u>Under Lock and Key</u>

I thought to go on,
But I was too exhausted.
It was too difficult
for me to make fresh tracks.
So I stood there,
in silence and listened.
Even under the blanket
the earth moaned.
The silence fed an urge
to make noise,
fill the void,
the emptiness.

Spring 1994, New York City

I was on my way to constructing the prototype for an electronic book. Not the type that emulates the metaphor of the book interactively on the computer screen. Who wants to read all those words off a glowing piece of glass. I was constructing an actual book. By turning the pages of this book a slide projector moved forward or backwards depending on the direction of movement through the pages. I wanted to make this prototype out of metal. With a pauper's pension, I quickly remembered that aluminum foil is metal. Binding cardboard covered with foil, my first prototype was made. Each page a live feed to the stamp. In my excitement I forgot that human flesh is conductive. I plugged the stamp into the AC outlet and the IBM computer for programming. But every turn of a page was erratic. And eventually I blew the stamp. Three basic stamps later and a rapid evolution of the book construction my prototype worked.

April 9, 1993, Peterborough, New Hampshire

In the distance I heard a group of crows. They were following me. So I walked, trying to find them. They found me first — way above in the mammoth trees. They are so tall, five or six stories high with most of their greenery at the top. Above these magnanimous pines three crows fly — calling and following — sometimes flying blindly until the call of its mate sets her in the right direction. The most incredible sound — their wings beating the air like a whip.

Spring 1994, New York City

The sculptural book was made out of plexiglass, leather, rubber and scratched text. It sits embedded in an old fashion wooden music box. When I found the music box at a thrift store the pink ballerina was still placed at it's center, spinning continuously to the tune of the mechanical music maker. I broke her off and laid her to rest at the bottom of the music box next to my breadboard. The music maker a work of mechanical genius almost more interesting than any computer chip ever made.

Dec 12, 1990, Star Gazing, Banff Centre for the Arts, Alberta Canada

Last night she and I walked quietly down the dark road that circles the centre. It was snow covered and cold — too slick for automobiles. While walking down that private road, I thought of a scene I've been wanting to put to film. It's of me walking alone down a dark road. Slowly other people appear from the woods and join me in my silent journey. I felt like she and I were as one walking down that dark road. Walking quietly through the pine forests, filled with wild animals, our eyes were peeled to the sky — to the billions of stars floating above. We talked about the beauty of landscape viewed upside down.

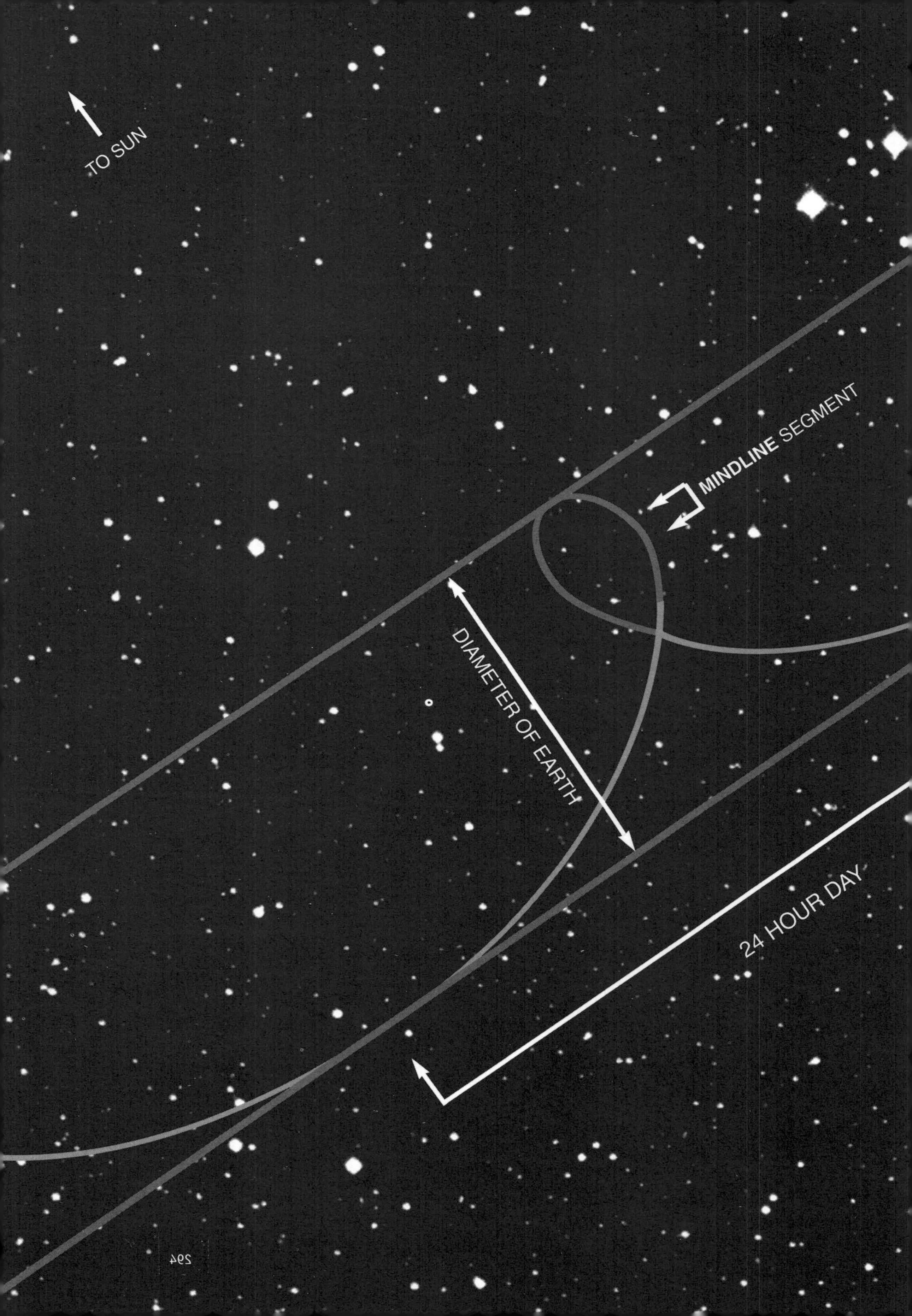

TO SUN

MINDLINE SEGMENT

DIAMETER OF EARTH

24 HOUR DAY

294

HORIZON

The above curve is a MINDLINE, or the path a human brain traces through space as the planet Earth rotates during a 24 hour period. The parallel lines indicate a portion of the Earth's orbit around the sun.

The following page is a magnification of the MINDLINE SEGMENT (pictured above) which illustrates a woman's private thought pattern as she sits in her living room just before noon.

MINDLINE SEGMENT

artist: SHARI FRILOT

production consultant: Christina Wheeler

June 4 09:05AM 1 page received From025950137 Korea 00:00:50
Transmission OK

To My Amerikanized and Humanized Friend:

Nothing is new under the Heaven
except the surface of the artificial
landscape surrounding our weakened
human reality.
In Korea, we already have begun
the second Korean War
in the televised landscape.
In your mother land, Korea,
the fear of the nuclear war has become a
soap opera in a non-fiction history.
Nobody can direct and edit this Errol Morrisian
documentary-like chaos
except the satellite and CNN.

From the distance, in my imagination,
we have already begun the destruction of Korea with
these two words: North and Nuclear.
Maybe this time, South Korea can easily win
over the North, because we have more TV stations.

From Korea, Seoul, Doe-Woo Park
6/4/94

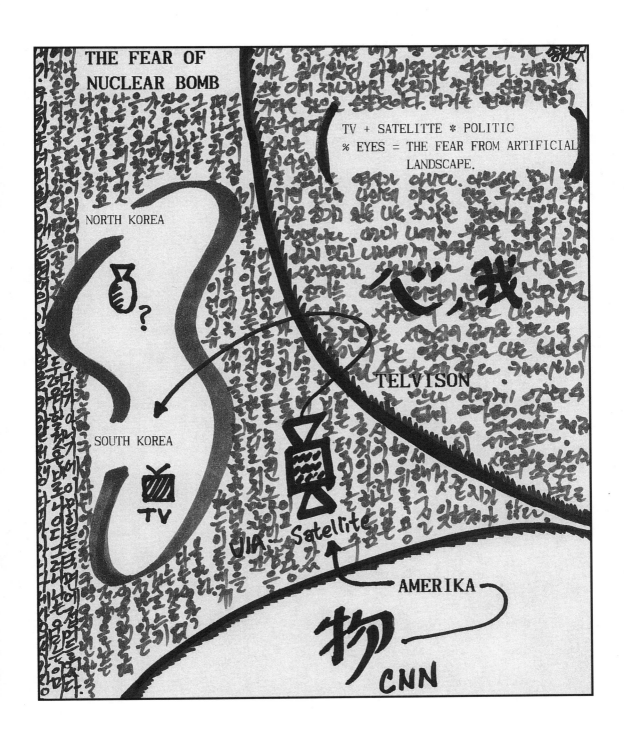

To My Televisionized Friend:

I don't exactly have the same fear as yours.
However, I hardly can deny that
the fear of the possibility
of actual war is any less strong for me
than the fear of the word "nuclear."
I have never seen the actual bomb on TV.
I have only heard the word "nuclear"
spoken by people on the TV.

Right now, I strongly suggest that you
have to overcome this fear of television
and design a new television
incorporating a parallel vision.
This television system has to
have two different monitors:
one is for the actual footage of the location
without any comment-language, no voice-over,
and without any cutting,
or interpretation of the time and of the events.
It is a pure artificial language presented
through an electronic reality.
And the other shows an illusion
as in any war movie.
It could be a movie like Rambo,
The Day After, Platoon, or
the footage of the Gulf War on CNN
CNN CNN CNN CNN CNN CNN CNN CNN
CNN CNN CNN CNN CNN CNN CNN CNN.
The reality is yours and the other,
the illusion, is harming your vision.

Turn off your TV.
And make your own television.
So that you can always separate
reality and the illusion.

But TV and my mind's eye don't see
the dark side of the moon.
So this new war begins in your mind,
on TV, and even in cyberspace.
And, as a result,
this Korean War will then become real.

From NY, Amerika, Jong-Won Park
6/9/94

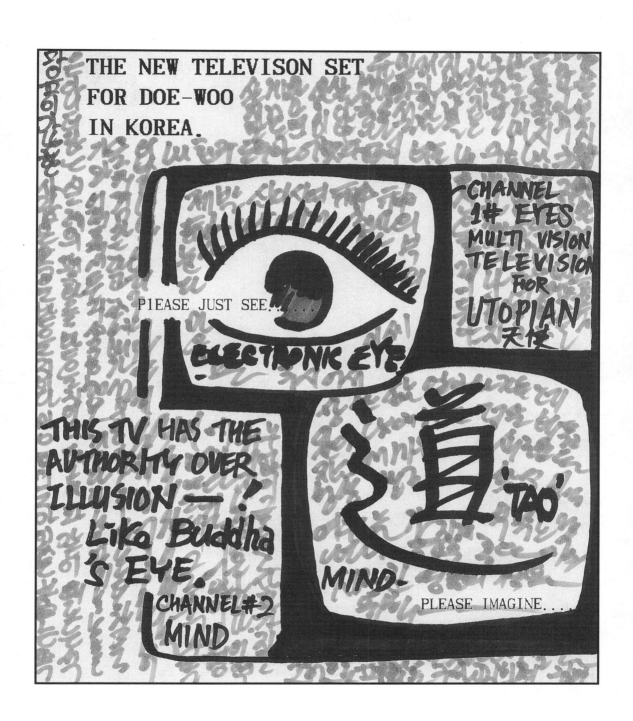

JONG—WON PARK

ParkBench

ParkBench
- Internet
- Videophones
- Electronic Bulletin Board

ACCESS **ParkBench** is a network of kiosks installed in locations in Manhattan which are accessible to the public. At each kiosk, users are given the option of browsing the internet with Mosaic, beginning with the ParkBench home pages. They may read and contribute to ongoing conversations on topics of local interest in **CHOICE** the BBS (electronic bulletin board service). By choosing to use the videophone, they can share audio/video space with someone at another site. The kiosk is child-and wheelchair-accessible, and has two complete interfaces, so two people can engage simultaneously. Each is constructed from stone and stainless steel and is designed to remain a permanent part of the site.

CONNECTIVITY

Videophone installation in the front window of Acme Gallery, London **installation by Nina Sobell 1977**

NINA SOBELL/EMILY HARTZEL

LANDSCAPE

New York is a set of landscapes stacked one on top of the other: geological, ecological, historical, architectural, political, economic, cultural, media. ParkBench is a rabbit-hole where you can fall from one layer of this landscape through to another. While ParkBench gives users access to the vast textual landscape of the internet, it also facilitates their excavation of the City's resources. Users will find pictures and stories which elucidate the history of the sites of each kiosk. They can learn about current cultural activities at each site, and can contribute their own stories and lore. Meanwhile, they remain in contact via videophone with user(s) at the other sites. ParkBench roots users in their own locality, while connecting them to users currently at other sites in the city, while offering access to information relating to sites all over the world. This combination of information-cruising with real-time video-assisted conversation reinforces both parts of the activity. By enabling users to talk about the information they are discovering, it helps to lodge that information more deeply in their minds. And by giving them something to talk about, it helps to facilitate their conversation.

With Cellular Videophone Watch and Magic Wand

TRAVEL

Living on earth makes us animals; our desire to travel across it makes us human. From travel we learn, and one of the freedoms we cherish is the freedom to travel when and where we choose. Cruising the internet puts one in the driver's seat on a discovery trip. Having no access consigns a person to parochialism. ParkBench provides public access to the internet via Mosaic, an internet browsing tool based upon hypertext links. This system enables the user to be an engaged learner, following his or her own interests to move from one information source to the next.

MAP

ParkBench is designed to help keep discoveries in context. Toward this end, its interface is based on a map of Manhattan, and users navigate by joystick. After logging onto the machine, they find themselves represented on the map by a colored bicycle, and they can see all of the other users' bikes as well. First they ride along city streets toward the location of the site they're most interested in investigating (Museum, Subway Station, Community Cultural Center, or University), and from that point they launch their internet voyage. If another user "arrives" at the same site, they can open up a videophone connection.

Neighborhoods appear as collages of photos and video clips, and users can access listings of local restaurants and clubs, find maps to neighborhood gardens, and discover sites of historical interest nearby. The Mosaic pages contain links to other cultural institutions in New York. A user at the St. Mark's Church kiosk, for example, might choose to read about the Church's history, in which case they would be transferred to the relevant page. That page in turn might contain links to documents on other buildings of the period, and to the New York Historical Society's listings. While they navigate through this information, users continue to share the same audio/video space.

The videophone feature includes the capacity for a shared notebook, in which users who are connected can draw, type, and paste in pictures which originate either on the screen or from the video camera which sits atop the monitor. Anything one user enters in the notebook can be seen and manipulated immediately by either user. Imagine a pair of people separated from one another by a window fogged by condensation. Though they're not together, they can see one another's drawings evolve in real time.

ParkBench offers a visitor to the city the chance to get a feel for each neighborhood before actually making the trip there. It enables a resident of the neighborhood to discover new destinations and happenings. And it gives the two the chance to share information, drawings, and images with one another. When they are ready to return to earth, they hit the eject button and find themselves back on the streets of New York.

GLOBE

The ParkBench model is modular, adaptable to cities in any country in the world. Just about any institution is an appropriate site, and its history, community, and current activities become the contents of its homepage. The key to a healthy network, in turn, is its diversity. It should include sites which are geographically separate, and which attract a diverse range of people. In New York the sites are St. Mark's Church in the East Village, a Museum of Art, a subway station, the Center for Advanced Technology/Media Research Lab at New York University, and New York University's cable television station.

As more cities join the ParkBench network, users can access the homepages of sites all over the world, while videoconferencing with people there.

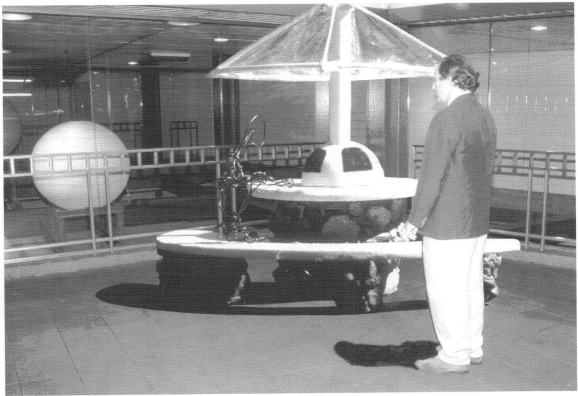

ParkBench installation at Herald Square MTA station   photo by George Kondogianis

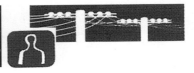

parkbnch@large.cs.nyu.edu
xzentrx@echonyc.com
hartzell@echonyc.com

THANKS

NYU Center for Advanced Technology in Digital Multimedia
NYU Department of Telecommunications
Bill Van Duesen of Ion Computer NY, for Intel Video Proshare 200 videoconferencing system
NYNEX
JHWintner Designs

(pre)view

Introduction by Reese/Ligorano

If you were to pose the question, "Will the book ever die, ever disappear?" We would have to say, "No." The book as a carrier of words is evolving, its intentions are shifting. It is a human form, as well as an artifact of information. It is genetic in character and variations of it have evolved and developed in all cultures from the Egyptians and Coptics, the Chinese and Japanese, the Mayans, through to the Europeans.

Yet, our generation is witnessing the metamorphosis of the printed word into an electronic form of information. This transformation is comparable to the paradigmatic shift during the 15th century when movable type supplanted the holographic text and manuscripts became *incunabula*. The book and its associative use as a form for cultural authority and validation is undergoing enormous change.

Under these conditions, the books has become a sculptural icon, symbolic of the loss of auratic significance. It also is symbolic of the shift and topological drift of how print and ultimately the world is visualized.

> If you burn a book, it opens unto absence
> in the flame. If you drown it, it unfolds with
> the waves. If you bury it, it quenches the
> thirst of the desert...
> — EDMOND JABES FROM <u>THE BOOK OF QUESTIONS,</u>
>   <u>YAEL, ELYA, AELY</u>

Review

The Book Talks Back:
The Video Books of Ligorano/Reese

by Jason Weiss

Despite their apparent similarity in form, the artist's book turns out to be quite a different animal than the literary artifact. The book that is mass produced serves a functional role — ultimately to make money or to win converts — but it also may be said of the loftier products of literature that they all play down the cover for what is inside. Whatever aesthetic considerations go into the design, it remains subordinate to the book's content. The artist's book, by contrast, radically alters this relationship.

Often presented as a unique object, and so distinguished from the infinitely reproducible text where only copies exist which can be owned by everyone, the artist's book draws attention to the mixed media of its construction. Even when it may be touched, its pages turned, it poses its own conditions in terms of reading. These conditions, however, only apply to that singular object, according to its blend of visual and sculptural elements, and its use of forms of writing, as well as the position it occupies with regard to the viewer. Text here may be largely de-emphasized or even absent, yet to read this book sets up a fruitful tension with our more usual habits of reading.

The video books of Nora Ligorano and Marshall Reese complicate this process by incorporating the most popular medium of our time, the moving image. Cut into the space of the page is a screen, which in effect screens out the text around it. The book becomes more like a theatrical object, the frame for the artists' strategy, or the proscenium arch itself, and the whole apparatus plays upon that central enchantment which looks strangely like television. But here the language of television is turned inside out to reveal the artifice of its illusion.

Installation view of **The Bible Belt**, 1992-1993.

Amid their other activities as artists, Ligorano/Reese have produced three video books to date. Each tackles issues in the ongoing cultural debate in the United States. Their latest work, *Acid Migration of Culture* (1994), stands as their most ambitious and their most public. A large and elaborate installation, throughout the month of January it occupied the main windows of the Donnell Library, the branch of the New York Public Library directly across from the Museum of Modern Art. The piece concerns the hot topic of censorship and the arts, and includes statements from about fifty artists, critics, politicians and religious leaders. The frame in this case is a 45-foot long photo mural that shows the open pages of dictionary which was composed on a computer, since the words defined on these two pages cover the entire alphabet: terms such as "art," "blasphemy," "civilization," "diversity," "family values," "freedom," "representation," and so on. Set into each page like portholes or wormholes are two video monitors, without sound, that present a range of opinions in scrolling text, accompanied by a photo identifying each speaker as well as intermittent images, such as flames over landmark legal texts and once-banned books spinning across the screen, to dramatize the issues. The doors to the library are at the center where the book's pages meet. The viewer finds upon entering the book (the door) that the entire piece has been left behind, literally out on the street. Here, at least, the insomniac could discover that this particular book never sleeps.

The title of the installation, according to the artists,

> ...is a pun on the problems of library collections and, in a larger sense, on our society's own cultural reference and identity. In a library collection, acid migration is irreversible and leads to the complete destruction and deterioration of a book. It occurs when a material containing acid comes in contact with one containing less or no acid.

The left and right video monitors, repeated in the pages facing the doorway, alternate statements that correspond roughly to left and right political viewpoints. The piece challenges its audience, by turning the private act of reading into a public event, aprticularly when considering what is being said about censorship and the arts. But the implication is clear: it seems hard not to see the attacks by conservatives as shrill and paranoid, particularly against the NEA; they are the acid that could destroy the culture.

This section of the video is then followed by a second part, comprising responses from people in the arts to three questions: How would you define culture today? What is the role of art and artists in today's society? Should artists consider the public and the public's reaction when creating their artwork? A. B. Spellman, for instance, points out that "culture is more fluid

than ever before," and he remarks that the categories of both identity and genre have become harder to define. Edward de Grazia would see this as a hopeful sign, since for him "the role of the artist is to rob us of the limits to our vision." The responses presented are kept to a few lines, but they show quite divergent attitudes even among figures of a similar political stripe. The book thus becomes a genuine reference work, by opening its very composition to a small multitude of voices.

Straightforward as it may seem, the piece occupies a curious technical position. The book itself is reduced to a matter of surfaces, where its nature as object is almost canceled out. What's more, the video component is also pared down, in that sound is dispensed with and the dominant image is a series of texts. Yet by layering the information in a visually compelling way, the book gains a certain dimension through the viewer's gaze. The passerby sees this unusual display and stops a moment to take it in. Registering that it is a sort of dictionary, one notices the changing images and moves closer to see what it says. Standing right next to it, one loses track of the mural — just as, from across the street, the video images seem only a blur — but is struck by the picture of this giant book. The full duration of the tape is about forty minutes, but since it is not dramatically structured like a movie and the season precludes loitering, a person is likely to read the book only in snippets — to browse as it were. This does have its advantages: given the elements of the piece, its impact is immediate; one doesn't really need to watch the whole thing. Still, if a person passes by there repeatedly, he or she is offered the prospect of finding the book always at a different moment. In a sense, the book turns its own pages.

Installation view of **The Acid Migration of Culture** at The New York Public Library, 1994, by **Ligorano/Reese**.

The issues at stake in this work recall the two previous video books by Ligorano/Reese, which employ the medium of television through more familiar routes. *The Bible Belt* (1992-93) reflects the slick hard-sell approach of televangelists, but taken to extremes. The piece consists of an open Bible mounted on a wide leather belt with a large gold-plated buckle that says "Jesus." Cut into the middle of the chapter "Proverbs," the video monitor shows a salesman hawking the Bible Belt as an affirmation of traditional values. The sales spot seems genuine with its requisite zeal, but gradually it becomes clear that actors are involved. However, this video segment alternates with other material taken directly from television, as though channel surfing, where excerpts of real televangelists are followed by glimpses of scrambled porn: the juxtaposition of this material produces a disturbing logic, to suggest that the marketing of desire is really a clever shell game. On display in a gallery, the Bible Belt sits on a pedestal in the middle of the room surrounded by a number of other such belts which are hung along the walls. In the words of the artists, the work "alludes to the wagon train of family values encircling the body politic."

As a book, the Bible is rendered almost irrelevant by the piece. What counts is its presentation, converted into a strange article of clothing, like a fanny packs, as well as its representation — in the hands of such preachers it might sooner be snake oil. But what does it mean to wear a book, to wear it in good health? Does it become transformed, or even diminished, when subordinated to a function? The way the Bible Belt is constructed, the book that looms as founding text watches out for the rear; at any rate, the person who wears it cannot read it, though he smiles in blank satisfaction as shown by the happy family modeling the belt in the video. By putting it on, he seems only to invite the unwelcome intruder to hover too closely in a frustrated effort to follow the word.

On a more quotidian level, the first video book by Ligorano/Reese also treated the deceptions of the word, in that it tracked the manipulations of the mass media at the time of the Persian Gulf War. *Breakfast of Champions* (1991) portrays a typical American scene with ironic grandeur. Here the text as prop is a newspaper rather than a book — *The New York Times* — whose composite headlines trace the military and economic buoyancy of the moment. Laid upon a square breakfast table, it is surrounded by a bright array of other props: a placemat and coffee mug emblazoned with American flags, a slice of toast with a yellow

patty of butter, a small vase of yellow flowers, a yellow folding chair, and above it all hangs a huge, ominous yellow ribbon. Cut into the paper, like another news photo, a video monitor offers a frightening blitz of non-information. The video begins with George Bush's "kindler, gentler" presidential ad from 1988, following him amid a backdrop of surrendering prisoners of war, explosions, tanks, and

paratroopers. Gradually, through a sampling of tv news coverage from the Gulf War, the screen itself seems to explode into many little screens. Thousands of disjointed fragments in effect cut up the military's press conferences, to show that this veneer of journalistic realism is really all packaging and no content.

If reading a daily newspaper, according to Marshall McLuhan, is "like taking a warm bath," the empty news concentrated in this installation accumulates with chilling effect. Everything seems dead here, even the generals talking on like machines — the butter will never melt on the toast, the leftover coffee will not be drunk, the newspaper will continue to fade and there is no point in turning the pages for nothing will change. It reminds us that, contrary to the sunny scene depicted, yellow is also the color of illness and of death. Ligorano/Reese show that what is missing in these pictures is a sense of dialogue, the free flow of information and ideas. And that is precisely what brings their latest work alive.

Above:
Detail of the installation of **Breakfast of Champions**, 1991.

Opposite:
Detail from **The Acid Migration of Culture**, 1994.

EDGE OF THE CONTINENT

The thing about Florida is that people leave their homes
And families
All over the country
And come here looking for the sun
They think life will be easier
Because it's warm
Whatever was wrong
Will change because the sun shines
All these fat assed white people
Wearing flip flops
Pretending they're Adam and Eve
In the Garden of Eden or something
Palm Beach, beautiful sunsets, fancy houses, expensive cars
Behind the good life is a lot of low class trafficking
Prostitutes on yachts
It's a revolving door situation down here
There aren't any boundaries
People aren't attached to roots

Margie Strosser

IN THE HOUSE

I don't know how much fun you can say it is
When you're sitting in a crackhouse all boarded up
No lights
Sweating like pigs in the heat of summer
In Ft. Lauderdale Florida
98 degree temperature
In the evening
Half the time no air coming through the windows
Because the place is all boarded up
And mice running
Across your feet
Because you're sitting on the floor
With candles for a source of light
Until they burn down
Then all you can see
Is the light from the lighter lighting the pipe
Sitting around a bunch of guys
And all you do is sit there
You're so paranoid
So paranoid there's nothing enjoyable
About it
You're high for 5 seconds
That's all it lasts
And then you think about doing another one
Don't even enjoy it when you do
Another one
That's the sad part about it
Then you wonder why you want to do more

Strange Weather, 1993, is a videotape made collectively by Peggy Ahwesh and Margie Strosser. Photographs here are from footage shot by Peggy Ahwesh.

THE HEIST

J. was out on a 1/4 million dollar bond, slowly but surely killing herself.
After she smokked her last rock on the outside and finally went to jail,
I got pushed off the gravy train.
I never went back to my regular job.
M. was still working on and off as a temp.
I started doing heists.
I was never one of those scumbag girls
who would suck on anybody's dick.
I never get myself into that situation.
Some people are born low.
I was never that much into sex anyway.
Sometimes M. and I would go off on an adventure.

Once she was my partner on a heist.
We were deciding what we were going to steal today...
Car phones, copiers, a load of lap tops.
I knew some guy who worked in a U Store It.
He let me know what was up.
We get in to my Datsun Z
and go out to this place
look at the warehouse doors
and cruise up and down
I said its just like the Monty Hall show
Let's Make A Deal

What's behind door # 1?
Door # 2? Door # 3?
So M. said lets go for a couple of laptops.
Usually I had my magic wand.
Incredible tool that could unlock any master lock
but some bitch had snatched it
so I had to use the crowbar
But that was OK
No one even noticed
We threw the stuff in the car
Headed back to civilization
We sold those things for $1500 bucks each

to a guy I knew in Lauderdale
Not bad for a days work
We thought we were getting pretty good at this
So we stayed up all night
Planning what to do next

OLD YELLOW NUMBER 2

So there I was
Sitting in the Broward County Jail
I had just gotten moved
From the felony to the misdemeanor department
I was waiting for my lawyer to post bond
As I walked down the hallway with the guard
I tried to keep my tennis shoes from falling off
Because they had taken my shoe laces
So I wouldn't hang myself
I said you gotta be kidding me
The new community cell was pretty empty

It was about 9 at night
I sat down and started watching TV
Everyone else was in bed
But this one girl came up
Started talking to me
Looked like she had smoked crack
Since the day she was born
I was afraid to sneeze
She might blow off the bench
She was really scarry looking
Unhealthy
Her eyes were sunken back to her earlobes
We were watching Miami Vice on TV

Pretty funny from the Broward County Jail
I smelled a burning smell
I turned around
Saw 2 girls sitting in the back corner smoking
Looked like a rolled up cigarette
"What are they smoking that smells so bad?"
She turned to me and laughed
"Oh that sweet smell of old yellow # 2"
"What's that? Some kind of tobacco?"
"Girls get so desperate in here"
She said

"They raided the pencil sharpener
And rolled the shavings with paper
Torn out of the telephone book"
I laughed so hard I peed myself

Pearl of the Orient
Jewel of the Levant
Garden Without Fences
The Most Developed of the
Underdeveloped
The Last Sanctuary
The Levant
Land of Welcome and Tolerance
The Playground of the Middle East
City of One Thousand & One Nights
Tangiers of the Levant
Land of the Cedars
Le Pays du Miel et de L'encens
Land of Milk and Honey
City of Eternity
City of Bliss
Levantine City
Paris of the Orient
Alexandria Quartet North
Oriental Favorite of the West
Playground of the Arab World
Switzerland of the Middle East
Hong Kong of the Levant
Window on the West
Gateway to the East
Gateway Between the East and West
Gateway for the West
Crossroads of the Middle East
Crossroads of Three Continents
Crossroads of Civilization
Cultural Crossroad
A Polyglot World
A City of Middlemen
A Crazy quilt of Minorities
The Suckling Child
The Precarious Republic
A Trojan Horse
Improbable City
City in Crisis
Bastard French
City of Regrets
City of Strife
City of Fear
A Broken City
Forbidden City
A World No More
Trojan Horse
A Country Held Hostage
A City That Will Not Surrender
The Impossible City

The Thornbush
The Fractured Country
A New Barbarity
An Open Wound
The Open Heart of the Arab World
Neither Victors Nor Vanquished
Nightmare in Beirut
Death of a Nation
Hell by the Sea
Lebanam
Land Beyond Redemption
Land of Cruelty and Hatred
A Byword of Barbarity
Une Ville Qui Refuse de Mourir
Mille fois Morte, Mille Fois Revécue

© JAYCE SALLOUM, 1994

Appendix:

- Gateway for the west to the Arab hinterland.
- Switzerland, Tangiers and Casablanca all rolled into one.
- The most developed of the underdeveloped countries.
- ...dialogue of the deaf...
- "natural Lebanese proclivity for divisiveness and wrangling.."
- Lebanese penchant for violence' *D. Urquhart, British, 1857 JR*
- the Levant expired in Beirut in 1975 · *Jonathan C. Randal, GATW*
- "..violence itself has never worried the Lebanese....." *p.42 JR*
- 'What were Israeli soldiers doing in West Beirut, this city laden with hatred
  devoured by resentment, weighted with mysteries we cannot penetrate?'
  Shimon Peres p.228
- to live in Beirut is to learn to die without reason..
- Lebanized
- every one of them is always ready to set his country on fire to light his cigarette
  French Consul-Gen on eve of WWII.
- ...in a country the size of Connecticut, at times held together only in their
  paranoid fear and loathing of each other...
- "I left for the complicated Orient with simple ideas"   *General de Gaulle, WWII*
- Tango in Beirut
- Exit Lebanon
- Photo Finish   *Time Ag 26'85*

JULIA SCHER

Don't Worry, 1994,
site-specific installation
in Kölnischer Kunstverein,
in Cologne, Germany.

MACABRE ART. WORKS MADE WITH FLESH BY MODERN FRANKENSTEIN.
IRATE PIARA TRAUMATITZED THE ARTIST.
LIFE IS AN IMITATION OF ART: DEFORMET BABIES ARE STILL BEING BORN
THE DEAD RECOMMEND NOT IMITATING THE PAST. FATHER CYCLOPS
CONCLUDES: DWARE IN ART, GIANT IN THE SRTIFE FOR POETRY.

AIXALÀ-ANTÚNEZ, POETIC PUS, RETRATS.
"I STOP A FLESH BABY; I SPIT ON IT, I DRUG IT,
I GIVE MY LEG TO EST AND KILL IT"
ASSERTS PLUMBER J.SIMO.

FRONTON
PASTOR
ASTRONAUTA

MARCEL.LI ANTÚNEZ

ABSURD TITLE: THE MAN FROM NAVARRE GOES TO THE MOON.
BESTIAL CINEMA WITHOUT SCRUPLES. ABOMINABLE.
AIXALÀ-ANTÚNEZ, DESTROYING FOLKORE AND CALLING
THEMSELVES ARTISTS."I WAS REFERTILIZED IN NEO-MOTHER
AND WAS BORN ON THE MOON": TIED UO AND DRUGGED
SHEPHERD FRONTON TELLS IT ALL.

YAU CHING • CONTINUED FROM PAGE 65
Western communists have been obsessed
with how the Chinese "liberated" themselves in 1949, and sinologists continue to
give positivistic readings of ancient Chinese
texts, there has been very little study about
how the flourishment of modernist Chinese
literature in the '30s and the '40s, (including
the fiction of Shen Zhong Wen and Eileen
Chang, the poetry of Mu Dan and Xin Di)
was truncated by the takeover of the Com-
munist Party. (It goes without saying that
there is even less serious concern about the

There were rumors about the Police Department of China keeping a blacklist of Hong Kong's "anti-revolutionaries." Here shows a guy looking at a Hong Kong Phone book, and the cop says, "How come you have that 'Hong Kong Blacklist' too?"

literature and the arts of Hong Kong and Taiwan, because they appear so
"unChinese." The only cultural products from Hong Kong circulating in this
part of the world are, ironically, from its entertainment industry, i.e. the
gangster and kung fu films. This perverse phenomenon we'll have to talk
about next time I see you).

Because I am writing to you from this part of the world, I can imagine the
essence of me as its irreproducibility. But because of where I came from, I
am very aware that this irreproducible me is not an abstract, natural, taken-
for-granted condition. This privileged side of the world, which makes my
desires possible, is in itself, a product of an ancient and ongoing process of
colonization, which also deprives others of their desires for irreproducibility.
My friends in Hong Kong currently know only how to channel their desires
to be as reproducible as can be, so as to maximize their intervention into the
(rapidly changing) socio-political formations. And this political self, this
desire for power, is like a virus that you want to introduce into the system as
quickly and as pragmatically as possible. But before it gets into the social
order, it first gets into your order of being and inhabits you... The difference
between "me" and "them" at this point is that, to me, being an activist is a
choice and to them it is not.

HI FRIEND,

Thanks for expressing concern of my status. I just became legal to work here
as long as I stay in the same job. I waited 3 months to get this piece of
paper. Let's look at what it says: "Approval of an immigrant petition does
not convey any right or status. The approved petition simply establishes a
basis upon which the person you filed for can apply for an immigrant visa..."
This paper means I have successfully completed one step towards immi-

Still from **Is There Anything**, 1991 by **Yau Ching**.

grating to this country. It is legal for you to be physically inside this country, but you are still, politically, an outsider. What it is warning me is that along the many other steps I have to pursue in the future towards that end, there is no guarantee. *They* can change their mind whenever *they* feel like it. The strategy of exclusion is to keep the border (which defines the territory) an unnegotiable but obscured fact. Your Other cannot exactly tell when she is out, when she is in, what the rules of the game *really* are, or how long she has to wait. She will live in this state of perpetual insecurity until she wears out and gives up. Then nobody needs to take her.

Yes, I'm still investigating different ways to get a green card. Chances are I may have to find a *man* to marry. If I apply through my job, my employer has to put an ad in the *Times* and then argue that I am better than all the applicants who are citizens! I can't believe the extent of institutionalized racism and heterosexism I am dealing with in this country, which after all, you may say, is of my "choice." (Why don't American ethnographers and anthropologists study the intriguing minds and exotic cultures of their public policymakers? Why didn't the direct cinema film/videomakers document how illegal immigrants were created instead of the "lives" of the illegal immigrants? O well...) Frankly, I don't know how people survived immigration. Either way, the figures on the lawyer's bill are astronomical.

Yes, you are right to say that I am dealing with an extremely protectionist/exclusionist socio-political system. I am, once again, reminded that "basic human rights," instead of being transcendental existential conditions as we are sometimes led to believe by the U.S. media, are, in fact, bounded by historical constructs like political territories. Obviously, there are millions of people who live here and have donated their lives to keep this system going, but do not share the rights conferred upon U.S. citizens, including the rights to express, shall we say, in art (when all the major grants are for citizens only), or to vote. Yes, I want to particularize the case of the exiled/migrant artist because the very limited options available to this poor creature help to illuminate how this country is run, and what American imperialism is partially based on. While an engineer from abroad can apply (usually successfully) for U.S. citizenship by proving to have continued the profession of an engineer in the States, a foreign artist cannot become "naturalized" as an artist. The U.S. immigration policy can be read as: 1. Artist as a profession is of no significance, and/or, 2. There is no artist outside the U.S.

Writing from this side of the world, I tend to think of Hong Kong as the colonized, the oppressed. But Hong Kong's economic success (or "miracle" as the Hong Kong media likes to stress) is in part built upon its easy access to the labor and materials of its "others" — the population in Mainland China, who experienced exclusions, exploitation and discriminations of various kinds in the (dependent) territories of Hong Kong. While Hong Kong people are being denied entry to countries all over the world since the "problem" of 1997 (if you have big bucks, you may buy yourself a citizenship from countries which you only heard of from stamps), Mainland Chinese have been denied entry to Hong Kong since 1841 (when Hong Kong became a colony).

The case of Hong Kong has highly problematized the theoretical dichotomy of the colonized versus the colonizer, or, the oppressed versus the oppressor. As a colony, Hong Kong has historically been used to perform as a mediator between China and Britain, and in maintaining that role, violates the voices from within Hong Kong and China. One of the most long-lasting effects of colonization is that the colonized have been led to identify with the colonizers. The history written *for* them would *look like* the history they themselves want. For those who cannot identify, history has taught them that their

Chinese Prime Minister Li Peng, the delegate of Chinese Kung Fu Troupe to the UN, performing an "Xtra-Special Skill: The Kung Fu of Super Thick Skin," swinging sacks which say "Human Rights" and "The June 4 Tian An Men Massacre."

Chinese Prime Minister Li Peng to Hong Kong British Governor Wilson: "For the sake of smooth transition, don't let me down, OK?" Wilson holds a list of the Appointed Members of the Legislative Council. Li Peng wears a band saying "Vote Pro-China-Say-Only-Yes Party."

The punishment of those trying to esacape from China to Hong Kong circa 1900.

history has been spoken, before they speak. Ten years ago, on September 26, 1984, the Draft Agreement on the Future of Hong Kong was signed between the British and the (Mainland) Chinese Government. While an Assessment Office was set up to "gather opinions" on the Agreement, it was also announced that "no changes could be made." It was obvious that the fate of some six million people were decided entirely without their participation. The real choice for Hong Kong people was to accept China's takeover in 1997 with the agreement as writ (and subject to change, as we witnessed during the past ten years), or to accept China's takeover in 1997, *period*.

How has life treated you otherwise? The worst part of living in diaspora is we all become more self-obsessed than we wish. How can you deal with someone who talks about themself, their anger, their frustrations, their anxieties all the time? It is like, I guess, having a lover who has AIDS. Lately I decided to change AIDS back to a metaphor and say Diaspora is just like AIDS. How about that? Take Care.

Love,

y c

THERE IS NO GREATER CRIME THAN LEAVING

Bertolt Brecht

There is no greater crime than leaving.
In friends, what do you count on? Not on what they do.
You can never tell what they do. Not on what they are.
    That

May change. Only on this: their not leaving.

He who cannot leave cannot stay. He who has a pass

In his pocket — will he stay when the attack begins? Perhaps

He will not stay.

If it goes badly with me, perhaps he will stay. But if it goes

Badly with him, perhaps he will leave.

Fighters are poor people. They cannot leave. When the attack

Begins they cannot leave.

He who stays is known. He who left was not known. What left

Is different from what was here.

Before we go into battle I must know: have you a pass

In your coat pocket? Is a plane waiting for you behind the
    battlefield?

How many defeats do you want to survive? can I send you
    away?

Well, then, let's not go into battle.

An earlier version of this paper was presented at a "Nomad" meeting at Banff Centre for the Arts, Canada. Drafted in November 1993. Revised in August 1994.

Thank you (just for the sake of legitimizing me - I know, many of you hate what I said anyway)

I would like to thank the writers who have inspired me, but it is an impossible task. (Besides, you take it and make it your own - I collect words and conflate them. Third world girls are known to be unscrupulous after all.) Nonetheless, for those people who like names, I am grateful to the following whom I am consciously addressing as I write: Rey Chow, Slavoj Zizek, Su-Ellen Case, Andrei Codrescu, Ian Rashid, Leung Ping-kwan, Stuart Hall, Trinh T. Minh-ha, Frantz Fanon, Gregg Bordowitz, Judith Butler, Gayatri Chakravorty Spivak, Homi Bhabha, Eve Kosofsky Sedgwick, Diana Fuss, and the unnameables.

KELLY COYNE • CONTINUED FROM PAGE 227

a template for her surgeries. The variety of interpretation is impressive:

> A truly radical idea would be more along the lines of emulating a figure from a Bosch painting, or replacing your eyebrows with fingers (like windshield wipers). — KEITH SEWARD, ART FORUM

> In her effort to represent an ideal formulated by male desire, she does not strive to improve or rejuvenate her original appearance (she has never had a face lift) but instead uses her body as a medium of transformation.
> —BARBARA ROSE, ART IN AMERICA

> Because of its collusion with the traditional cultural hatred meted out against the female body and its stated goal of an achieved "idealised" female form drawn from the conventional canon of art historical representations, Orlan's *Reincarnation*..., if it means anything, shows that misogyny is so engrained in our social ideology that we don't call violence in its name barbarism — we call it art. —LAURA COTTINGHAM, FRIEZE

I appreciate that Roberta Smith, reviewing Orlan's multi-media spectacle, *Omnipresence*, for *The New York Times*, brings up Vanna White, the ultimate media-born(e) creature:

> The distance between undergoing surgery in hopes of looking like Vanna White and submitting to it to resemble a high-art, highbrow ideal like "Mona Lisa" is ultimately only a matter of taste, the underlying element of self-loathing and self-destructive perfectionism remaining the same.

Unfortunately, she closes her mind to the possibility that, depending on the context, constructing yourself to look like Vanna White, or the Mona Lisa, could be used as an act of empowerment or subversion. Even though I am guilty of it, obsessing over Orlan's choice of features precludes more complex questions about her work.

The oddest review, hands down, comes from Jerry Saltz, whose piece in *Art in America* follows Barbara Rose's thoughtful article by several months. However, Saltz has a big burr up his butt about Conceptualism, and rather than concerning himself with any of the content of Orlan's show, uses his review to grouse about art which "is fiddling while Rome burns." The review is so wonderfully overwrought that I feel compelled to quote it at length. First he describes how, in the last eight years, a whole generation of art school artists, "weaned on the doctrine of art-after-art and itching for a place in the text books" have "washed up on Conceptualism's shores." Then he turns to Orlan:

> On May 1, the decadent phase of late-Conceptual art reached a terminal

stage in Orlan's show at the Penine Hart Gallery, where the artist could be seen on videotape undergoing plastic surgery and/or liposuction. In some misguided — if deeply sad — attempt at feminist appropriation, Orlan is having her face and body rebuilt by cosmetic surgeons... By the time she is through (only 14 more operations) she is to have the chin of Botticelli's Venus, the forehead of the Mona Lisa, and so forth... One work is titled *Reliquary #9, I Gave My Body to Art.* If you ask me, she should give her brain to science. It's upsetting to see Conceptualism come to this place.

Saltz's neurosis aside, why the great discrepancy in interpreting Orlan's work? There are some holes in this idea of the composite image. She is not trying to become an ideal beauty (and if you see her that much is clear), but if these mythological figures supposedly represent character traits she admires, how would she hope to express that through grafting together single features from each?

Orlan is using the vocabulary of a 19th century phrenologist as the basis for this high-tech transformation, in much the same way she combines religious iconography with liposuction. Furthermore, she is engaged in romantic notions of art making ("I give my body to art") while physically acting out a post-human discourse. In other words, when Orlan talks about art she means Art, art as a religion, art as philosophy, art as something for which she is willing to die. At the same time, the process of her transformation, the radical reconfiguration of her body which she is enduring, speaks to the disintegration of the Body as the measure of all things, reflecting more recent thinking about the body as a subject, loosely categorized as "post-human." In addition, she considers herself a feminist, but seems enchanted with biomedical technology, a field which other feminists keep under close scrutiny. Orlan is a bundle of contradictions, and the complexities of following her esoteric logic through to its conclusion is more than most critics are willing to do, much less the media. Yet the sensational nature of her project is hard to resist for any opinionated critic or news hound. In the end, the confusion surrounding her work leaves her intentionality up for grabs.

> People say I'm insane. They say it's not art,
> but I think that every time there is a significant rupture in art, people say its not art.
> They said that about the Impressionists. 3

Sylvia Rubin from the *San Francisco Chronicle*, freed from the terrible burden of being an art critic, tells it like she sees it:

Orlan says she has given her body to art. She says she wants to look like a
composite of prominent women in art and mythology, including the Mona
Lisa, Venus and Diana. But the 46 year old woman with a dark blue tuft of
hair, unnaturally high forehead and strange protrusions over her eyebrows
looks bizarre, as if the last surgery had gone horribly wrong.

Has something gone horribly wrong? Like many, Rubin does not seem
quite convinced that Orlan's only goal is art production:

What drives Orlan to surgery again and again - *aside from calling it art* - she
isn't saying. "What is important to me is a complete transformation; to have
the old image erased. At the end of all the operation, I'm going to get a new
name and change my identity." (italics mine)

Later she cagily adds:

If there is a painful childhood she is trying to erase, she isn't saying anything.

Laura Cottingham from *Frieze* blames the media for goading Orlan into
"repeatedly submitting her body to pain and distortion:"

...artistic and gallery self-promotion are an obvious aim of the Reincarnation
of Orlan and if the media weren't so encouraging this central motivating factor would disappear, and so might the bodily mutilations ...the self-hatred
that goads Orlan into medical barbarism is only further encouraged by the
media's eager willingness to exploit this self-loathing into a sensation.

Questioning Orlan's mental stability is standard procedure in almost all
readings of her work. She is regularly referred to as a narcissist, a masochist,
an exhibitionist and a hysteric. A French medical journal devoted an entire
issue to her, and concluded (reassuringly) that she is sane. The constant
questioning of Orlan's sanity functions in many of these discourses to de-
legitimize Orlan as an artist in a way which does not de-legitamatize the
outrageous behavior of our Art Heroes and Bad Boys. This is enough of an
issue for Barbara Rose that she is compelled to defend Orlan's work as art.

I call it art because after considerable reflection I do believe that Orlan is a
genuine artist, dead serious in her intent and fully aware of the risks and
consequences of her elaborately calculated actions. In the end, the two
essential criteria for distinguishing art from non art, intentionality and transformation, are present in all her efforts.

Speaking of art heroes, I was surprised to find that the artist most often
compared to Orlan is Chris Burden. Stelarc, an Australian practitioner of

high-risk body art, was mentioned by a couple of critics, and the less imaginative brought up the ubiquitous Duchamp. Few attempted to position her
in relation to other women artists. A smart friend of mine compared Orlan to
Annie Sprinkle, in that she searches for transformation and empowerment
though means not traditionally accepted as empowering. I'm still chewing
on that idea. Meanwhile, I do understand the Chris Burden comparison in
terms of masochism, although I would question the context of that
masochism, in terms of gender and institutions. But for some, Burden's
brand of masochism is more palatable than Orlan's.

> While Chris Burden reduced the agony of this various performances to
> single shocking instants that years later still have the power to make a searing
> impression on the mind, Orlan's travail goes on and on, becoming a tedious
> blur of needless suffering laced with a narcissistic stoicism and a desperate
> need for attention. —ROBERTA SMITH, THE NEW YORK TIMES

> *If it's too cold you die. If it's too warm, you die. If there's*
> *too much pressure you die. Eighty years on earth is frankly*
> *not enough . If I wanted to take a trip to another planet*
> *and see other ways of living, I would not be able*
> *to do that. Our bodies are not keeping up with the times.* [4]

Orlan is enthusiastic about the possibilities of bio-medical technology.
This may seem at odds with a critique of cosmetic surgery, but apparently
she is only critical of the *standardization* of beauty. Jim McClellan, writing
for *Life*, hooks Orlan into the discourse of the post-human:

> Her performances arguably make most sense if seen as an examination of
> the fate of our bodies and even our identities in an age of ever more sophis-
> ticated technologies of the self — from lifestyle advertising and psycho-
> analysis to cosmetic surgery, smart drugs and steroids.

He quotes her as saying:

> ...the whole core of this work has to do with the status of the human body in
> our present society and in the future. We're changing, mutating. We'll
> change even more with genetic manipulation. The body is obsolete.

Barbara Rose, however, reads Orlan's intentions with a different twist:

> Her program... provides a devastating critique of the psychological and
> physical consequences of the distortions of nature implied in the advanced

technologies discovered by scientific research, from microsurgery to organ transplants to potential genetic engineering.

And Susan Gerhard of the *San Francisco Bay Guardian* brings up the hip notion of the cyborg in relation to Orlan's work:

> It's not the final morphed version she wants to celebrate — not right now, at least. It's the process and its icon: an un-"womanly" cyborg, a bloody, exposed collection of skin and fat.

Gerhard attempts to weave her way through Orlan's philosophy, outlining Orlan's disdain for the body, disdain for standardization, and her almost perverse faith in technology. In their interview, Orlan asserts her critique of the beauty industry, but goes on to say:

> In general feminists tend to be very strict about plastic surgery. Why wouldn't you take advantage of advances in technology in order to make yourself more comfortable?

Gerhard questions what she means by "comfortable:"

> Does she mean psychologically "adjusted, " as Michael Jackson must have thought he would become, or does she mean, somehow better physically "fit" for living in this world?

I found a possible answer to this question for Gerhard. Penine Hart asserts that one of the most important ideas in Orlan's work is her belief that this transformation will reduce the difference between her outer appearance and inner being. Orlan sees this split as being a part of the human condition, and a split which technology can heal. I found only one print reference to this idea, in an article by Cynthia Robins of the *San Francisco Examiner*, and I do not remember Orlan mentioning that idea during her presentation. Why isn't this idea of unifying interior and exterior one the central points of criticism around Orlan's work? Why doesn't Orlan make sure it is one of the central points in publicity about her work? Conceptually it provides ample ground for discussion, and so is more useful than a lot of prurient interest in her evolving features. Apparently, Orlan begins every surgery by reading the following preamble, here as quoted by Robins.

> The flesh is deceiving... it is unnecessary, because the being and the appearance do not coincide, and this possession is a cause of misunderstanding in all human relations. I have the flesh of an angel, but I am a jackal; the flesh of a crocodile, but I am a pup... the flesh of a woman, but I am a man. I never

have the flesh of who I am. There is no exception to the rule because I am never who I am.

I imagine Madonna dressing in nun's robes and delivering the same words as an affirmation of her own mutability. For Orlan, though, these words are a declaration of discomfort and dissatisfaction with the limitations of the flesh. I understand now that she really does consider herself a martyr, ill at ease in her earthly flesh and willing to suffer to reach transcendence. Technology and Art, her two-headed god, offers her salvation through transformation. She plays the role of the misunderstood martyr well. But I think instead of giving her body to art, she has actually given it to the media. If the media tried to invent the perfect artist to write about, they could have not done better than Orlan. Her more accessible ideas, including the morphing of classical beauties and the plastic surgery angle, combined with her flamboyant, haughty image, play beautifully into cynical sound bites: "Orlan, the artist who literally suffers for her art." John and Jane Public read about her over breakfast, and wonder why artists don't paint anymore. Supposedly she is more interested in the process of her transformation than her final image, but I wonder if she ever considered how this process of transformation would be read, and remembered.

1. Cynthia Robins,*San Francisco Examiner*, Friday, February 4, 1994
2. Jim McClellan, *Life* , April 17, 1994
3. Sylvia Rubin, *San Francisco Chronicle*, Friday, February 4, 1994
4. Sandra Gerhard, *The San Francisco Bay Guardian*, February 2, 1994

BIBLIOGRAPHY: Laura Cottingham, (review) *Frieze,* January- February, 1994

Margalit Fox, "A Portrait in Skin and Bone," *The New York Sunday Times*, November 21, 1993

Susan Gerhard, "The Beauty Morph," *The San Francisco Bay Guardian*, February 2, 1994

Michele Greppi, "Like A Surgeon," *New York Post*, Thursday, December 23, 1993

Jim McClellan, *Life*, April 17, 1994

Cynthia Robins, "An Artist's Changing Face," *San Francisco Examiner,* Friday, February 4, 1994

Barbara Rose, "Is It Art? Orlan and the Transgressive Act," *Art in America*, February, 1993

Sylvia Rubin, "Her Face Is A Work of Art," *San Francisco Chronicle*, Friday, February 4, 1994

Jerry Saltz, (review) *Art in America*, September 1993

Keith Seward, (review) *Art Forum*, October 1993

Roberta Smith, "Surgical Sculpture, The Body As Costume," *The New York Times*, Friday, December 17, 1993

Contributors

MARCEL.LÍ ANTÚNEZ is from Barcelona, Spain. He is a multimedia artist and a founding member of LA FURA DELS BAUS (a Spanish performance group) and also LOS RINOS (a conceptual art group). He works in plastic arts and with audiovisual material. Marcel.lí works with film director, J. M. Aixalá, who has won numerous awards for his publicity film work.

BURT BARR is a New York City artist who works in video and photography. His work is widely shown in a multitude of venues. He is the recipient of numerous grants, both public and private. His video installations as well as particular works are handled by the Paula Cooper Gallery, and his tapes are distributed by Electronic Arts Intermix.

ROBERT BECK is an artist and videomaker living in New York. This October, he had a solo exhibition of his *True Crime* series at I.C. Editions. He is currently at work on *"Girlfriend" In A Coma*, a half-hour videotape focusing on the music of the 1980s band *The Smiths*, and their lead vocalist, Morrissey.

SALLY BERGER is a Curatorial Assistant with the Video Program in the Department of Film and Video at The Museum of Modern Art, New York. This past summer she initiated and co-curated with Victor Masayesva Jr. and Beverly Singer *Traveling with the Ancients,* an exhibition on indigenous media held at the Museum. She was Executive Director of International Film Seminars for the Robert Flaherty Seminars between 1989 and 1994.

DIANE BERTOLO lives and works in the intersection of a Venn diagram composed of art, design, and cyberstuff.

JORDAN BIREN was born and raised in Los Angeles, CA. For reasons of health, he and his wife of eight years moved to Seattle, WA in July 1987. A son, Max, was born to them on April 8, 1988. Disappointed with Seattle, they moved in August 1990 to San Francisco, CA where they continue to live.

PAUL BRENNER is the Exhibitions Director of Randolph Street Gallery and Project Director of The File Room.

KAUCYILA BROOKE and **JANE COTTIS** live and work in Los Angeles. They co-produced the videotape *Dry Kisses Only* which screened at national and international film/video festivals and in various solo screenings in U.S. and Canada. Jane Cottis produced the videotapes *This Is Not Not a Blank Tape, Dear* and *War On Lesbians* and other collaborative tapes with Paper Tiger Southwest. Kaucyila Brooke makes photo and text narratives (*Making the Most of Your Own Backyard: The Story Behind an Ideal Beauty, Thirteen Questions, Tit For Twat: Madam and Eve in the Garden*) for exhibition and publication and teaches at Cal Arts. Brooke and Cottis are currently researching the well known site of the lesbian crying room.

BUCK BURNS has, for three years, lived with an extraterrestrial who occupied his body, wore his face, used his voice. Now at last the theorist, who has created a formidable persona, tells his reaction to the many aspects of Buck, the struggle within himself, and the final acceptance of the mixed blessings the alien brought to him. Through sensitive illustrations Buck weaves a powerful and very personal life story! "This is the most passionate and personal statement that I've ever made. It is totally my own. As a theorist who always interpreted the words of others, I'm filled with a sense of relief at finally expressing my own thoughts and images."

YAU CHING is a writer of experimental essays, poetry and fiction in Hong Kong. She worked as the editor-in-chief for *Film Biweekly*, and has produced works in various media including installation, performance, video, film and audio. In 1990, she moved to NYC to study at New School for Social Research and the Whitney Independent Study Program. Her films and videos have been awarded at festivals nationally and internationally. She has also received several grants including awards from Jerome Foundation, Center for New Television, Visual Studies Workshop, Asian Cultural Council and Banff Centre for the Arts.

SEOUNGHO CHO was trained in Graphic Arts in Seoul, Korea, and came to the U.S. to study video art. Lyrical and striking, Seoungho Cho's

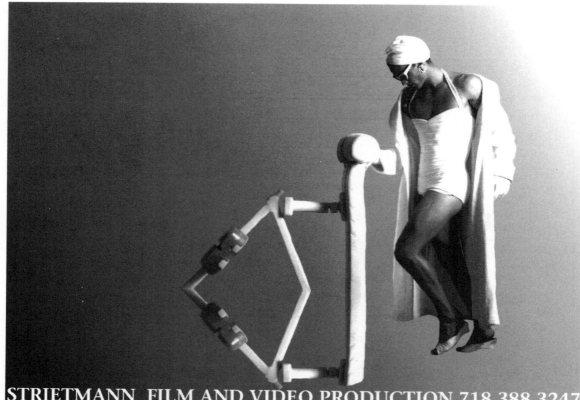

IFS
International Film Seminars, Inc.
presents

THE 41st ANNUAL ROBERT FLAHERTY SEMINAR

AUGUST 5 - 10, 1995

Wells College
Aurora, New York

Who's looking at who?

Film and videomakers, scholars, students, and film enthusiasts are all welcome
to join this diverse, yet intimate group who gather three times a day
to view and discuss films and tapes with the artists who made them.

Marlina Gonzalez-Tamrong and Bruce Jenkins
of the Walker Art Center present

"THE CAMERA RE-FRAMED: TECHNOLOGY AND INTERPRETATION"

A program examining the politics of ethnography, the camera as intrusion,
and the impact of new technology on film and video

who are you looking at? Who's looking at you?

Register Now!
Space is limited

Grants-In-Aid Deadline: April 28, 1995

IFS
Michelle Materre, Executive Director
Shari Rothfarb, Seminar Coordinator

305 West 21st Street   New York, New York 10011-3001   tel 212.727.7262   fax 212.727.7276

work uniquely blends image processing and sound collage to produce formal, painterly and highly metaphoric explorations of subjectivity and the subconscious. His tapes have been exhibited internationally, including at the Robert Flaherty Film Seminars and at Artists Space in New York.

CYNTHIA CHRIS is a writer and sometime artist. Her criticism has appeared in *Afterimage, The Independent,* and *High Performance,* among others.

KELLY COYNE, a techno-dominatrix, enjoys a glamorous and enviable lifestyle in San Diego. However, she is willing to entertain suitably prestigious job offers. Sincere inquiries only, please.

SARA DIAMOND is a television producer/director, video artist, curator, critic, teacher and artistic director who has represented Canada at home and internationally for many years. She has recently been appointed the artistic director of the Media and Visual Arts Department at the Banff Center for the Arts, and continues as the executive producer for television there. Her television productions include *The Lull Before the Storm,* a four part series using fictional and documentary strategies which explores the history of Canadian women during and after WW II, and *On To Ottawa,* a re-examination of the 1935 trek to Ottawa by Canada's unemployed.

TONY DOVE is a performance and installation artist who works with electronic media. Her performance/installation *The Blessed Abyss - A Tale of Unmanageable Ecstasies* debuted at the Whitney Museum of American Art at Philip Morris as part of the performance series *Performing Bodies and Smart Machines,* which Dove co-curated with Helen Thorington and Jeanette Vuocolo. Dove developed a collaborative virtual reality world at the Banff Centre for the Arts in Canada with Michael Mackenzie, a British playwriter and director living in Montreal. She is working on an interactive film project and an installation for 42nd Street sponsored by Creative Time.

JUAN DOWNEY (1940-1993) moved from Chile to NYC in 1965. Since that time he produced a major body of media work that interweaves a sophisticated multicultural discourse with an idiosyncratic search for identity. Merging the subjective and the cultural, the diaristic and documentative, Downey investigated the self through the historical texts of Western arts and culture, and the heritage of his native Latin America. His work was exhibited world-wide and he was the recipient of numerous awards throughout his life. Downey was one of the most original voices of contemporary media arts.

JESSE DREW is an independent video producer, media-activist and writer based in San Francisco and Texas. Having abandoned a career as an electronic technician, he now spends much of his time agitating for popular access to new technologies.

SANDI DUBOWSKI's *Tomboychik* won The Golden Gate Award for Best Short Documentary at The San Francisco International Film Festival, has screened at The Rotterdam Film Festival, The N.Y. Film Festival, The New Museum's *Bad Girls* show, and is distributed by Video Data Bank. He is a co-curator of MIX: The N.Y. Lesbian & Gay Experimental Film/Video Festival. He just completed a residency at The Experimental TV Center and the Film/Video Arts Mentorship Program with Shu Lea Cheang for his project-in-progress — a Hasidic go-go drag featurette shot from Israel to Berlin to Brooklyn.

DYKE TV is a stylish, energetic weekly TV magazine, mixing news, arts, sports, political commentary, health coverage, music videos and much more. After a little more than a year of broadcasting, DTV airs in fifteen cities throughout the country, with new cities joining the roster on a regular basis. The goal of DTV is to place television at the service of lesbian visibility and empowerment, with positive and truthful images. Inclusion of all members of the national lesbian community is part of the goal of DTV, through viewership as well as participation in the means of production.

KELLER EASTERLING is an architect, teacher and writer. She is co-author of *Call It Home,* a laserdisc history of American suburbia from 1934-1960 and author of *American Town Plans,* a book and Hypercard diskette. Easterling recently authored an on-line Mosaic version of *Call It Home* which assembles and narrates stills contained on the disc. She is a full-time faculty member of the Columbia Graduate School of Architecture, and joined the Carleton faculty for a special studio this past Fall.

FRANCES SALOMÉ ESPANA is a media artist-writer based in Los Angeles, California.

MINDY FABER is originally from Kentucky, where she produced her much acclaimed work *Suburban Queen.* Now living in Chicago, her work has garnered many prizes and

has screened extensively at national and international museums and festivals. Grounded in biting humor and engaging narrative, her tapes are informed by the complexities of political and feminist thought, exploring the construction of female identity as a result of traditional expectations and limitations. Blending personal stories with an investigation of broad social forces, Faber's tapes chart the complexities of female psychology in mother/daughter and interpersonal relationships.

RAUL FERRERA-BALANQUET is an Afro-Arab-Latino multimedia artist, writer, and curator. His writings have appeared in *ArtPapers*, the *Cinematograph*, the *Radical Teacher*, and *El Junglar*, among others. His works and performances have been exhibited at the Whitney Museum of American Art, MIX-New York, Randolph Street Gallery, Video IN-Canada, Museo de Arte Actual-Columbia, Galeria Fort-Barcelona and other venues in Europe, North America and Latin America. He currently teaches at Columbia College in Chicago.

NORA FISCH is a visual artist. Born in Buenos Aires, Argentina, she has lived in NYC since 1988. She graduated from NYU (1991) and attended the Whitney Museum Independent Study Program (1994). She works in a variety of media and has exhibited in the U.S. and in South America; among these: at the Bronx Museum of the Arts, Sidney Mishkin Gallery, Artists' Space (NYC), the Museo Nacional de Bellas Artes, and Centro Cultural Recoleta (Buenos Aires).

SHARI FRILOT is a video artist, independent producer and Director of MIX: The New York Lesbian & Gay Festival. After spending 5 years pro-ducing television in Boston and New York, she began to work with independent projects. Her works *A Cosmic Demonstration of Sexuality* and *What is a Line?* have been translated into several languages and shown around the world. Her primary artistic interests involve investigating the relationship between physical and emotional terrains by using, as theoretical aids, new directions in mathematics and science.

RICHARD FUNG was born in Trinidad and lives in Toronto. His videotapes have been screened internationally and his essays have been published in several anthologies, magazines and journals. He'd really rather be gardening and cooking, though.

HARRY GAMBOA, JR. is a Los Angeles based video artist/writer. His work *L.A. Familia* will be exhibited at the 1995 Whitney Biennial.

MOLLY HANKWITZ has been writing criticism, history, architectural theory and fiction since 1983. Her current interests include film/video, technology and space. She attended Barnard, Yale, and the Whitney Program; she teaches, lives, and works in California.

EMILY HARTZELL is a student in the Master's Program in Computer Art at the School of Visual Arts in New York. Originally an artist in photography and writing, she has extended her skills to include video production and multimedia production on the Macintosh. She received her undergraduate degree in Environmental Studies from Harvard College, after completing extensive course work in math, physics, and the History of Science.

DALE HOYT has been involved with new and alternative media as a maker, curator and critic since he was eleven years old. He has exhibited internationally since he was nineteen and his work is included in the permanent collections of many museums, galleries and private owners. His most recent acquisition was by the Anne Frank Foundation of his 1986 video work *The Complete Anne Frank*. He is currently working on a feature length piece entitled *The Orphan*.

ADRIENE JENIK is a media artist/ curator/educator currently spending a lot of time in the basement of the Integrated Electronic Arts (iEAR) Program at Rensselaer Polytechnic Institute pursuing her M.F.A. degree.

PAM JENNINGS is a photographer, video and electronic media artist based in New York City. She has been a MacDowell Artist's Colony Fellow, recipient of NYSCA Media Arts grants, and an Artist-In-Residence at the Banff Centre where she completed her video *the silence that allows...* Her video *Sleep Now Variations* is touring with the AFA and MoMA's exhibition, *Video Art: The First 25 Years*. Her most recent work involves the manipulation and programming of interactive computer technology in a work-in-progress interactive game, *Solitaire: Dream Journal*, and an interactive installation *Under Lock and Key: The American Art Song Project.*

MONA JIMENEZ works with computers, video and other tools to create both time-based work and prints. Work from a recent series of computer prints titled *Between the Lines: Mothers, Sons and War* was exhibited in Buffalo, NY and Portland, ME.

ROBERT KINNEY is a MFA graduate from the Visual Arts Department at the University of California San Diego.

WARNING: CULTURE AND THE ARTS ARE IN DANGER!

Federal support for culture and the arts is under attack. The new Congress will soon vote on whether to **eliminate** the National Endowment for the Arts, the National Endowment for the Humanities and the Institute for Museum Services.
THE LOSS OF THESE FEDERAL AGENCIES COULD MEAN THE END of local museum exhibits, dance and theatre companies, symphony orchestras and cultural programs across America. The only way these programs could be saved is through the support of people like you. Please contact your Senators and Representatives TODAY.

CALL 1-900-370-9000

For $1.99 per minute (9 am to 10 pm Est), which will appear on your next phone bill, **emergency mailgrams will be sent to your Representatives in Congress within 72 hours**. Total estimated cost: $6 to $8. Make your voice heard! Send a message that this funding is a good use of your tax dollars...a boost to local economies, jobs and community development....important to the quality of life. Urge your friends to call!

EMERGENCY COMMITTEE TO SAVE CULTURE AND THE ARTS
a project of the American Arts Alliance, 1319 F Street, NW, Washington, D.C. 20004

ELECTRONIC ARTS INTERMIX

ARTISTS' VIDEOTAPE DISTRIBUTION SERVICE
One of the world's leading resources for artists' video. Over 1,850 works by 155 international artists. Screening Room available by appointment. Comprehensive catalogue and 1995 New Artists/New Tapes/ Special Series now available.

EQUIPMENT LOAN SERVICE
Equipment rentals to artists and nonprofit organizations for video installations, exhibitions and screenings.

EDITING/POST-PRODUCTION FACILITY
3/4" off-line editing and duplication services at low rates. ($15/hour or $25/hour with an editor)

536 Broadway -- 9th floor -- NY NY 10012 Tel. (212) 966-4605 Fax (212) 941-6118

DONALD KINNEY has actively pursued his own program of studies in theatrical arts and has performed with a variety of touring repertory companies. Together, the twin brothers have collaborated to create a body of video art that has been presented in solo and group exhibitions throughout the U.S., Canada, and Europe. They are recipients of residency awards and grants from the Wexner Center for the Arts in Columbus, Ohio and the Lyn Blumenthal Memorial Fund in New York.

JUDITH RUSSI KIRSHNER is a critic and Director of the School of Art and Design at the University of Illinois at Chicago.

JASON LIVINGSTON is a recent domestic immigrant from upstate New York to Manhattan.

MARY LUCIER became involved with photography and media arts in the mid-1960s. Since 1973 she has concentrated on video installation, producing some 35 works dealing with landscape and the human psyche. A major theme in her work is the scarification of the land and the body, and how the mapping of these scars as physical terrain serves to link human topography with geographic landscape in such a way as to suggest a unified and shared history. A new installation, *Last Rites (Positano),* will be shown March 18 to April 22, 1995 at Lennon, Weinberg, Inc., New York.

MING-YUEN S. MA was born in Buffalo, New York, and raised in Hong Kong. He is currently based in Los Angeles, and works primarily in video, multimedia, and installations. His videos *Toc Soree, Aura,* and video installation *Between the Lines; Who Speaks?* have been screened and exhibited in the U.S. and abroad. Ma has curated exhibitions for venues such as the Los Angeles Festival, the Asian American International Film Showcase, Mix: N.Y. Lesbian and Gay Experimental Film and Video Festival, and the Los Angeles Center for Photographic Studies.

LAURA U. MARKS is interested in how independent media pulls audiences together. She writes frequently for art, academic, and alternative publications, programs independent film and video, and is working on a Ph.D. Laura currently lives in Rochester, NY.

VICTOR MASAYESVA, JR. is a widely recognized independent producer who has been making video art and television for over 12 years. His critically acclaimed *Itam Hakim Hopit* was produced in his native language and this and other works, including *Ritual Clowns,* have been the focus of special exhibitions at the Museum of Modern Art, the Whitney Museum and in Japan, the Netherlands, France and the Soviet Union. He has won numerous awards including the Gold Hugo at the Chicago International Film Festival and most recently the Maya Deren Award from the American Film Institute.

MERATA MITA was born and raised in Maketu, New Zealand, where she received a traditional Maori upbringing. After she taught school for over twelve years, she became a filmmaker in 1976. Her work has been commended around the world for its courageous presentation of Maori issues. Her documentary features include *Bastion Point: Day 507, Patu!* and *Mana Waka.* In 1987 she completed her critically acclaimed feature film *Mauri.*

SHANI MOOTOO is an essayist, a cottage industry manufacturer of olfactory stimulants, and a decathlete. In the summer of '89 she and seven other women stowed away for 21 days on a shrimp trawler from the Panama Canal to Tierra Del Fuego. She is an ardent fan of Richard Fung's culinary abilities.

ALBERTO MUENALA is a filmmaker from the Quichua community of Otavalo, Ecuador. He is a graduate of Centro de Estudios Cinematograficos, CUEC of the Nation Autonomous University of Mexico, UNAM. He directs documentary and dramatic videotapes on subjects pertaining to the Otavalo community and important to all indigenous peoples. His works include *Inti-Raymi, Yapallag, Allpamanda* and *Mashikuna Companeros.*

MUNTADAS was born in Barcelona in 1942. He moved to the United States in 1971, and now lives and works in New York. His videotapes and installations often explore the transmission of information through systems and have been shown in numerous exhibitions worldwide. He has taught and lectured widely at institutions including MIT, Cambridge; the University of California at San Diego; the Universidade at São Paulo, Brazil; and the Ecole Nationale Supéricure de Beaux-Arts, Paris.

THE MUSEUM OF JURASSIC TECHNOLOGY in Los Angeles, CA, is an educational institution dedicated to the advancement of knowledge and the public appreciation of the Lower Jurassic. Like a coat of two colors, the Museum serves dual functions. On the one hand, the Museum provides the academic community with a specialized repository of relics and artifacts from the Lower Jurassic,

with an emphasis on those that demonstrate unusual or curious technological qualities. On the other hand, the Museum serves the general public by providing the visitor a hands-on experience of "life in the Jurassic."

MAYA NADKARNI's recent works include *A Time of Her Own* and *Romanian Holiday*, which was produced through the Film/Video Arts Shu Lea Cheang Artist/Mentor Workshop. She currently attends the Whitney Independent Study Program in New York City.

MEENA NANJI is an independent videomaker and curator living in Los Angeles. She is currently working on an autobiographical video entitled *A Net of Jewels*.

MICHAEL O'REILLY is a Philadelphia native. He is responsible for the aural, verbal and visual components of his installations, films, videos and performances, including the technical aspects of mounting such works. *Snack Bar Open* was originally performed as part of the American Music Theater Festival's performance cafe in Philadelphia. He is currently working on a piece about his father's incarceration in Allenood Federal Prison Camp.

FLORENCE ORMEZZANO was born in Paris in 1965, and has been living in New York since 1989. She has realized several videos, among them are *Cut cut cut Codec* , 1986, *Heads or Tails*, 1991, as well as a few artist books. She is currently working on a video to be called *Anaxilea*, the journey of a woman warrior from 2500 B.C.

CHRISTOPHER ORTIZ is a graduate of Vassar College. He is currently a doctoral candidate in the Dept. of Film and Television at UCLA. He is writing his dissertation on contemporary Mexican cinema. He has published articles on a wide variety of subjects including Latino/a media arts and contemporary Spanish literature. In addition, he is an independent video and film curator and has curated for a number of organizations such as LA Freeways and Film Forum of LA.

NAM JUNE PAIK is a major contemporary artist and seminal figure in video art. His sculptures, installations, performances and tapes encompass one of the most significant bodies of work in the medium. From his Fluxus-based performances and altered television sets of early 1960s, to his ground-breaking videotapes and multimedia installations of the 1970s and 1980s, Paik has made an enormous contributions to the history and development of video as an art form. Paik currently lives in New York City.

DOE-WOO PARK is a member of cyber-punk movement group in Korean universities and has published several books about current political and cultural theories.

JONG-WON PARK is an independent film and videomaker from South Korea. Currently, he has two work-in-progress projects, one is a scenario about multi-national relationships in New York, and the other is about the experiences of young Korean Americans in New York. He is also trying to start a post neo-realism movement in the Korean film industry with several other young filmmakers.

LISS PLATT is a video artist and photographer currently residing in Brooklyn, NY. Her works have been exhibited and screened in the U.S., Canada, and Europe. She sometimes teaches, curates, and writes (only under duress), and most recently has taken up playing ice hockey.

RICK PRELINGER runs Prelinger Archives in New York City. He is presently working on *Our Secret Century*, a CD-ROM series on twelve millennial themes to be published by The Voyager Company.

RANDOLPH STREET GALLERY is an artist-run center in Chicago, IL, that generates and supports activities at the intersections of art and society. Believing that art and creative expression are social as well as personal in nature, RSG provides a forum for people to engage in art and contemporary issues. Ongoing programs and special projects promote artists and public access to art through exhibitions, performances, video and film screenings, public art, education programs, grants to artists and arts advocacy.

JAYCE SALLOUM has been working in video since 1984, and installation, photography, and mixed media since 1975. His work deals with a variety of contexts critically engaging itself in the representation of cultural manifestations and other cultures. The videotapes in particular question the construction of culture in the media, its pervasive influence in the political and personal realms of one's life. Salloum's videos have been shown throughout North America, Europe, the Middle East and other regions. Tapes distributed in the U.S. by Video Data Bank, Third World Newsreel, Drift and Facets Multimedia.

JOYAN SAUNDERS is an intermedia artist whose work has been exhibited internationally at venues including the Berlin Film Festival, LACE and the American Film Institute in Los

Angeles, the New Museum and the Museum of Modern Art in New York. She currently teaches and directs the New Genre Program in the Art Department at the University of Arizona in Tucson.

JULIA SCHER's work is really about "looking at looking." Through installations, poetry, performance, video, computers, and most recently an audio CD, she tries to be vigilant in a world where no one is vigilant. Further questions can be directed via the internet to bil@echonyc.com.

SUZIE SILVER is a videomaker. Her tapes, including *A Spy (Hester Reeve Does the Doors)* and *Freebird*, merge her fascination with performance, video, queer sexuality, pop culture, visual pleasure, and gender disarray.

NINA SOBELL is an artist who pioneered the use of interactivity, video, and computers in art. Her first work in interactivity, in 1968, was a group of sculptures which were designed for the undirected play of participants. Her work went on to include a videotelephone installation for Documenta in 1977, a storefront installation called *Six Moving Cameras, Six Converging Views,* and an interactive television show which broadcast on NYU's Windows show on cable TV in 1992. She has also taught at UCLA and was an artist in residence at the Interactive Telecommunications Program at NYU in 1991-92.

MARGIE STROSSER is a media maker who produces and directs programs for the non-broadcast educational market as well as produces independent work. Her most recently completed independent video work (*Strange Weather,* 1993, with Peggy Ahwesh) premiered at the Museum of

Modern Art in December, 1993, and has been screened at many festivals throughout the world including the AFI Festival in Los Angeles and Kijkhuis World Wide Video Festival at The Hague.

SUSAN STRYKER was born in 1961 at Fort Still, Oklahoma, and grew up on army bases all over the world. Stryker finished a Ph.D in U.S. History at the UC/Berkeley in 1992 after beginning the process of changing her sex from male to female. She specializes in interpreting the cultural construction of marginalized identities and has supported herself for more than a decade as an educator, lecturer, freelance writer, and independent scholar. She has published fiction, political commentary, and academic articles in several journals and 'zines and has been instrumental in helping to build a national transgender rights movement. She started thinking of herself as an interdisciplinary gender artist a long time ago, but discovered only in the past couple of years that other people were willing to take that self-identification seriously.

ELISABETH SUBRIN is a media artist, writer and curator living in Chicago. She is currently completing a new work titled *Swallow.*

ERIKA SUDERBURG is a multimedia artist and writer who lives in Los Angeles. Her works in photo, film, and video have been exhibited internationally.

JOCELYN TAYLOR is an activist and independent videomaker who lives in New York City. Her productions, *Father Knows Best, Looking For LaBelle, 24 Hours A Day,* and *Frankie and Jocie* explore issues of coming out, sexuality, and eroticism and have

screened at museums and festivals in the U.S. and in Europe. In her present position as Screening Director at Downtown Community Television, Jocelyn develops and promotes three yearly video festivals and a weekly screening series. She will be contributing to the black lesbian anthology, *Afrekete,* which will be published by Doubleday in 1995.

AYANNNA M. UDONGO is an independent video maker, performance artist, photographer and free-style dancer. She is the Director of Outreach Development at Video Data Bank. She has been a video maker since 1991. Her first video *Edges* was released in 1993 and has been seen in numerous exhibitions and festivals in the U.S., Canada, England, Germany and Australia. She is presently involved with two video projects: *Lypsus Rising* (completion date: December 1994) and *Moon Song of the Nubiants* (available in April 1995).

MICHELLE Y. VALLADARES has worked on documentaries with producers Victor Masayesva, Jr. and Lourdes Portillo. She is currently co-producing a Brazilian feature film with filmmaker José Araújo and trying to complete her first short film *Tina and Nora.* She was born in India and raised in Kuwait. She has lived in the U.S. since 1976.

MARIA VENUTO is a media artist originally from Buffalo, New York. She currently works as Program Director of the Standby Program, Inc.

JASON WEISS is the author of *Writing at Risk: interviews in Paris with uncommon writers* (University of Iowa Press 1991). His writings, creative and critical, have appeared widely on both sides of the Atlantic.

VIDEO DATA BANK PRESENTS

tapes on

Landscape
Body Language
Territory

VIDEO IN THE VILLAGES
BY VINCENT CARELLI

BURIED IN LIGHT
BY JEM COHEN

TOMBOYCHIK
BY SANDI DUBOWSKI

DELIRIUM
BY MINDY FABER

A.R.M. AROUND MOSCOW
BY JEANNE C. FINLEY AND GRETCHEN STOELTJE

BORDER BRUJO
BY GUILLERMO GOMEZ-PENA AND ISAAC ARTENSTEIN

MOSCOW X
BY KEN KOBLAND

GREETING FROM OUT HERE
BY ELLEN SPIRO

FORMER EAST, FORMER WEST
BY SHELLY SILVER

FREEBIRD
BY SUZIE SILVER

EDGES
BY AYANNA UDONGO

WORK IN PROGRESS
BY LUIS VALDOVINO

**For more information call 312.345.3550
or fax 312.541.8073**

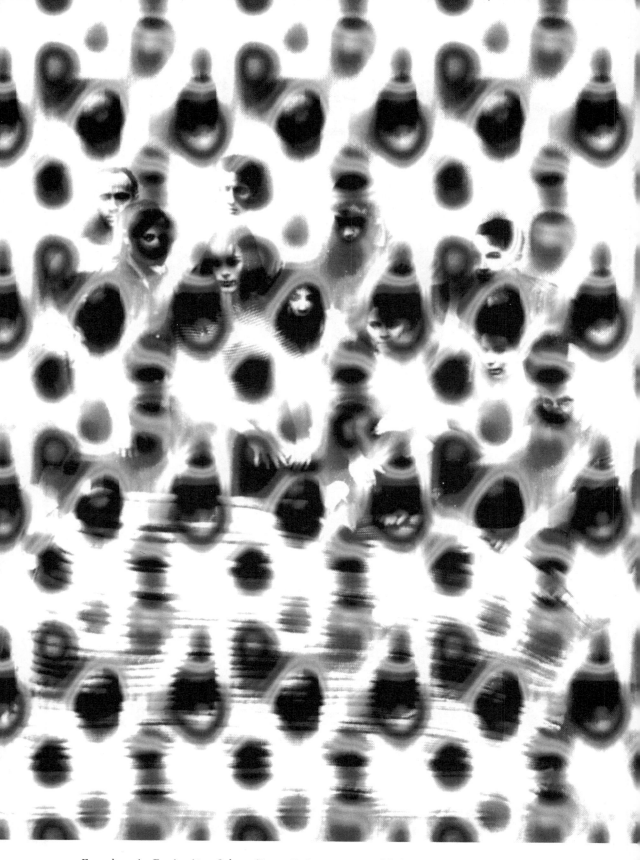

From the series *Fascinación y Cultura (Epocas Excitantes, Lugares fabulosos): Finale of **Parts of Some Sextets**, 1965*

S U B S C R I B E !

Editions are limited.

$12 per issue if ordering just one.

FELIX

A Journal of Media Arts and Communication

Philo Farnsworth's first Image Dissector tube, ca. 1926.

O **INDIVIDUALS: $30 FOR THREE ISSUES**

O **INSTITUTIONS: $34 FOR THREE ISSUES**

Subscription should begin with Issue # (specify issue):

Vol.1 #1 Censoring the Media. 1991 (Sold out. Available as collector's item only, please inquire).

Vol.1 #2 Shot/Reverse Shot: Cross-Circuit Videologue. 1992

Vol.1 #3 Post-Literate. 1993

Vol.2 #1 Landscape(s). 1995

Vol.2 #2 End Century Micropolitics: MediaLiterature/ Media Literacy. 1996

Vol.2 #3 The Southern Cone. 1996

Name/Contact

Institution

Address

City   State   Zip

Become a friend to FELIX. Tax-deductible donations:

$25 $50 $100 $250 $500 $1,000   _____Other

Checks or money orders should be made payable to The Standby Program, Inc. Payment must accompany order (in US currency). Foreign postage add US$30 per subscription or US$10 per issue for airmail / US$15 per subscription or US$5 per issue for surface mail or Canada and Mexico. Please contact us for retailer and bulk rates. Correspondence regarding subscriptions, back issues and change of address should be sent to:

FELIX, PO Box 184, Prince Street Station, New York, NY 10012-0004 USA.
Tel: (212) 219-0951 Fax: (212) 219-0563. FELIX is published by The Standby Program, Inc./Kathy High, Editor. It is published irregularly once a year.

Above: still from
**Hard Times and
Culture: Part
One: Vienna
'fin-de-siecle'**,
1990, by
Juan Downey.